MELVIN BELLI

MELVIN BELLI

KING OF THE COURTROOM

MARK SHAW

BARRICADE
BOOKS

Published by Barricade Books Inc.

185 Bridge Plaza North

Suite 308-A

Fort Lee, NJ 07024

www.barricadebooks.com

Copyright ©2007 by Mark Shaw

Library of Congress Cataloging-in-Publication Data

Shaw, Mark, 1945-

Melvin Belli : King of the Courtroom : Lawyer, Legend, Legal Revolutionary / Mark Shaw.

p.cm.

Includes bibliographical references.

ISBN 1-56980-324-2 (alk. Paper)

1. Belli, Melvin M., 1907-2. Lawyers—United States—Biography. I. Title.

KF373. B44S53 2007

340.092—dc22

[B]

ISBN 1-56980-324-2

First Printing

Manufactured in the United States of America

[Melvin Belli] made it perfectly permissible to be flamboyant. He was like a leading artist, one you think about in terms of Van Gogh and Picasso. They did things that gave other artists permission to try new things. They had the heart and soul to push others. Belli was like that, like a great artist who kept pushing and other lawyers like me said, "Hey, we can be like that."

Gerry Spence, trial lawyer

It was said that Shakespeare must have been a trial lawyer because he knew so much about everything. The trial lawyer's pursuit of facts and man's activity in a long professional career will take him from a study of submarines, to airplanes, to poliomyelitis drugs, to ballistics, to the identification of the head of a cricket, to problems of homosexuality in prison, to counterfeiting of old masters: indeed to the very ultimate of the philosopher's question "what is life itself," in some breach of warranty case where the question is (and this one I had), "Is there *living* virus in this vaccine?"

Melvin Belli, Modern Trials

He was like a big howitzer. You had to point him in the right direction.
Lawyer Frederica Sayre to Chicago Tribune

[Belli] was gifted by nature with a velvety hypnotic voice that could charm cobras right out of their baskets.

Time Magazine

The FBI director is a factious dictator who has assembled a platoon of storm troopers. . . . [He] is a dangerous, dangerous man whom we should have gotten rid of a long time ago.
Melvin Belli, Excerpts from Belli FBI file

Belli is obviously a mentally disturbed and intemperate attorney who served as defense counsel for Jack Ruby.
Agent C. D. Deloach, Belli FBI File, 1980

CONTENTS

Dedicated to Lyle Stuart,
a man who was never afraid to
stand up for what he believed in.

AUTHOR'S NOTE

WHO WAS MELVIN Belli? Was he a rogue, a lovable charmer, a scoundrel, a monster, an egotistical maniac, a shyster, or simply a flamboyant, misunderstood genius?

Was the San Francisco attorney, dubbed "The King of Torts" by *Life Magazine*, the ambulance chaser critics alleged, one who sacrificed legal ethics to snatch a client? Did he fit the outlandish profile of the bombastic madman fellow lawyers said should be disbarred?

Was Belli a womanizer whose six marriages proved he was more in love with the law than with any woman, or a publicity hound whose doomed representation of Jack Ruby proved he cared less about the facts of a case than promoting himself? Or was Belli the greatest attorney that ever lived, a true legend, a creative thinker with an extraordinary imagination, a pioneer whose legal philosophies revolutionized the way courtroom law is practiced today?

These questions show why Belli is worthy of notice and why his life should be chronicled start to finish. Few others were innovators like Belli, who practiced his trade for more than sixty years and left a legacy that seems more fantastic than factual.

Belli was dubbed the "Father of Demonstrative Evidence" and the "Father of Modern Personal Injury Law." He is also given credit for developing the "opening statement" at trial, creating "Day in the Life of" films for personal injury victims, and being the first to utilize aerial photographs and economic techniques to assess damages.

He was the founder and former president of the American Trial Lawyers Association and founder and dean of the International Academy of Trial Lawyers. He was among the first to advertise his law practice, the first lawyer to appear in a commercial advertisement, and the first to earn million dollar–plus jury verdicts.

To further understand Belli's impact on his profession, consider several of the seventy-two groundbreaking books he wrote or cowrote. They include the classic *Modern Trials*, a valuable resource in law offices and law schools today; *Trial and Tort Trends*; *Blood Money*; *Ready for the Plaintiff*; *Belli Looks at Life and Law in Russia*; *Dallas Justice*; *Belli Looks at Life and Law in Japan*; *Trial Tactics*; *The Belli Files*; *Reflections on the Wayward Law*; *Classics of International Law*; *Melvin Belli: For Your Malpractice Defense*; *Divorcing*; and his autobiography, *My Life on Trial*. His book *Everybody's Guide to the Law* is still popular today.

A Google Internet search finds more than 350,000 references to Belli, an indication of the scope of his legend. He is constantly mentioned by those familiar with his astounding court record, and the phrase, "That lawyer is as good as Melvin Belli," is a common compliment. Nearly *ten* years after his death, many people dial Belli's old San Francisco telephone number to hear a secretary answer the telephone, "Offices of Melvin Belli."

Belli's passing hasn't precluded several law firms in the United States from continuing to use his name on their letterhead. Belli, Weil, Grozbean, and Davis, a Washington, DC, firm, displays Belli's photograph first on their Web site. He is listed under "Our Lawyers" as if he continues to practice law from the grave.

I met this giant of a man in 1984 when he hosted a series of television segments titled *The World According to Belli*. Shortly thereafter the rambunctious barrister invited me to the Major League Baseball All-Star game at Candlestick Park. Under blue skies on a windy San Francisco day, we rode south on Highway 101 in his shiny gold Rolls Royce convertible. In a jolly mood, Belli told fascinating stories, his snow-white hair fluttering in the wind. During the game, we sat in the stands adjacent to third base as the American League beat the National League 2–0. Twenty-one strikeouts occurred, a major league record. Belli roared as the batters swung at the sky. How that man loved to laugh.

I remember the crisp banter between Belli and the beer-drinking, fun-loving fans. In groups of three or four, they paraded by to shake his hand or pat him on the back. Some thanked him for standing up for the little guy. To them he was the poor man's paladin, one whom had successfully sued the hometown Giants and their owner Horace Stoneham for a faulty seat-heating system. The lawsuit was Belli at his ornery best.

Belli, nearing seventy-five years old, had the pep of a preschooler. He was married to Lia, wife number five, and devoted to daughter Melia and son Caesar, as well as his beloved dog, Welldone Rumproast III.

As our friendship grew, I noted Belli's dedication to the law. Many believed the profession had passed him by, but I saw a razor-sharp mind still ripe with imaginative ideas. He was a true legal scholar whose historical knowledge of law was astounding.

When the flamboyant lawyer died in July 1996, I was greatly saddened. I felt that one of the true icons of the legal profession had passed. In my mind he was Clarence Darrow, William Jennings Bryan, Louis Nizer, Edward Bennett Williams, and F. Lee Bailey rolled into one. As dedicated legal associate and superior court judge Morris Beatus told me, "Mel was a true historical figure."

To be certain, Belli's contribution to modern civil and criminal procedure is incalculable. He extended the rights of consumers and influenced manufacturers to produce safer products. Without his efforts, opportunities for the wronged, especially the poor, to sue wrongdoers would have been severely diminished.

Belli's greatest gift to the legal landscape was the introduction of "demonstrative evidence," now common in our courts. The legal pioneer paraded enlarged X-rays, sophisticated models, blackboards displaying damage amounts, and detailed photographs into court. He proved that lawyers needed to "show" juries the evidence instead of simply using testimony to "tell" them. After *Roots* author Alex Haley interviewed Belli for a 1965 *Playboy* feature, he wrote, "He has had more effect on the law in the past ten years than any fifty lawyers in the last century." William Prosser, distinguished dean at Berkeley's Boalt Hall, called Belli a "Hollywood producer" and his trials "epics of the super-colossal."

In his prime, Belli's celebrity was like that of a rock star or sports icon. When he was in a courtroom, it was standing room only. He was hounded for autographs, and the curious public flocked to his famous Montgomery Street offices hoping to catch a glimpse of the genius at work.

Gerry Spence, a rambunctious Wyoming attorney and best-selling author known for buckskin jackets and colorful cowboy hats, appreciated Belli's brilliance. Flamboyant in Belli's mold, Spence told me that he was highly influenced by the older lawyer's reputation while he was growing up.

"I used to dream that I could be just like Belli," Spence explained. "As a young lawyer, I had no role model, but he paved the way for everything we do in the courtroom. He was truly a beacon of light that shone the way."

Spence considered Belli's contribution to the profession "in the top five of the twentieth century." "He made it perfectly permissible to be flamboyant," Spence said. "He was like a leading artist, one you think about in terms of Van Gogh and Picasso. They did things that gave other artists permission to try new things. They had the heart and soul to push others. Belli was like that, like a great artist who kept pushing, and other lawyers like me said, 'Hey, we can be like that.'"

Belli's pioneering efforts transcended the law and had a rippling effect on all segments of society. This became clear as I chronicled his life, one filled with fascinating experiences. His wisdom enriched the lives of those who, in turn, affected change in the worlds of business, entertainment, and politics. He was especially influential in medicine, a field Belli knew more about than most physicians.

His client list read like a *Who's Who* of twentieth-century celebrities. During the more than six decades he practiced law, Belli represented such famous personalities as actors Errol Flynn, Lana Turner, and Mae West; boxers George Foreman and Muhammed Ali; The Rolling Stones; evangelists Jim and Tammy Faye Bakker; comedian Lenny Bruce; Washington socialite Martha Mitchell; mobster Mickey Cohen; stuntman Evil Knievel; stripper Carol Doda; and murderess Winnie Ruth Judd. He brushed coattails with dignitaries such as tennis legend Arthur Ashe, opera star Rossano Brazi, financier Donald Trump, baseball great Barry Bonds, and President Bill Clinton.

To begin my search for the real Melvin Belli and to chronicle many of the significant moments in his life, I consulted books he wrote and researched others that mentioned him. I traveled to his Sonora, California, birthplace to learn about his early years and visit his grave site. I spent considerable time in San Francisco interviewing his friends, legal associates, partners, secretaries, and receptionists. I spoke with the trustee and attorney for his bankruptcy proceeding. Many loved him; some despised him. Everyone had a story to tell.

Most, I discovered, possessed an agenda, a motive for having been allied with the famed lawyer. Paranoia, distrust, and hatred for those who befriended Belli ran rampant. Many attempted to benefit from his death.

The highlight of interviewing Belli's friends and acquaintances was witnessing how much they enjoyed telling colorful stories about "The Boss," "MMB," or "Dr. Belli," as they called him. I laughed with them as they recalled special memories of his crazed antics.

While the facts Mr. Belli's life unfolded, I became fascinated with his representation of Jack Ruby, the assassin of Lee Harvey Oswald. Though he lost the case, his revolutionary presentation of the unpopular psychomotor epilepsy defense was unparalleled.

To better understand the history-making case, I visited Dallas and the Dallas County courthouse. I walked up the same steps Belli ascended when he entered the courtroom where Ruby was tried. Standing on the "grassy knoll" in Dealey Plaza, I listened as author and former FBI agent Bill Turner told of drinking escapades with Belli and New Orleans District Attorney Jim Garrison. Regarding Belli, Turner said, "Every move he made was theatrical. [He was] the theater of the absurd."

In 2005, when presidential advisor Harriet Miers was nominated for the Supreme Court, Belli's influence on the legal world was apparent when news quickly spread that the Texas attorney's first internship was with none other than Belli. No wonder this author was asked to write an article about the legendary barrister for the prestigious *Yale Dictionary of American Lawyers*.

Belli was featured in the April 2006 issue of *Vanity Fair* magazine. On page 142, he stood directly behind famed New York journalist Dorothy Kilgallen in a photograph taken during the Jack Ruby trial. Recollections of Belli also occurred when Paramount/Warner Bros. released the film *Zodiac* chronicling a bizarre killing spree in the San Francisco Bay area in the late 1960s. Actor Gary Oldman portrayed Belli, whose interaction with the alleged killer was front-page news.

So who was the real Melvin Belli? Opinions abound, but one thing is clear: He was one of the most fascinating characters the Good Lord ever permitted to walk the face of the earth. Here is his story, a balanced portrayal, warts and all.

Mark Shaw

PROLOGUE

Dear Melvin

This is the Zodiac speaking. I wish you a happy Chirstmass. The one thing I ask of you is, please help me. I cannot reach out for help because of this thing in me wont let me. I am finding it extreamly dif-icult to hold it in check I am afraid I will loose control again and take my nineth and possibly tenth victom. Please help me I am drounding. At the moment the children are safe from the bomb because it is so massive to dig in and the trigger mech requires much work to get it adjusted just right. But if I hold back too long from no nine I will loose complet [crossed out] all control of my self and set the bomb up. Please help me I can not remain in control much longer.

THIS CHILLING HANDWRITTEN note, ending with the famous Zodiac symbol (a flat zero with an off-center "plus sign" through it), was posted December 20, 1969, with six one-cent stamps to "Mr. Melvin Belli, 1228 Mtgy, San Fran, Calif." It continued the famed San Francisco attorney's involvement with one of the most unforgettable cases in history. He later wrote, "The San Francisco papers were full of a one-man crime wave called the Zodiac killer, a real loony who'd attacked three couples in lovers' lanes in the Bay area and a cab driver, killing five of them, and leaving his mark at the scene. The killer bragged about the killings in letters and cryptograms to the press which were laden with zodiacal nonsense—hence his name, the Zodiac killer. Most recently, he had threatened to shoot the tires out on a school bus and 'pick off the kiddies as they came bouncing out.'"

On October 22, 1969, Belli, a giant of a man described by the media as "silver-tongued and silver-haired," had been catapulted into the spotlight when Oakland police received a 2:00 AM telephone call from someone claiming to be the Zodiac killer. He demanded that either Belli or Boston-based attorney F. Lee Bailey appear on a San Francisco morning KGO radio program hosted by Jim Dunbar. Police hoped this meant the killer had decided to turn himself in, and perhaps wanted the negotiations to be handled by Belli.

AT 7:10 AM, as morning traffic congested the freeways, the studio telephone rang. The caller, described as having a "hesitant and drifting voice," hung up. Ten minutes later he called again. Belli, reluctant to call him "The Zodiac Killer," suggested using a more common name. The caller chose "Sam."

For the next fifteen minutes, Belli and "Sam" chatted. Listeners were riveted to their radios by the chilling voice of the man who had no compunctions about killing innocent people and threatening children.

Police listened to the exchange, sizing up the killer and searching for his motivation.

Belli: How and where can we meet you?
Sam: Meet me on top of the Fairmont Hotel. Without anyone else. Or I'll jump.

Sam hung up, but immediately called again.

Belli: Do you think you need medical care?
Sam: Yes. Medical, not mental.
Belli: Do you have health problems?
Sam: I'm sick. I have headaches.
Belli: I have headaches too, but a chiroprator stopped them a week ago. I think I can help you. You won't have to talk to a soul in the world but me.

Once again Sam hung up, calling back at 8:25.

Sam: I don't want to go to the gas chamber. I have headaches. If I kill, I don't have them.

Belli: No one has gone to the gas chamber in years. You want to live, don't you? Well, this is your passport.
How long have you been having these headaches?

Sam: Since I killed a kid.

After some banter about headaches, blackouts, and the death penalty, a scream was heard in the background.

Belli: What was that?

Sam: I did not say anything. That was my headache.

Belli: You sound like you are in a great deal of pain. Your voice sounds muffled. What's the matter?

Sam: My head aches. I'm so sick. I'm having one of my headaches.

After a cry and a pause, the caller resumed the conversation.

Sam: I'm going to kill them. I'm going to kill all those little kids.

Belli: You feel like you're going to flip out? Sam, what do you want us to do?

Sam: I feel an awful lonesomeness.

These short conversations would continue for more than two hours. Twelve out of thirty-nine calls were broadcast live.

Belli arranged a meeting, suggesting Old St. Mary's Church in San Francisco's Chinatown as a location. Instead the caller chose St. Vincent de Paul Thrift Shop in Daly City, south of San Francisco. Belli told him, "Take care of yourself," then left for the appointed destination.

With police, photographers, and various media in tow, there was little chance the killer would meet Belli. Forty-five minutes passed before Belli gave up and returned home to sleep.

Days after the radio conversation, Belli's housekeeper informed him the killer had called several times, and the lawyer's name was mentioned yet again in a note from the killer.

Belli's interaction with the Zodiac killer, still at large today, was symbolic of the bizarre nature of his law practice. During his six-decade career, the San Francisco barrister would alter the legal landscape like none before or since.

BOOK I

1

A LAWYER IS BORN

SONORA, CALIFORNIA, AN old mining town nestled in the western hills of the high Sierras, was best known for its gamblers, hookers, and gold-crazed miners. There, on July 29, 1907, Melvin Mouron Belli was born.

Sonora boasted a rich history. Once occupied by the Mi Wuk Indians, the budding town was ravished by an influx of invaders from Europe, South America, the South Pacific, and China when gold was discovered at nearby Coloma in the late 1840s. Seeking riches, the miners panned the rivers and streams in Tuolumne County.

The bustling town where young Melvin grew up featured Old Croco's Church, the C. H. Burden Undertaking Parlor, and the Yo-Semite Hotel. Charles Lang's Bakery sold bread for five cents a loaf, six loaves for twenty-five cents.

The future lawyer's father was Caesar Arthur Belli, son of a successful Nevada rancher. Caesar was an entrepreneurial man who prided himself on his appearance and began each morning with a barber's shave. He made it a practice to wear a vested suit and carry a pocketwatch attached to a heavy gold chain. Melvin would carry on the tradition.

Regarding his father's taste for sartorial splendor, Belli said, "When he went trout fishing, he would look as if he had just stepped out of the Abercrombie and Fitch catalog: straw hat, waders, and a split bamboo rod." As for his physical attributes, Melvin said, "He was one of the handsomest men I have ever known and he smelled of lavender or carnations, and, at times, of Sen-Sen and bourbon."

By the time Caesar, an extremely bright young man, reached his sixteenth birthday, he had studied at Bern College in Switzerland and become fluent in six languages. The Bellis were of Swiss descent, but there was evidence that the family was part of the original wave of Genovese families that left Garibaldi's Italy for the California gold rush. The name was originally pronounced "Bally" after the Swiss shoe. Later, Melvin refused to consider himself Swiss, saying, "Only money changers, cuckoo clock makers and hotel keepers call themselves Swiss."

Melvin's mother Leonie, a petite brunette with an engaging smile, was of French descent. Several ancestors had been doctors and surgeons; one served in Napoleon's army.

Leonie's father, Henri, became Sonora's town physician. He was a respected man who opened a family pharmacy, Mouron's Union Drug Store, on the corner of Washington and Linoberg, across the street from the *Union Democrat* newspaper. Melvin recalled him fondly in a book he coauthored titled *Divorcing*. "Grandma Mouron used to regale me with stories about how he would saddle up the team of horses in the middle of the night to visit a sick person. On what turned out to be his last ride, he was caught in the middle of a cloudburst; he survived the storm, only to die of pneumonia." He added, "The remembrance of my grandfather's dedicated public service to people in real need is one of the reasons [I became] a lawyer."

Melvin was born in a room above the pharmacy where his grandmother Anna Mouron was California's first woman druggist. Being an only child, Belli said later, greatly impacted his persona. He told author Arthur Sheresky, "I suffered from that. It makes for selfishness."

Early on, Melvin was called "Pete," but his mother, a prim and proper woman who was called "pretty" by those who knew her, decided "Pete" wasn't acceptable. Leonie tried to keep her son from becoming too rowdy by dressing him in Little Lord Fauntleroy velvet suits. He despised them, believing he looked prissy.

Belli's friends and colleagues later noted that he rarely mentioned his mother, a large-breasted woman dubbed "very Italian," despite her heritage. "He was much closer to his grandmother," said Joyce Revilla, longtime friend and secretary. Belli's daughter Jeanne said her mother, Belli's first wife, told her, "Dad hated his mom."

A subject of young Belli's affection was a worn plastic skeleton that his grandmother kept in a dark room underneath the stairs. He loved to play with the bones, wave the arms, and examine the skull. Sometimes he referred to himself as "Dr. Belli," a hint of later interest in the medical profession.

When Melvin's grandma Anna died, his uncle Otto continued the family business. The location became a Sonora landmark. A graduate pharmacist at the University of California, Otto was a Sonora fixture. In a biographical sketch published by the nearby *Columbia Gazette* in 1855, Otto had listed his "hobby" as "trying to understand life in its various phases."

When Otto passed away in 1949, a *Union Democrat* editorial praised him. It read, "Sonora has lost a well-loved citizen and shining symbol of integrity and dependability."

MELVIN HAD FOND memories of Sonora. He loved the countryside and the nearby mountains. During later trips to Scandinavian countries, he often reminisced about Sonora Pass, a gateway to skiing. He compared its beauty with passes in the Swiss Alps.

Belli would return to Sonora to be celebrated. He arrived in a shiny Rolls-Royce, complete with entourage, true to his larger-than-life image. Honored at the Tuolumne County Historical Society, he rambled on about boyhood days that featured "Buns at Hop Kee's, ice cream at Burnham's, and delicious meals at Gem Cafe."

Further evidence of Belli's fondness toward his formative years appeared in *Divorcing*. He wrote, "I see the logs sparkling and the fire reflected in the highly polished black high-buttoned shoes of my dad and my uncle. . . . Experiences such as these made me feel that family life was forever, and how wonderful that was."

He recorded more childhood memories in an article he penned for the Tuolumne County Historical Society in 1973. "I can remember, Jack, my Irish setter," he wrote in *CHISPA*, "trailing me up to school, then going home to wait for me." He added, "I remember on Easter how we always got one of Mrs. Lick's Easter eggs from the reverend as we came out of church."

He recalled seeing a stuffed quail hanging in one of Sonora's finest hotels. It was tied to a thin wire that extended through a hole in the ceiling. The wire was attached to the springs of a bed reserved for occupants of the bridal suite. When the quail shook, the patrons in the bar laughed and cheered. The newlyweds must have felt like they were performers at a sporting event.

Sonora Gold Rush stories filled Melvin's head as he grew up. He loved to hear tales about the outlaws who passed through town and the miners who shot first and asked questions later. Their legacy, he knew, was captured in the names they gave their claims: "Murphy's Defeat," "Dead Man's Bar," and "Blood Springs." He recalled a teacher who dismissed students from school to search the streets for gold nuggets. Belli would tell friend Alessandro Biccari that he wished he had been born during the Gold Rush days.

Those who wonder where Belli attained his flair for the dramatic need look no further than his father. Quite accomplished at mathematics, Caesar performed mathematical feats on stage when vaudevillians swept through Sonora. Melvin said his dad could multiply large numbers, such as $8,648 \times 1,342,765$, without pencil or paper. His defeated foes: Chinese merchants who used an abacus. "Dad even learned to speak Chinese," Melvin recalled.

Caesar believed in Sonora and its future. In 1904, after working as a timekeeper at the Standard Lumber Mill, he joined others in establishing The 1st National Bank. Caesar was twenty-four-years-old. To rally customers, the *Union Democrat* reported that Caesar, intent on proving the existence of gold in nearby mines, displayed gold specimens at the bank. They were, he swore, from "the Wilson and Means mine on Jackass Hill near Tuttletown."

In 1906, Caesar displayed the tough crust that would also be a signature quality of his son Melvin. When he learned that San Francisco had been nearly leveled by an earthquake, Caesar decided he needed to help. He stuffed gold bullion worth over twelve thousand dollars into a saddlebag and rode west toward the "City by the Bay." His destination was the Bank of Italy, operated by noted financier A. P. Giannini.

The now-famous earthquake occurred at 5:12 AM on April 18, 1906. Warnings had been issued prior to "the big one," but one reporter wrote that they were ignored because of the mind set of the "excitement-craving, money-seeking, luxurious-living, reckless heaven-earth-and-hell-daring citizens of San Francisco." The Great Fire raged through the city.

When Caesar arrived in San Francisco, he was shocked by the destruction. Firefighters and militia raced from street to street attempting to contain the blaze. Dark smoke billowed out of burning buildings as citizens raced through the streets carrying whatever belongings they could. The greatest damage occurred in the financial district and North Beach area. At the final count, more than 250,000 citizens were homeless. The city's fire chief had been killed. The Palace of Fine Arts, a Bay Area treasure, survived.

Undaunted, Caesar Belli, his gold bullion in a wheelbarrow, finally located Giannini at the corner of Kearny and California Streets. To the banker's surprise, his young counterpart said, "I suspect you'll be needing this." Giannini, who later became president of the Bank of America, was deeply impressed. Ironically, Melvin Belli's famous offices on Montgomery Street in San Francisco would be located within blocks of the A. P. Giannini Plaza.

The importance of helping others was thus impressed up Melvin early in his life. He spoke glowingly of his father as a man not afraid to stand up for things he believed in. History would prove that like father, like son.

BELLI FIRST VISITED the "City by the Bay" as an eight-year-old, in February 1915. He later admitted he was captivated by San Francisco, saying it "was love at first sight, the beginning of a romance."

The city was celebrating its resurrection from the nightmare ignited by the earthquake. The event, dubbed the Panama Pacific Exposition, featured patriotic music played by John Phillip Sousa. Marking the rebirth of San Francisco, the gala affair lasted for nine months and twelve days.

Belli said that two aspects of the Exposition mesmerized him. The first was a roller coaster called the Joy Zone that streaked along near the Exposition's twelve palaces. The second was hearing the spirited words of the great lawyer and orator William Jennings Bryan.

Childhood pal Irving Symons, whose family operated a successful lumber company, accompanied Belli to San Francisco. "We were both in grammar school," he recalled. "Melvin and I rode the street cars to see how far across the city we could go for five cents. We sat up front with the motorman."

Symons said young Belli was "unpredictable," liked to "do the unusual," and was one to "speak his mind." He remembered Belli stealing a handful of toothpicks from a restaurant: "We cut them in half and had sword duels with them. Sometimes we'd draw blood, but we were just having fun."

Two years after his first glimpse of San Francisco, the ten-year-old moved to Stockton. His father, as a major stockholder, assumed control of the San Joaquin Valley Bank. At one point, Caesar decided to sell his interest in the bank to A. P. Giannini, in exchange for nearly $500,000 worth of stock in the Bank of Italy. At the last minute, the elder Belli had a change of heart, deciding he could not sell out on the minority stockholders. Giannini condemned Caesar for "backing out," but Melvin learned a lesson regarding loyalty to those who were friends.

While Caesar's bank thrived, he began growing grapes, raisins, and pears on a farm near Stockton. When the Volstead Act of 1919 prohibited the sale of those commodities for use in making wine, Caesar decided to circumvent the law. Displaying his cantankerous nature, he produced "raisin bricks." The labels, according to Melvin, read, "Caution: Do not put this in water at 105 degree temperature and do not add yeast and sugar because this will turn into excellent wine."

Some days later, Federal agents appeared at the Belli farmhouse. Within minutes they had badgered Caesar into admitting his guilt. Later, Melvin swore that watching his father being intimidated without the assistance of a lawyer had a lasting effect.

According to longtime Tuolumne County resident Roy Brooks, the Belli farm was a lively place. "Some Saturday nights we would go to Caesar Belli's barn," he wrote. "It had a hardwood floor, and we would spread hay around and dance until dawn ... we played polkas, waltzes, quadrilles, and even jigs."

Young Melvin's sexual adventures began early. His educator was "Helen, a big girl with a pretty face who led me out to the back steps of the high school science building one balmy night during a school night and showed me a thing or two." He was fifteen at the time.

Belli said Helen's lessons about the birds and the bees gave him "an extra measure of confidence in myself." Prior to Helen he had trouble speaking in front of others, once telling a group, "It's not that I can't remember what to say, it's just that I have so much to tell you I can't decide what comes next." Post-Helen he was able to speak so eloquently that drama and speech teacher Minnie Howell said, "Melvin, you'll have a thousand and one audiences and they'll have a love affair with you." His newfound ability to speak, he said, "was like swimming in a pool of warm oil."

Being able to articulate didn't mean Belli always had his facts straight. During his college days, he delivered a speech that triggered profound comments from his professor. His evaluation read, "His historical facts were infamous—Belli's got the Russian before the American Revolution. He's got Genghis Khan going through Africa. All of which is horrendous." To Belli's credit, the instructor added, "But he's a spellbinder."

The type of books young Belli read provide some insight into the development of his "show, not tell" mind set. Without television to impede his intellectual growth, he read constantly.

The most compelling book, he said, besides those by Robert Louis Stevenson and Edgar Rice Burroughs, was *The Book of Knowledge.* "[The authors] didn't just tell me how many miles it was to the moon, they told me in terms I could visualize for myself," he wrote in his autobiography, *My Life on Trial.* "If you could put X million railroad boxcars end to end, then the moon would be that many boxcars away from the earth. Miles I couldn't understand, boxcars I could."

During high school, Belli the speaker became Belli the actor. He played the part of Donald Swift, a loquacious film director, in the play *The Whole Town's Talking.*

Belli was also a member of the debate team and sports editor of the school newspaper, *The Guard and Tackle.* He did well academically, achieving valedictorian honors. His anticipated address, titled *Respect for Life and Order*, was a hint of things to come.

But Belli, not unlike his father, had a bit of rascal in him. Shortly before graduation, he and several close friends attended a showing of Cecil B. DeMille's *The Ten Commandments.* Belli said, "It was pretty impressive seeing all ten of the commandments coming out of clouds and lightning and all, but after that smashing opening it really was more fun watching Gloria Swanson taking a milk bath right on the screen."

After the film the boys flocked to the Belli home. They popped the corks on several of Caesar Belli's finest bottles of wine and helped themselves to his collection of liquor. Belli later said, "I was brutally attacked by a bottle of whiskey." Drunk to the point of falling down, the boys lumbered over to the offices of *The Guard and Tackle,* where they decided that heaving wastebaskets out of a window was great fun.

Garrison, the principal, didn't agree. The next morning, he telephoned the Belli house and was told that because "he isn't feeling well, little Melvin won't be in today." Exasperated the principal informed Melvin's mother of his exploits and told her that her son was suspended. That meant no valedictorian honors, and worse, no diploma.

Though Caesar attempted to save his son by pleading with the principal, his efforts were fruitless. But Melvin was about to learn a lesson. The next stop in the pursuit of his diploma was the office of Judge Rutherford, who Melvin described as "red veined," with a "whisky nose and a beer belly."

"You have been wronged," he told the boy. Since the judge obviously had a soft spot for those who liked to take a sip or two, he was sympathetic to Melvin's plight. "[He] started rummaging around the whiskey bottles in his rolltop desk," Belli recalled, "looking for a bunch of legal forms. He hauled out a couple of writs, a replevin, a bench warrant, a subpoena duces tecum, a habeas corpus, a habeas diploma, and a handful of bail bonds. He stuck them all together with notary public seals and a red ribbon . . . and served them on the principal. I got my diploma on the spot."

Belli was amazed at the result, saying, "It was the most majestic legal encounter of my entire life." Whether the encounter led him to become a lawyer depends on when Belli told the story.

"In truth, I really don't know when I decided," he explained. "I think I always wanted to be a lawyer. . . . Lawyers were leaders. Lawyers would settle disputes. Lawyers would do the talking. Lawyers would square things for those who didn't have the heat to do it for themselves."

A MODEL-T FORD transported eighteen-year-old Melvin Belli to his college of choice, the University of California at Berkeley. Two days later he was nearly sent home.

Belli, by then a strapping young man, and four childhood chums were walking through campus when they noticed older students harassing one of Melvin's friends, a Chinese student named Sooey Ng. To humiliate the boy, the older students were dabbing war paint on his body.

Belli and friend Harry Cobden unsuccessfully attempted to persuade the troublemakers to cease the hazing. A fight broke out, and before long, other students joined the melee. "They finally had to call out the campus gendarmes," Belli recalled, "and the local fire department, who used high-pressure hoses to break it up."

The dean of students wasn't pleased, stating, "You men aren't even an official part of the student body and already you've started a riot." He sent them directly to the home of the university's president, General Barrow. Taking pity on the boys, he placed them on probation with the stipulation that they care for Thunderhead, his snow-white mare. The altercation demonstrated Belli's distaste for anyone taking advantage or making fun of another.

Back home his father was experiencing financial woes. With his investments spread too thin, Caesar lost his bank holdings and was forced to become a salesman to make a living.

Witnessing his father's financial demise provoked interesting emotions in young Belli. Asked later to comment on Caesar's troubles, he said, "My father must have gone through a couple of million dollars. I don't know exactly how he did it. But he did it with aplomb. I didn't understand money then, and I still don't."

Caesar's monetary woes meant Melvin had to seek employment. In addition to the fifteen dollars a month he earned for participation in the ROTC program, he made money by selling Real Silk hosiery door to door. He also waited tables at his Delta Tau Delta fraternity house and spent time as a soda jerk at a local drug store. Displaying the savvy that later marked his legal career, Belli wrote to companies soliciting free samples of soap and shaving cream. He then sold the goods to his fraternity brothers.

Belli boasted that a great source of income during this time was produced by his willingness to eat, of all things, moths. "I would pop one into my mouth and swallow the dusty little creature," he explained. "Then I'd take up a collection and pull in a couple of dollars [for them] to see Belli eat another moth. I would down a shot of whiskey afterward in the fervent hope that the whiskey would kill any plague virus, but I lost my job as entertainment captain the night that Joe Chase . . . topped my act by eating a slug."

Belli was an average student, earning Bs and Cs. Despite his lack of academic excellence, he was gaining quite an education, albeit away from the classroom. One instructor was Colonel Edward Pettis, an Army Air Corps reservist who loved to fly. He took Belli up in a DeHavilland plane and presto—a daredevil was born.

"Once Ed tried to see how much I could take," Belli recalled. "He did a series of stunts: Immelmans, barrel rolls, loops. I loved it. Then he did a dizzying spin down, down, down, right straight toward Alcatraz, and pulled out at what I thought was about the nick of time. It seemed I could have spit in the yard."

On the ground Belli was just as daring as he was in the air. When the suggestion was made during a late-night party at his fraternity house that someone run around the block bare naked, Belli volunteered. Ten dollars was quickly solicited to bolster the dare.

When Belli dashed from the fraternity house, he did not realize that his brothers had called as many other fraternity and sorority houses as possible to warn them of the show. Within minutes a line of cars was stationed along the route with headlights glaring. Police who learned of the escapade chased Belli the last hundred yards or so, but he ran into the fraternity house, grabbed his clothes, and kept right on running out the back.

On another occasion, he wasn't so lucky. Striding through Chinatown with a classmate, he suddenly grabbed a live turkey, yanked it from its cage, and sped away on foot. The shopkeeper screamed after him in Chinese. Bystanders who understood that the screaming meant "Stop thief, stop thief, he stole the bird" collared the youngster and his friend.

The dean of students decided Belli's actions were "conduct unbecoming a student of the university" and placed him on probation for a year. He was just as upset that he was not allowed to defend his actions as he was with the punishment. He believed it was "an example of how institutions supposedly dedicated to the higher arts of civilization have always been prone to deny such elementary rights as due process of law."

Irving Symons, Belli's grammar school buddy, said Belli wasn't afraid to try anything. "He and I double-dated in my Chrysler," Symons said. "We took the girls to San Francisco, but there were no bridges in those days and we missed the ferry boat home. When we arrived on campus, it was 2:00 AM and the girls couldn't get in their sorority house. To gain the attention of the housemother, Mel knocked on the door and said in a dark tone, 'It's the strangler,' and then ran away. I'm sure he scared her since there was a strangler loose in Oakland. But she let the girls in, and Mel, who always did the spectacular, had saved the day."

According to Belli, studying was never a priority. He did, however, continue to read voraciously, and much of his time was spent in the Emerson Shakespearean Library. Belli was always curious, and the knowledge he gained from books became fodder for many of the great speeches he gave in the courtroom.

Having graduated from the University of California in June 1929, at age twenty-two, Melvin Belli knew for certain he wanted to study law. He just wasn't sure where.

BEFORE CHOOSING A law school, Melvin Belli was determined to see the world. Learning that the S.S. *Kentuckian* was seeking twenty-five-dollar-a-month seamen, he applied and was hired. Their destination: New York City.

Belli said that he matured as much during the voyage on the *Kentuckian* as he had in all his previous days on earth. When word leaked out that he was a "college boy," superiors made certain that he received the dirtiest jobs on board. He was given the task of reeling in a heavy anchor chain while standing in what was called the "chain locker." Belli said he was required to grab the chain with a "big steel hook" as it came tumbling in. The more the chain draped, the less room there was in the locker.

"There were stories all over the seven seas about guys who had been mangled by the slipping chain," Belli said. "And my partner Ernesto, a Chilean, didn't make me feel any safer. He was a wild man flailing around in that hot locker with his hook. After the ordeal was over, Ernesto hugged me and kissed me on the neck. You would think we had just gone over Niagara Falls together in a barrel and survived."

Belli hoped to see the Panama Canal during the trip, but the boatswain kept him below deck. Regardless, a photograph he displayed in his book *The Law Revolt* portrayed a skinny kid standing on the bow of the ship with two oil drums behind him. He wore gloves, a sleeveless T-shirt, and grubby jeans that had been rolled up above the ankles. The caption to the photo read, "Melvin Belli, as an able-bodied seaman, 1929, Panama Canal Zone."

Days later the young college graduate was standing in the middle of Manhattan. "I just stood there taking it all in," he recalled. "The buildings, the billboards, the theater marquees; God, the people—all kinds of shapes and faces, some of them hurrying along, some taking their time, some extremely pretty girls [actresses, I imagined], some hard-looking hookers, some street types trying to sell everything from mechanical dogs to hot watches, and lots of cops."

At Yankee Stadium, Belli watched Babe Ruth hit a two-run homer to beat the Detroit Tigers. That evening, he enjoyed "the nose that knows," Jimmy Durante, at the piano.

Not satisfied with simply sampling the largest city in the United States, Belli the adventurer boarded a ship for Europe. After docking he rode the train to Berlin, then bought a motorcycle and raced across Germany. Train and bus trips provided days in Budapest and Prague as well. He sailed up the Danube as far as Belgrade.

A more experienced young man arrived in San Francisco as the summer of 1929 lapsed into fall. A brokerage house hired him as a board marker until the stock market began to fail.

Returning to adventure, Belli sailed to the Orient on the S.S. *McKinley*. He docked in Tokyo where he recalled "buying Johnny Walker for fifteen cents." At the Astor Hotel in Shanghai, Belli and a friend from Massachusetts feasted on "caviar, oysters, lobster, crab, venison, guinea hen, pheasant, steak, and crepe suzettes," while enjoying "fine wine, champagne, and music," all for two dollars each.

When the maître d' mentioned "desserts," Belli's eyes lit up. For an additional five dollars, a beautiful woman would appear for "companionship." Later he said, "Ludmila and Natasha were White Russians; they were almost too much for us. Beautifully coifed and dressed in long, white gowns, full-breasted and long-legged, accomplished during dinner in the art of good conversation, inventive later in the art of love." Natasha suggested that Belli commemorate the occasion by having a tattoo artist imprint a rose on his derriere. After considerable thought, Belli refused the offer.

In a short period of time Belli had experienced the world beyond California. Now he was ready to tackle law school, and become the attorney whose brilliance would astound those who witnessed his courtroom magic.

2

YOUNG BELLI

IN 1930, AS the United States wallowed in the first year of the Great Depression, Melvin Belli walked through the gates of one of the most prestigious law schools in the nation. The school, Boalt Hall, was located at the University of California at Berkeley.

Belli floundered at first, earning Cs in torts and contracts. These poor grades stiffened his resolve, and from that point on, it was nothing but high marks for the driven young man. The carefree, don't-give-a-damn-about-studying Belli metamorphosed into a workhorse. "I worked from eight in the morning until the library closed at 11 PM," he recalled. "I worked Saturdays and holidays and right through the summers." By the time he graduated, Belli ranked fourteenth in a class of forty-nine. He was most proud of the straight As he earned in criminal law and property.

Legal history was particularly fascinating to the budding attorney. Belli learned the rule of law from several of the finest professors in the country: Ballantine on torts, McBain on evidence, Kidd on crimes. He also studied international law and bills and notes. "I took every course they had to offer," he said. "[And] I spent my spare time in the stacks, perusing old books on common law history, Roman law, and oddities of the law. I loved a well-turned legal expression from medieval times—when the profession was classical and esoteric."

Surprisingly, Belli swore that at the time he had little interest in courtroom legalistics. "I had no desire to see a trial or haunt the courtrooms," he recalled.

By 1933 he danced the night away armed with a law degree. He was twenty-five years old.

Instead of studying for the bar exam, Belli opted to accept a job that would further educate him about the trials and tribulations of the common man. He would see firsthand what suffering was all about.

The job, which paid $75 per month, gave him a chuckle when he first heard about it. "We're going to be bums for the NRA," classmate Warren Olney told him.

"The NRA?" Belli asked, bewildered.

"The National Recovery Administration," Olney replied, "It's one of those new agencies in Washington. Roosevelt says we've got nothing to fear but fear itself. But the NRA is scared of a revolution in this country and they need more information."

Belli and Olney jumped a freight train toward San Jose. They adopted new names and wore old clothes to give them the "bum" look. Belli was Louis Bacigalupi, "Slim" for short; Olney was Bill Brucker. Belli later quipped, "I was loath to become a 'government spy,' and if there was a revolution, I might just have joined up. But I needed the dough."

Spying on the "Okies," as Belli dubbed them, was a clandestine mission. Working undercover meant he was given a secret Los Angeles telephone number to report incidents of violence. He said he never used it, though he witnessed Los Angeles police clubbing "black, poor Okies" for simply attempting to include their names on the relief rolls or begging for food.

Hopping from train to train, Belli joined the ranks of Clark Gable, James Dean, Ernest Hemingway, and other famous personalities who rode the rails. He saw poor souls out of work and suffering. With no homes and no jobs, they were a common sight along the railroad.

Years later Belli recalled lessons learned while working for the NRA. "I guess that might have been the time when I started identifying with the underdog and the outcast in a real way." Later, he echoed those thoughts in *Playboy* magazine: "Moving out and about then, riding in and on and underneath freight cars, 'bumming,' standing in soup lines, sleeping in skid-row 'jungles,' I developed my deep strong sympathy for the underdog and the outcast."

★ ★ ★

SHORTLY AFTER HE left the NRA, Melvin Belli married his first wife, Elizabeth "Betty" Ballantine, a pert Kappa Alpha Theta at Berkeley and the daughter of Henry Winthrop Ballantine, one of Belli's tort law professors.

Betty was an attractive lady with happy eyes and high cheekbones, who developed an affection for plumed hats. She was described by daughter Jeanne as "very feminine, a gentle soul." She told Jeanne she was attracted to the debonair young lawyer like a "magnet."

The lovebirds drove to Reno, Nevada, in a Model-T and were married before a justice of the peace. The year was 1933. Betty accepted a job with Traveler's Aid that paid twenty-five dollars a month.

Belli barely passed the bar exam on his first try in 1933, having decided that he didn't need to study. Soon after he was hired to work for a lawyer he dubbed "Winston." The position, which paid fifty dollars a month, required that the budding lawyer represent the interests of insurance companies.

Belli quickly learned that Winston was basically incompetent, and worse, a crook. When the old lawyer was forced to win a case or risk losing insurance company business, Belli heard him tell the doctor involved in the case, "Where it says six months disability, put three, instead of saying muscle spasms, put feigned muscle spasms, where you say the woman had some pain, say she 'simulated' pain and then add our old clincher: when you watched her put on her coat after the examination, she showed no evidence of pain."

After learning of Winston's crooked practices, Belli quickly quit the job. He packed up and joined a noted criminal defense attorney. The pay was twenty-five dollars a month. At Christmas the attorney presented the young lawyer with a five-dollar bonus. Belli said he and another associate "got drunk, spent all our money except eighty-five cents, and returned that to our boss as our Christmas present. He was delighted."

By 1936, Belli had set up an office at the California Racing Board. "I had two orange crates for a desk with a plank between them," he recalled, "and an old campstool for a chair—and no one to represent."

Belli's first solo case came as a referral from his father. Realizing his son was sinking into financial hell, he told a young couple charged with murder that Melvin would gladly take their case.

The accused were Hazel Terman, the foul-mouthed wife of a rancher, and her boyfriend, David Pike. They had allegedly hired a hitman named

"Happy Ed" Williams to shoot Hazel's husband square between the eyes. Happy Ed's aim with a 30–30 rifle was perfect.

Belli's first challenge was to decide whether he could represent clients who had committed the acts for which they were charged. He knew that many lawyers declined to represent the "guilty." In his mind, that determination wasn't proper. "It is the jury's problem to determine the degree of legal guilt—not mine," he said.

David Pike's defense would be waged on the grounds that he was insane at the time of the killing. "He had to be nuts to be in love with Hazel," the young lawyer surmised, "and so I had psychiatrists examine him."

The shrinks agreed, and so did the jury. David was shipped off to Mendocino State Hospital. Belli's first case was not only lost, he failed to earn a fee. The struggling lawyer took on a second client, Donald Streeter, also charged with murder.

Belli won with a "not guilty by reason of insanity" verdict, but again, the Streeter case produced no income. However, the publicity surrounding the trial caused Father George O'Meara, the Catholic chaplain at San Quentin prison, to contact him. Little did he know that meeting Father O'Meara would change the course of his legal career.

The Catholic priest wanted legal representation for the killers, robbers, and thieves that inhabited San Quentin. Surrounded by barbed wire, the dirty yellow prison in Marin County, California, housed the worst of society's scum.

Father O'Meara made it clear that defending convicted men would neither ingratiate the young lawyer with those of moralistic attitude, nor provide him with any income. But he caught Belli's attention when he said, "Some of the cases you'll likely get here will help make your name known, maybe bring you some business, who knows? To get people into the church, you've got to ring the bell."

Instantly the first publicity of his career came Belli's way.

Several convicts had rioted in the prison, intent on escaping. Using guns that had been smuggled into the fortress, the prisoners took their guards hostage.

Two of the inmates, Alexander McKay and Joe Kristy, decided they needed a more important hostage. They barged into the warden's office where he was meeting with the parole board. One inmate hit the warden on the head, then forced him and two parole board members into a car. They raced away from the prison before order could be restored, but were quickly captured.

Shortly thereafter, Belli was leaving San Quentin when Father O'Meara whispered, "Mel, they don't have much of a chance and sure as the Pope's in Rome they'll hang. But you'll fight for them, hear?" Belli nodded and shook the priest's hand.

Belli's growth as a lawyer was noticeable not only in his choice of cases, but also in his courtroom demeanor. Early on he had been reserved, unwilling to challenge the court even when he felt his clients were being unfairly treated. This all changed during the defense of the "San Quentin Two."

The trial's defining moment came during Belli's cross-examination. While he was heatedly questioning a witness, he noticed that the judge, a man named Butler, had risen from the bench and was pacing back and forth behind it. Upset at the discourtesy, Belli told Judge Butler, "Very respectfully, your Honor, this is very disconcerting to me and the jury. I know you may be uncomfortable during this cross-examination, but it is very distracting to me, a young lawyer trying to do his best."

The judge was known for being bombastic toward irreverent attorneys. Seconds passed in silence as the room awaited a response. The judge simply sat down, saying softly, "Mr. Belli, would you please see me in chambers after we adjourn?"

At day's end, expecting a tongue-lashing or contempt of court citation, Belli stood before the judge. Judge Butler began by saying, "Mr. Belli, of all the young men who've been before me in the past twenty years. . . ." Then he hesitated, continuing with the words, "You, Mr. Belli, have the makings of a great trial lawyer."

Belli swore he didn't smile at the unexpected compliment, but surely his heart began beating again. Armed with confidence, he marched out of the judge's chambers ready to free his clients from the clutches of the law.

It didn't happen. The jury ruled the defendants guilty on several counts and sentenced them to death.

Belli was determined to go the extra mile for his clients. Not only did he file the applicable appeals, but when they were unsuccessful, he placed a transatlantic telephone call to the London office of British Foreign Minister Anthony Eden. He requested that Eden intervene on behalf of

McKay, a British subject. To Belli's surprise the foreign minister did just that, placing a call to the governor of California.

That act brought media attention to Belli's doorstep. He did not attempt to fight it off. He held the first of his thousands of news conferences at his sparse offices at the California Racing Board. The next day a photograph with the caption "Melvin Belli, Attorney at Law" ran in the *San Francisco Examiner*.

Nevertheless, there was nothing Belli, Anthony Eden, or anyone else could do to save the San Quentin Two. Belli and Father O'Meara met with the condemned men the day before they were to be hanged. While O'Meara comforted them, Belli stood transfixed as he watched carpenters finish building the gallows and check the nooses to make sure the knots were tight. To the side, he spied two wooden coffins, ready for use.

THE NEXT DAY, Belli returned to San Quentin for the hangings. "There was a smell of death and sweat and uneaten meals in the air," he recalled. "The rain was still beating on the roof and an old scratchy phonograph played *Clair du Lune*, one of the last requests of the condemned."

Belli, to the disdain of a prison guard, said a final good-bye. "So long Mac. So long Joe," he uttered as the two men were positioned on top of the trapdoors. Moments later the trapdoors opened, and the two men fell to their deaths. Belli would admit he experienced nightmares after the death of his clients.

Days later, during a San Francisco Press Club dinner, he was introduced to the district attorney of Alameda County, a man named Earl Warren. Warren was running for attorney general of the State of California and would eventually become chief justice of the U.S. Supreme Court.

Warren delivered a lengthy speech to the press club, in the preface of which he described Belli as "a comer." He joked that when the two inmates at San Quentin had been hanged, "Belli had lost half his law practice." Reacting immediately, Belli said, "Mr. District Attorney isn't telling the truth. I had my whole practice wiped out." He later told reporter Ken Kelley that his early defeats caused him to have "a batting average worse than Willie Mays with the crabs."

Belli would become a staunch opponent of the death penalty. "There was already too much brutality in the world," he said. Belli also told *Playboy* magazine, "I don't favor institutional vengeance under *any* circumstances. Who in God's name has the right to pass judgment on the life of another human being?" He added, "Who is to usurp this divine pre-rogative? Only primitive minds sanction this kind of barbarity. Just look at the creeps who are in favor of it; you get the feeling they want to be the ones to pull the switch."

True to that credo, he later filed a writ for a death-row inmate named Billy Smith. He witnessed the insensitivity of a Supreme Court judge when he encountered him at the Senator Hotel in Sacramento and pleaded for Smith's life. Belli said the judge told him it was too late; the young man had already been executed. He then added, according to Belli, "'Have some of these wonderful bacon and eggs.' And then he laughed."

Based on early experiences like this one, Belli decided to become a crusader for those who needed a sturdy ally. In the years ahead, he was determined to build a reputation as a lawyer never afraid of a challenge.

IN 1938, JUST before Christmas, Caesar Belli passed away. A career in criminal defense might have been in store for the young lawyer had it not been for the circumstances surrounding his father's death.

Officially, Caesar died of pneumonia, but the cause of death troubled Melvin. Further investigation revealed that a local drugstore had filled a prescription for Caesar shortly before he died. The medicine, a new drug called sulfanilamide, was correct, but the dosage was wrong. Surprisingly Belli did not take action. "I should have sued," he said later, "But I did what most people did then; I let them get away with it."

Regardless, the incident planted a seed in Belli's mind. He had decided that being a criminal defense lawyer, while it had merit, wasn't precisely what he wanted to do for the rest of his life. The stress and strain of the occupation had caused severe stomachaches (later diagnosed as a duodenal ulcer) and migraine headaches that threatened to incapacitate him. These would continue as the years passed.

In an interview with author Arthur Sheresky, Belli explained, "I got to the point in criminal law where I realized that if I stayed in it I would have ended up in the bucket [jail] because everybody was bribing every-body. The cops in San Francisco were arresting people and then going to jail bond brokers and lawyers and telling them for five hundred dol-lars, they would swear that it was so dark that they couldn't really see what happened. The defendant then got off."

"I really wanted to get into the civil side [of the law]," Belli said. "Specifically into the field of personal injury. I felt that our economic system [like our criminal system] was stacked against the little man." He knew that he could best serve the public by targeting what he saw as its biggest problems: insurance companies. Belli later wrote, "The insurance companies . . . took in unbelievable amounts of the public's money—billions of dollars each year. Ostensibly, the public was buying protection. But the insurance-company executives seemed to forget they were holding other people's money in trust. They had come to regard that money as theirs and they would be damned if they'd give it up without a struggle, or even account for it."

Belli was enthusiastic, but realistic when he considered a career as a personal injury attorney. "It just didn't pay," he explained. "In personal-injury cases, the lawyer got one-third if he won the case and nothing if he lost—a real gamble, in which the payoffs were low and late coming." He soon found a way to increase his chances for success—and in the process, made legal history.

3

A COURTROOM REVOLUTION

IN 1940, ADOLF Hitler invaded Norway and Denmark; Winston Churchill gave his famous "blood, toil, tears, and sweat" speech; and Franklin Delano Roosevelt was elected to a third term as president of the United States. And on a rainy day in San Francisco, another man was about to make history.

Few realized it at the time, but when thirty-three-year-old attorney Melvin Belli accepted the Ernie Smith murder case, he was poised to permanently affect how evidence was presented in criminal trials and personal injury cases.

The charge against Ernie Smith, a young black inmate with a record as thick as a telephone book, was murder one. Prosecutors alleged he had brutally murdered fellow inmate Arthur "Artie" Ruis in the prison exercise yard by repeatedly kicking him in the head.

Belli first met Smith in a San Quentin visiting room. His initial reaction was to typecast him. "I didn't know what a killer 'looked like,'" Belli recalled, "but this guy fit the stereotype: glowering eyes, overworked maxillaries, pouty lips. I thought I could see R-A-G-E in every pore of his being."

When the attorney asked Smith for his version of the confrontation, the convict insisted that he acted in self-defense. He defiantly told Belli that when Ruis attacked him with a makeshift knife, he yanked it away, and in the ensuing struggle, stomped Ruis to death to protect his own life.

Smith swore his version was true, but Belli had his doubts. The lawyer informed his client that unless he told the truth, their defense was doomed. More than likely, he believed, a jury would find his client guilty and sentence him to be executed in the gas chamber. So certain were prison officials of the outcome that they had already transferred Smith to death row.

While exiting the prison after the visit, Belli asked one of the guards if it was possible for an inmate to possess a knife. To his shock, the guard said, "We let them have the little ones, but . . ."

The guard then opened a drawer full of what Belli later characterized as "the most evil collection of weapons I'd ever seen: broken saw blades, files, tire irons that had been sharpened down, bedsprings made into twisted daggers." At trial Belli would add "makeshift knives" and "pig-stickers" to the list. He immediately subpoenaed the drawer.

The revelation convinced Belli to change his opinion of his client's chances. "Ernie Smith's defense suddenly became dramatically plausible," he later told reporters.

Midway through the trial, a San Quentin prison guard's face glistened with sweat as stone-faced Belli peppered him with rapid-fire questions, educating the jury on life at America's famous home for society's misfits.

Having established a "kill or be killed" atmosphere, Belli turned to his counsel table and picked up a large wooden desk drawer. He continued questioning the guard as he approached the jury. Ever the showman, he hugged the drawer to his chest as if it was his client's only chance. It was.

The key to the trial, Belli knew, was to shock the jury into agreeing with Smith's self-defense claim. To make his point, he asked the guard whether inmates had easy access to weapons. When the guard said, "No, but we find them anyway," Belli stepped ever closer to the twelve men and women whose eyes were suddenly focused on the mysterious desk drawer.

Spectators held their breath, the prosecutor craned his neck in anticipation of a strenuous objection, and the judge peered down from his bench. Belli neared the railing. Just before he reached it, he stumbled. The drawer catapulted into the air. When it landed, knives and other makeshift weapons clanged on the hardwood floor and ricocheted in every direction.

Jurors gasped, spectators oohed and aahed, the prosecutor bellowed, "I object," and the judge pounded his gavel to restore order. All while Belli, beaming with satisfaction, emphasized his point by slowly retrieving each weapon as if it were a priceless heirloom. He carefully dropped them back in the drawer as jurors leaned over the railing to have a closer look.

The next day the front page of the *San Francisco Chronicle* featured a photograph of Belli accompanied by an article detailing his courtroom victory. A media star was in the making. More important the use of what would be dubbed "demonstrative evidence" had been born.

Regarding his experiences using demonstrative evidence, Belli said, "I had learned a valuable lesson: That jurors learn through all their senses, and if you can tell them and show them too, let them see and feel and even taste or smell the evidence, then you will reach the jury."

Belli sought an opportunity to challenge the theory in civil court. He got the chance when Edmund "Pat" Brown, San Francisco's district attorney, requested that Belli represent Chester Bryant, a gripman for the Market Street Railway Company. Bryant had been severely injured when the iron grip that held his cable car to its power cable snapped and hit him in the stomach.

Belli called veteran gripmen as witnesses to detail what had occurred at the corner of Powell and O'Farrell streets. But Belli, recalling the Ernie Smith case, had bigger ideas.

He argued that the cause of the grip snapping was malfeasance on the part of the gripman operating on an adjacent run. When he had improperly released his grip, Belli theorized, it had caused Bryant's grip to shoot back at him. The challenge was to re-create the accident.

"I spent three hundred dollars to have a craftsman build a big scale mock-up of the Powell-O'Farrell intersection, cable cars and all," Belli recalled. "The model was bigger than a king-sized bed, but I brought it into the courtroom, and a full-sized gearbox too."

Judge Griffin, presiding over the case, ruled for Belli when defense counsel objected to the model. Days later, Belli knew he had a winner.

"When I saw the jurors leave the jury box and pore over the model and examine the gearbox and the grips," Belli said, "I saw frowns turn to smiles of understanding. The light dawned on me, too. Now I saw how demonstrative evidence in a personal-injury case could turn the tide in favor of the injured."

Once again, over the objection of what he called "the railroad lawyers," the spirited barrister rolled a blackboard into the courtroom. Realizing he had captured the attention of the jurors, Belli, for what was believed to be the first time in history, "chalked up" his client's medical expenses, adding an amount for current and future suffering. The budding lawyer's mind set after the Bryant case was, "What else can we offer a personal-injury victim but money?" He said, "We have nothing that will make the man or woman who is permanently injured whole again, nothing that will help him walk without a limp, nothing but drugs to let him sleep without pain."

The jury awarded Chester $31,883.25. More important, Belli had proven that demonstrative evidence was a critical part of any lawyer's arsenal.

The effects of Belli's exploits in the courtroom reached beyond San Francisco as far as New York City and Dallas. Despite his youth Melvin Belli was becoming a force in the legal world.

In 1944, the thirty-seven-year-old barrister published an article titled, "The Adequate Award and Demonstrative Evidence," in the *California Law Review*. Judges and lawyers across the country read of his trial court achievements. The impact was immediate: Both plaintiff and defense lawyers incorporated the California attorney's ideas into their trial strategies.

Most important, Belli's use of demonstrative evidence permitted juries to better understand the case being litigated before them, significantly improving the machinations of the legal system. Soon a bevy of legalistic "helpers"—enlarged X-rays, color photographs, wooden scale models—began to appear in courtrooms. This change in courtroom procedure was becoming a most important element of Melvin Belli's legacy, and he had not yet reached his fortieth birthday.

WITHIN MONTHS BELLI found another occasion to experiment with his new strategy. This time the legal weapon was an L-shaped package, and the client was not a convict but the sad wife of a Navy commander.

Belli was representing Katherine Jeffers, a rotund young mother with pigtails. She had been severely injured while stepping off a cable car on Market Street in downtown San Francisco, in an area where four trolleys ran side by side. Struck by a trolley, her right leg had been shattered and was amputated below the knee.

During trial, Belli ran his fingers through his thick black hair and pondered what the case was worth. Models had been built to depict the accident. Jurors could clearly see liability on the part of the Municipal Railroad and the city and county of San Francisco for inadequate safety precautions. Based on his observations, Belli believed a jury verdict might warrant $50,000.

He was $15,000 short: The jury decided poor Katherine's injury was worth $65,000. "Nobody has ever gotten that much for a leg," Belli told the press.

But the insurance company representing the Municipal Railroad disagreed with the "clearly excessive" verdict and appealed. To Belli's chagrin, they won.

Belli believed that during the first trial he had not been able to impress enough the incredible physical and emotional damage that the loss of the leg caused Katherine. He believed he had let his client down and was determined not to do so a second time.

Sitting in his office, Belli envisioned the answer. Again, he decided to "show," not "tell" the jury what the future held for his client. Summoning his secretary, he made a most unusual request.

While his secretary searched for the item, Belli stopped at a local grocery store, where he procured a length of butcher's paper. When he returned to the office, the secretary had saved her job by locating the object Belli requested. He wrapped it in butcher's paper and walked briskly toward the courthouse.

The package was a daily sight for the remainder of the trial. Each day Belli entered the courtroom with a briefcase, law books, and the two-foot long package. He placed the package on the table in front of him, within full view of the jury, judge, and opposing counsel. "What is that?" everyone wondered. It couldn't possibly be the remnants of Katherine's leg, they whispered. Could it?

For three days, Belli kept the courtroom guessing, fussing with the package, but never mentioning to it. Having piqued their curiosity, he decided it was time to act.

"I knew the package was drawing more attention," Belli later recalled. "I could see the jurors sizing up my client, dressed in demure gingham, her one good leg in a black stocking, and then shifting their gaze to the L-shaped package and whispering among themselves."

The defense argument Belli faced had been predictable. Opposing counsel John Moran explained that while the injury was tragic, modern technology permitted those who had suffered the loss of a limb to lead a normal life. Downplaying the significance of her emotional trauma, he maintained that Katherine could dance, work, and even make love.

When it was time to rebut defense claims, Belli slowly picked up the package and moved closer to the jury box.

Belli cut the string dramatically. Then, as he spoke in hushed, emotional tones about his client and what her future might really be like, he began to unravel the paper.

One layer after another fell to the floor. Belli paced in front of the jurors, their eyes following him back and forth. Not a sound was heard as Belli's voice held the room in thrall. He milked the moment for all it was worth.

As Belli uttered "Ladies and gentleman of the jury, this is what my pretty young client will wear for the rest of her life," he violently ripped off the final sheet of paper. There, for all to see, was Katherine's off-white artificial limb.

The jurors gasped at the curious object, but Belli, ever bolder, dropped the artificial leg squarely in the lap of juror #1. As she winced in shock, he said, "Here, take it. Feel the warmth of life in the soft tissues of its flesh, feel the pulse of the blood as it flows through its veins, feel the marvelous smooth articulation at the new joint and touch the rippling muscles of the calf. Don't be alarmed by all of the laces and harnesses and straps and the grating of the metal. My client is no longer alarmed."

Tears dotted Katherine's eyes as she watched Belli's performance. The jurors stared at her as they passed the prosthesis between them. From their startled looks, Belli knew he had hit a home run.

Hours later the jury awarded Katherine $100,000, a huge sum at the time. When a reporter asked, "What were you thinking when she [Katherine] had her head bowed and the tears dropped on her cheeks," Belli, his legend spreading already, quipped, "I could hear the angels sing and the cash register ring."

Those cash registers rang again and again as Belli, the crusty barrister with a little-boy grin, continued to build his legal practice.

Following the Jeffers case, Belli represented Jeanette Gluckstein, a dress designer with an English accent. To improve her appearance and charm potential beaus, she had decided to increase the size of her breasts.

Unfortunately, Jeanette employed a surgeon who had the artistry of an auto mechanic. "I had plastic surgery on my breasts, and they're ruined," she sobbed to her counsel.

When the lovely, young Ms. Gluckstein removed her blouse and brassiere, the lawyer's face stiffened. "She looked like a Picasso nude," Belli recalled. "Both breasts were almost square. One was obviously larger than the other, the nipples had been sliced off and transposed higher than they should have been and the nipples looked inward. In addition, she had a large gash running from her breasts to her pubes." The doctor had assured his client she would have "the breasts of a virgin."

Belli decided to sue for a quarter-million dollars—an unheard of amount of money at the time. Lloyds of London, the doctor's insurer, balked at the amount. A trial was scheduled.

Expert testimony indicating the physician's incompetence was provided by a gentleman whom Belli referred to as "Clean Him Up" Smith, a reference to Dr. Smith's affection for liquor and Belli's need to sober him up. He was known at the time as a "plaintiff's doctor," having testified against physicians in twenty-odd trials. He was either an asset or a liability, depending on his level of sobriety.

Though Smith proved to be a valuable witness, Belli wasn't convinced that his testimony had riveted the jury. Nor was he convinced that the color photographs of Ms. Gluckstein's mangled breasts had the impact he intended.

But Belli had an idea. If he could bring a drawer full of weapons from San Quentin into court or wave an artificial leg in front of a jury, why couldn't he display Jeanette's breasts? The more he thought about it, the more he liked it.

The next morning, Belli marched into the judge's chambers. Without even a "good morning," he boldly stated, "Your Honor, I want your permission to have my client strip down in open court."

As the judge nearly choked in shock and the defense counsel made objections, Belli waited for a decision. After reviewing both sides of the argument, the judge said, "A jury maybe, but not an entire courtroom."

Belli was jubilant; Jeanette was not. She had been humiliated and embarrassed having photographs of her breasts displayed in court. She finally agreed when she was issued an ultimatum: If she didn't follow Belli's instructions, she could find herself another lawyer.

When the time came, Jeanette was led into the judge's chamber. As a female bailiff stood by, she removed her blouse. She was then covered with a sheet, which was lowered each time a juror passed by. Belli noted each juror's expression. Several, he noticed, winced as they saw the damage done to naked, shaking Jeanette, who had tears running down her cheeks.

The end result of Jeanette's display was another $100,000-plus verdict. Belli told *Time* magazine, "I figure the case was worth $30,000 a tear." He had struck again.

* * *

IN A CASE involving a young man dubbed "The Fattest Man in the World," Belli didn't even wait to get into the courtroom before employing demonstrative evidence. His client weighed 682 pounds. Belli said, "I couldn't see where his face left off and his shoulders began." The padding didn't help him when he fell off an extra-extra-extra-large chair in Long Beach, California. An hour, five firefighters, and extensive grunting later, the "Fattest Man" had been righted, rolled into a large van, and transported to the hospital. It took several orderlies to maneuver him into a room on the first floor.

When Belli entered the hospital, he asked a nurse where he could find his client. "Is he in a bed?" the barrister asked. The nurse replied, "No, he is in *two* beds." Belli checked, and sure enough, his client was lying on two beds that had been wired together.

Belli suspected his client had a herniated disc, but hospital officials denied the obese man X-rays, arguing that they wouldn't be able to penetrate his thick layers of flesh. The manufacturer of the X-ray table also warned, "We advise against tilting the table with this ponderous person on it."

Doctors decided exploratory surgery, to be performed by Dr. Peter Lindstrom, was needed. Belli's description of the event was classic: "The doctor couldn't take the man into the operating room because he would fall over the sides of the operating table like butter on a hot day. . . . The incision was a foot and half long. It took eight hours, and the man was administered a local anesthesia during the surgery, sitting up, because they couldn't lay him down on the operating table. Later, Dr. Lindstrom said, 'It was like a mine down there.'"

Dr. Lindstrom's analysis was that Belli's client suffered from "evidence of glioma or a possible malignancy." The insurance companies being sued offered $1,400. Refusing the sum, Belli prepared for trial, and with it, the adventure of transporting his client to the courtroom.

"It was like landing in Okinawa," Bell said, "We couldn't get him there by ambulance [so we] got a large moving van. We put the nurse and all the equipment and the bed pan and everything else in it."

When the squeaky-voiced insurance adjuster saw the moving van stop in front of the courthouse, he found Belli and increased the settlement offer to $3,500. Belli said, "nothing doing," and moved on to "Phase Two" of his plan to squeeze every cent out of the insurance carrier.

"Phase Two" involved a crane with a fifty-foot boom. As the poor fat man stood before the courthouse steps, golfball-sized beads of sweat dripping off his frame, a seventy-foot-long flatbed truck rounded the corner. The insurance adjuster's eyes nearly popped out of his head. He raced to where Belli was standing surrounded by reporters.

"Seventy-five hundred," he whispered, but Belli simply shook his head and moved toward a stately man who carried a briefcase. He was "Phase Three": A San Francisco city architect who carried the plans for the building. As the adjuster looked on, his suit now stained with perspiration, the architect checked the width, length, and height of the elevators to see if the fat man could fit. He couldn't.

That possibility eliminated, the architect and Belli began debating how to hook the fat man to the crane, lift him six stories to the courtroom floor, and then safely deposit him inside a window that was wide enough to permit entry of his bulk. Halfway through the conversation, the exhausted insurance adjuster opened his briefcase, hurriedly wrote out a check, and said to Belli, "Here's your $10,000. Please let me go home."

BELLI WOULD LATER employ his now-famous technique during a late-1950s run-in with the San Francisco Giants and their owner, Horace Stoneham.

Stoneham had the ingenious idea of installing radiant-heating systems in the Candlestick Park's box seats to keep season-ticket holders warm. Belli had purchased season tickets after seeing the new feature advertised in the Giant's yearbook. The ad promised that the temperature at ground level would be eighty-five degrees.

During a night game Belli attended with lawyer/economist and friend J. Kelly Farris, the stadium's heating system malfunctioned. "I was miserable and so was Mel," Farris said. "I was so fucking cold we left after the third inning and had a hot rum."

Determined to right the wrong and assist his fellow fans, Belli filed suit against Stoneham and the Giants for fraud and breach of warranty, acting as his own client. To prove that asses were freezing, Belli paraded several fans, including Farris, before the court. Each was decked out in long underwear, heavy coats and stocking caps—usual attire, they testified, for a Giants' game.

To emphasize his point, Belli donned an Alaskan parka. "This is the same one I wore to Siberia," he exclaimed. "But I couldn't keep warm in Box 4, Section J, at Candlestick Park."

He summoned officials from the heating company that operated the seat warmers. They helped his case by stating that while the mechanisms worked, the Giants wanted to cut costs, so they made the heaters unworkable.

One witness said, "I've been swimming in the ocean for forty years and I thought I could stand anything, but in those seats it was infernally cold. I nearly froze." The Giants' counsel chastised Belli's grandstanding while the witness testified, stating that "Mr. Belli has been gesturing like a band-leader" throughout the testimony.

The Giants' legal counsel said that it wasn't cold seats that kept fans away from the ballpark, but a bad team. Belli quickly replied, "We're concerned with bad heat, not bad pitching."

During the twenty-seven-minute final argument, onlookers could barely keep their faces straight. There was Belli, still wearing the hooded Alaskan parka, arguing that he was not interested in the fraud count. He just wanted his money returned. The jury, after deliberating only twenty minutes, returned a verdict for $1,597, the cost of his season ticket.

Belli's triumph was front-page news. The *News-Cal Bulletin* ran a story under the headline, "Chilly Belli Beats Giants, 1597–0." The case should have ended there, but Stoneham, described by Belli as "frugal," refused to pay the money. When an appeal was threatened, Belli quipped, "They'd appeal the second serving at the Last Supper."

Determined to collect his bounty, he filed a lien with the court demanding that he be awarded custody of the Giants' "Say Hey Kid," centerfielder Willie Mays, and that Stoneham's prize collection of Scotch be confiscated. Armed with court papers, Sheriff Matthew Carberry ordered deputies to Candlestick Park to guard the liquor and to 344 Spruce Street, where they informed the future Hall of Fame ballplayer, "You have been attached."

The great #24 was dumbfounded when the papers were served to him, telling a reporter, "If Mr. Belli owns me, I hope he has a good ball club." Stoneham, under protest, finally paid—in dollar bills. Belli donated the money to charity.

Chronicle columnist Charles McCabe observed the proceedings. Under the headline "Belli Boffo at City Hall," McCabe captured the true essence of Belli in his prime. He wrote, "Like several other bastions of the San Francisco Bar, Mr. Melvin Belli feels impelled to get on the blower to one or another of the local chatter columnists whenever he makes a pilgrimage to the washroom. He's the kind of guy who would perform in Macy's window, if the wire services were there." Regarding Belli's summation, McCabe said, "It was the greatest bit I've seen since Walter Hampden tore passion to tatters in Richelieu. Never had so much legal talent been wasted on such a minuscule issue. But it was great fun."

McCabe gave an entertaining description of Belli in action: "Mr. Belli, who has the round shrewd face of an Italian lay cardinal, is what you might call a pedantic dresser. He was wearing a staggering gray herringbone double-breasted number with slanty pockets and a magnificent doubt vest in back. His tailor is Anderson and Sheppard of Seville Row. . . . He wore a black tie and matching goggles. He waved the goggles at the jurors like Lennie Bernstein leading the New York Philharmonic."

BELLI'S REPUTATION SPREAD when he represented a fire captain named Fred Williamson, injured when a twelve-ton tractor-trailer rig crashed into his fire truck. He had been standing on the back step with two other firefighters. At impact the captain was thrown sixty feet onto the pavement. A fellow firefighter had to pry open Williamson's broken jaw to free his tongue and prevent suffocation. After being treated at a local hospital, he was transferred to a sanitarium.

The jury was to decide whether the fire truck's siren was on when it passed through the intersection. If it was, the fire truck had the right of way and the tractor-trailer was at fault. If not, liability was considerably weakened.

To bolster his case, Belli enlisted the assistance of Vince Silk, an ex-Vaudeville comedian. "Vince's job called for tact in dealing with people," Belli recalled, "and Vince had plenty of that. I put him to work circulating through the neighborhood . . . finding witnesses who could swear that they had heard the siren blowing clearly, loudly, and without stopping from the moment the engine left the firehouse to the moment of the crash."

Though Belli paraded twenty-nine witnesses before the jury, he believed that having people swear they heard the siren wasn't tantamount to hearing it. The night before his final argument, the imaginative attorney decided to do something about this.

Later that morning, as Belli delivered his final argument to the jury, close friend and president of the Firemen's Union Bob Callahan telephoned a local fire station. "This is it," he said. "Belli's on now."

On cue, a fire truck whizzed by the courthouse, its siren piercing the air. Belli backed away so the jury could gain the full impact of how loud the siren was. "I didn't even have to ask the jurors: How come this truck driver couldn't hear a fire siren?" he said later.

Though the siren enhanced chances for a monumental verdict, Belli had delivered what opposing counsel Paul Dana called "the finest final argument I have ever heard . . . The effect was not lost on the jury," he said. "Belli in some manner and with considerable skill had actually put himself in the place of Williamson. He actually at some time had suffered in his very vivid imagination whatever Williamson had suffered. I have never seen a man do it that well."

Belli spoke in hushed tones, raising and lowering his voice as emotion dictated:

Of what avail are Fred Williamson's limbs? Of what utility his eyesight? Of what significance the fact that he is a strong, physically able man in the prime of life, when we realize that his brain can make no profitable use of his limbs, that his eyes can communicate no pleasure to his spirit; that every day must be for him a day of confusion, of torture, and of a feeling of the most unjust persecution. Through no fault of his own, he has been rendered insane. Everything is out of perspective; nothing has meaning; his world is that of the psychotic, the madman.

The jury awarded Williamson $225,000. At the time, it was the single highest personal injury verdict, a fact Belli noted in an innovative publication he created called "The Adequate Award." It documented large amounts awarded across the country and acted as a reference guide for lawyers gauging the value of their clients' injuries.

The accident had put Fred Williamson into a permanent vegetative state. But each year, Belli attended a luncheon in his honor. At the luncheon the youngest lawyer in the firm would have to make a speech. The associate prepared like crazy, but thirty seconds into his talk, the firemen threw olives at him and erupted into a chorus of "FUCK BELLI, FUCK BELLI, FUCK BELLI," drowning out the dumbfounded speaker. Belli laughed until his cheeks hurt.

The thriving law practice cost Belli at home. By this time, the famous barrister had four children with Betty: Rick, Johnny, Jeanne, and Suzie. Though he loved Betty and the kids, they rarely saw him. Most nights he slept in his office, preparing for trials.

Betty warned him he was becoming an absent husband and father.

Deciding he could no longer tolerate their arguments, he packed the family up and headed for Europe.

Betty and Melvin stashed the kids at a Swiss school and headed for Rome. Aided by a monsignor from Sonora, they were given an audience with Pope Pius XII.

A photograph from the trip shows the family standing in front of their Trans World Airlines airplane. His three youngest children, smiles on their faces, flanked Belli, wearing a black fedora and two-piece suit. To their left stood Betty, gazing at Belli, and oldest son Rick, also smiling pleasantly.

A Rome holiday was just what Betty and Melvin needed to save their marriage. After a quick trip back to the States to lend his support to the National Association of Claimants Attorneys, Belli promised Betty another whirlwind tour of Europe. Though he had good intentions, personal chaos lurked around the corner.

4

ADVENTURES WITH ROBIN HOOD

BEFORE RETURNING TO the United States, Belli traveled to Paris to visit with famed actor Errol Flynn. They first met when Belli appeared in Hollywood prepared to take Flynn's deposition in a case involving actor Wallace Berry's son. Berry's son claimed he sustained injuries to his foot while crewing on Flynn's yacht, the *Zaca*.

Belli appeared on the Warner Brothers lot wearing a white linen suit and a proper Homburg. "At first, Flynn wouldn't see me," Belli recalled, "but when he saw me, he threw back his head and laughed. 'Now that's the way a lawyer ought to look,' he said."

Like Belli, Flynn lived a life full of rumors. When a book titled *Errol Flynn, the Untold Story*, alleged that the actor was both "a homosexual and a Nazi spy," Belli filed a defamation suit against author Charles Higham and Dell Publishing.

Allegations were also made that Flynn pursued underage girls, though he was acquitted of statutory rape in 1943. The questionable accusation was made that he was bisexual, but this was never proven. It was true, however, that he counted various Hollywood mobsters, including Mickey Cohen, as close friends.

Flynn was born Leslie Thompson in Hobart, Tasmania. Born in 1909, he was two years Belli's junior. The dashingly handsome actor sported wavy black hair, a pencil-thin mustache, and high cheekbones. He married actresses Lili Damita, Patrice Wymore, and Nora Eddington, and had four children. He was best known for his films *Captain Blood, The Charge of the Light Brigade, Dodge City,* and *The Adventures of Robin Hood.*

In his appropriately titled autobiography *My Wicked, Wicked Ways,* Flynn wrote, "I was hoaxed by life." Film legend Jack Warner described his friend as "charming and tragic," and said, "to the Walter Mittys of this world, he was all the heroes in one magnificent, sexy, animal package."

Belli told *Playboy* magazine, "[Flynn] was great company. He lived life to the fullest; he was up at all hours; he drank vodka before he got out of bed in the morning." He added, "And he had the Devil in him. He loved pixy tricks, and played more than his share of them. In a dresser drawer, I remember Errol kept about fifty emerald-looking rings, which he'd give to girls, telling them with great feeling, 'This belonged to my mother.'"

In Paris, Belli and Flynn stayed at the George V hotel for three days before traveling to Switzerland to join Betty. Flynn left the group to return to Hollywood while Betty, Melvin, and their children celebrated Christmas in the Swiss Alps. The family stopped in England before sailing for New York on the *Queen Mary.*

Though the vacation appeased Betty for a time, she rarely saw her husband once they returned to the States and he resumed running his practice. Discontent was brewing, but Belli refused to put his family ahead of his career.

Betty was less than pleased when her husband announced he was returning to Paris without her. Flynn had asked for Belli's help in resolving a spat with his producer regarding shared revenues for *The Adventures of Captain Fabian.*

Belli flew to Paris in 1950, leaving Betty to mind the children and decide whether or not to stay married.

Meanwhile, Belli and Flynn partied in Paris. Belli said he and the famous actor sat outside at the Belle Aurora and entertained tourists. While drinking bottles of Calvados that Belli said "would chase white lightning out of business," they dreamed up murderous legal cases in which they played principal roles. The inebriated men interrogated one another as if they were on the witness stand. Some of the onlookers couldn't speak English, but that didn't keep them from cheering on the pair. "One night," he recalled, "we drove over to Les Halles in Flynn's big Cadillac and tried to eat all the oysters in the market district and then walked up and down through the market singing and drinking and telling stories."

The duo traveled south to the port city of Nice. The *Zaca* was docked a few miles down the coast in Cannes. In preparation for a night of gambling, Flynn went to the bilge of the yacht and returned carrying several gold ingots. The swashbuckling actor rowed to shore and traded them for cash.

In Nice, Belli became smitten with an exotic woman named Franka Faldini. "Franka was eighteen, olive-skinned, full-breasted, teeth that shone, eyes that flashed," Belli recalled.

A photograph taken at the time shows Flynn, dapper as always, standing behind a smiling Franka. She was smartly outfitted in white tennis togs, her dark hair pulled back in a bob. Flynn grasped her tanned left arm at the elbow. To their right was Belli, a glint of silver in his otherwise black hair.

Flynn saw the attraction between the two, and cunningly decided he needed someone to go "location scouting" in Sicily. The next day, Belli and Franka left for the island. Belli said, "It may have been the temples, the moonlight or the Marsala wine, but when we returned to Nice, Franka and I were the closest of friends."

Defending Flynn in Paris once again, Belli learned that the French legal system was a bit different. When he asked his French cocounsel what chance they had in court, he replied, "We can't lose. I have given the judge one hundred thousand francs." Worried about the opposition, Belli inquired, "What did the other side give him?" Nonplussed, the French lawyer replied, "Mr. Belli, we are dealing with a respectable judge. He is a man of honor. He would not think of taking [money] from *both* sides."

Both Belli and Flynn were fun-loving pranksters. One night, after Flynn collapsed in their room at Paris' Hotel Prince De Gaulle, he charged admission for those who wished to view his drunken companion. The "customers" were a flock of streetwalkers he and Flynn had transported to the hotel in their Cadillac.

"I picked up some unused bar chits, asked the bartender for a pair of scissors, cut them up and wrote a bunch of 'Flynn tickets'," Belli said. "I sold each girl a ticket for fifty francs, went out on the Champs-Elysees and found a dozen more girls still on the street and sold them tickets, too. Then I took all the girls to Flynn's suite and paraded them through 'to see more of Flynn'—which they did—because he was lying there sound asleep on top of his bed, balls-ass naked."

Flynn finally woke up when a sexy French "broad" with "breasts that stuck out like toy cannons" jumped on him, yelling "Fleen, Fleen, Fleen." Belli escorted the other girls out of the room while "Fleen" entertained the lady.

Receptionist Maggie Quinn recalled that Flynn returned the favor. "They partied on his yacht, the *Adequate Award*, which he docked in San Francisco and later at the Sausalito harbor," she said, "and Belli passed out dead drunk down below. I was told that Flynn then sold tickets for a buck apiece to see Belli in the buff." Apparently, the sight didn't draw many patrons. Only two purchased tickets.

When Belli's frolic in Paris did not sit well with Franka, he and Flynn devised a scheme to win back her heart.

"We dismissed flowers and champagne as too unimaginative," he said. "The boutiques were all closed and the only thing that was open were the fruit and vegetable stalls at Les Halles. So we took a taxi there, and loaded it up with beautiful vegetables, cabbages, celery, lettuce, turnips, potatoes, rutabagas, carrots, eggplant, squashes of all kinds, cauliflower, radishes, onions, leeks, and lots of beautiful ripe tomatoes, all the extravagant bounty of the French countryside."

With the assistance of the fruit stand owner, the two drunken paramours tossed their bounty into the taxi and headed for Franka's hotel. When she opened her door, Belli said, "the half-ton of vegetables tumbled into the room [and] her laughter rang up and down the hotel corridor. Naturally, she forgave me. Good women always forgive."

Belli spent more than two months in Europe as Betty languished at home. It appeared the globe-trotting Belli had abandoned his family. Even those who worshipped him as an attorney did not condone his conduct as a husband.

FLYNN WROTE THE foreword for *Belli Looks at Life and Law in Japan*. The book eventually became a classic, though Belli appeared to be more taken with Japanese women than Japanese law. This was especially true in the chapter titled, "Mama-San, Papa-San, and the Geisha Girl." Belli wrote that "the Geisha girl holds a position in Japanese society unique throughout the world" and that he loved names such as "Miss First Snow," "Miss Little Bud," and "Miss Plum Blossom." He added, "Not only is [the geisha girl] a singer, dancer, and instrumentalist, but often a romanticist. . . . She has also functioned as a spy."

He detailed the geisha girl's capacity for what he called "companionship," noting with glee that "ninety percent of the cost of geisha girls is paid by business and industry treasuries. Under the Japanese government tax policy they are as much a legitimate tax deduction as is a bar bill in America for an out-of-town buyer, and his other even more romantic expenses."

Flynn's foreword was entertaining, containing comments such as "Insurance companies mutter darkly that Belli is as much a menace to the land as Khrushchev or Jesse James"; "There were men who sought the Holy Grail, Belli clobbers insurance companies"; and "It is easy to understand why Belli is labeled a prankster, eccentric, erratic, unpredictable, and, by insurance companies, a bastard, a public concern akin to cholera."

Flynn visited Belli shortly after penning the foreword. The actor was taken with the library his friend had accumulated. "Next to sixteen volumes of *Corpus Juris*," he wrote, "you will find *The Girl with the Swansdown Seat*. Alongside the Gideon *Bible* is a volume called *Madcap's Progress*, supported by *Justice Musmano Dissents . . . Lawrence's Seven Pillars of Wisdom* stands beside *Hitler's Gunman*, which lies against a fat book called the *Epitome of History*."

He was less impressed with Belli's decorating. "Anyone but Belli," he wrote, "would think it impossible to mix tasteful modern furniture and a fourteenth-century samurai helmet and a white chaise lounge for the dog to sleep on and a sixteenth-century Italian chair for you to hang your clothes on. Next to a Shinto Buddha is an old-time, crank telephone; when you pick up the receiver it gives you a shock and turns on the radio."

Flynn had recently divorced and swore to Belli that he would never marry again. He was keeping company with a voluptuous sixteen-year-old blonde named Beverly Aadland. And he was dying.

Belli described his facial features as "bloated and puffy," and suggested he take it easy. To this, Flynn replied, "Look, I've done everything twice. Why should I bother?"

Joyce Revilla said, "I was shocked when I saw him. His face was red, his nose bulbous, all from drinking. But he and Belli had similar personalities for having fun. They were both prankish little boys." Their friendship lasted until the final days of Flynn's life.

Shortly after the San Francisco visit, Flynn traveled to Vancouver to sell the *Zaca*. "That was like selling his life," Belli said. During the trip, the Hollywood legend died, and Belli lost one of his only true, close friends. Flynn had telephoned the night before his death. "He said [to my wife at the time], 'Tell the guy I love him,'" Belli recalled. "'Just tell him that for me.'" Reflecting on their friendship, Belli said, "I guess we *were* brothers. In a way—though I'm an only child. Like him, I was wild, enthusiastic; I love people. I'm a Leo, you see."

THOUGH HIS PHILANDERING didn't go unnoticed on the home front, Belli continued his affair with Franka. "I was settling down with Franka," he recalled. "I opened a Rome office and was running my San Francisco law business via long distance."

Belli's business interests had extended beyond the law. "I had a pumping oil well near Galveston, Texas," he said, "and a couple of hot movie deals besides. Franka and I had found this documentary on Mussolini that we thought we might sell to the *March of Time*. And I had invested $10,000 in a spy story that was being shot in Japan called *Tokyo File 212*, one of the first postwar films to be made in Japan."

Tongue in cheek, a New York columnist named Cholly Knickerbocker wrote, "Belli's first film . . . has been making box-office records and he is so happy he intends to make six more." Danton Walker, another journalist, said, "Others along the same line would be filmed in Iran, Iraq, and Turkey." The latter country's name, the columnist kidded, described the quality of the film. Belli, ever the optimist, panned the criticism, saying his film was perfect fodder for "television after eleven."

While Belli was immersed in the movie business, and a new career in Europe, Betty's unhappiness intensified. When she saw news clippings and photographs of her husband bandying about with Errol Flynn and "Belli's new love interest Franka," she decided to end the marriage.

"One of my investigators sent me a note saying he thought Betty was considering a divorce," Belli recalled. "I returned to San Francisco and tried to effect a reconciliation. It didn't work. Betty filed for divorce on January 8, 1951, and received custody of our four children. Rick was then fourteen, Johnny twelve, Jeanne nine, and Suzie six. That's when I lost them."

Belli said he had no one to blame for the failure of his eighteen-year marriage. "[Partner] Lou Ashe did his best to save my family for me," he stated. "I didn't listen to him."

Ashe's exact words, Belli recalled, were poignant ones: "God damn it, Mel. You work all the time. You never go home at night, but sleep in the office in your clothes instead. If I were you and had a family, I'd go home nights and spend time with my wife and kids. You'll be in trouble if you don't."

Daughter Jeanne said her father had a choice. "He could have either pursued his dreams in the legal arena, or stayed home and been a dad. He chose the former. And even when he tried to be a father, he wasn't very good at it." Growing up without a father had a lasting impact on Jeanne. "I had no dad, no role model," she said. "And it affected later relationships."

Joyce Revilla noted, "He just wasn't a very good father, didn't know how to be a father. That's why his kids were kind of dysfunctional like the old man." Jeanne Belli agreed, stating "even when we were with Dad for the summers, he didn't have much time for us. He was off writing a book, or trying a case."

Maggie Quinn recalled that one Christmas, Belli summoned her to his office and said, "Go buy four television sets and send them to the kids." "He was trying to show them that he cared," she said, "but I knew that he hadn't seen them in a long time."

Remorse didn't prevent Belli from having harsh feelings toward his ex-wife. "I'll never forgive Betty—or the children—for changing their last name from Belli to Ballantine," he said. This was a half-truth, as neither Jeanne nor Suzie changed their last names. Sons Rick and Johnny later reverted back to their father's last name.

Venting his anger toward Betty and her lawyer, Belli sent the lawyer's $3,500 fee to him in two sacks filled with pennies. Later he conceded that it was a mistake, saying the act left "a legacy of bitterness and hostility that enveloped me and my wife in a black cloud for years long after the divorce."

On the front page of the January 17, 1953, *San Francisco Chronicle* a headline read "Mel Belli Goes to Jail for Contempt." Above it appeared a photograph of Belli in black-rimmed glasses, peering out from behind bars.

Belli was jailed for failing to turn over Texas oil leases to Betty, though he swore they were worthless. Reporter Edd Johnson wrote, "It was a great day for everyone. [Belli was] making self-conscious jokes and flashing stock smiles at the newspaper photographers. Even Sheriff Dan Gallasher got into the act assuring Belli that he was not being placed in

'durance [imprisonment] vile,' but rather in 'durance chemically pure'—
that being the east wing of the county jail."

Belli complained that Betty hadn't permitted him to see the kids on
Christmas. "My arms laden with bundles—on Christmas day—I rang the
door bell," he said. "There was no answer. But I could see their little faces
pressed, grimacing against the windowpanes. I told them in pantomime
that I wanted to give them Christmas presents." Nearly weeping as he
spoke, he told reporters how he had been so lonely out in the snow as
he was told to "shove the presents through the window by an adult voice."
Belli, realizing he had gotten carried away, quickly backtracked. Betty's
house in Palo Alto hadn't seen a snowfall in fifty years.

The famed attorney was jailed from 12:40 pm until shortly after six
o'clock when the leases had been transferred. His final comment to
reporters was, "This is a bum beef. I'm writing a book on criminal procedure, and I started to write a chapter on how to keep out of jail, but
now I'll have to eliminate the chapter."

Decades later Belli and Betty forgave each other. During his final days,
she visited him in San Francisco along with Jeanne, Rick, and Johnny.
Both Jeanne and Johnny worked in Belli's offices. In a serendipitous turn
of events, Johnny met his future wife there. Belli had asked his son to sit
in on an interview with a prospective attorney named Beverly. While conducting the interview, Belli noticed the couple, seated side-by-side, was
paying more attention to each other than to him. He was right. Three
weeks later, Beverly became Johnny's wife.

After his divorce from Betty, Belli said, "From now on, I shall live with
Blackstone [English author of several legal books]. Women are out."

BELLI'S MARITAL FAILURE did not hinder his flourishing law career. In
the early 1950s, Sam Horowitz of the NACCA arranged speaking
engagements for him at Cornell, Princeton, Yale, and the Boston University Law School. His crusade at the time was to educate the American public and the legal establishment about the value placed on a
human life. He spoke frequently about the physical and emotional damage caused by injuries.

He emphasized that while baseball players were paid six figures, race-
horses valued at a quarter of a million dollars, and musical instruments
appraised at half a million dollars, juries were reluctant to award damages
in excess of $100,000 for loss of limb.

"The dignity of man," Belli wrote in an article, "had long since been heralded in the arts, literature, painting and music. Now, I said, the courts should be ready to acclaim in law the dignity of man with adequate awards for personal-injury losses to those with humble as well as gifted hands."

Belli knew that his techniques in the courtroom had successfully upped the ante concerning jury verdicts. He decided to share his knowledge and strategies with attorneys across the country. He said, "I visited thirty-five legal groups—bar associations and law schools—barnstorming all over the U.S. I felt as good as Mary-knoller bringing hybrid wheat and hospitals to southeastern Brazil."

Belli spelled out his credo in a speech he delivered to the Mississippi State Bar Association. "A doctor may bind up the physical wounds after personal injury," he said, "but it is only the plaintiff's lawyer who rehabilitates economically the client, his widow, his children. Let us speak frankly. Under our system of jurisprudence, compensation can *only* be allowed in terms of dollars. We've no system whereby a man, after personal injury, can be made whole again, can walk without a limb, sleep without pain."

He was fervent about his message. "The talks I gave were simply not money talks," he explained. "I loved the law and I was grateful to God for giving me the chance to practice the kind of law where I could help the poor and downtrodden."

He believed that courts around the country were listening to lawyers of the same mind and developing new laws on personal injury cases. To impress this fact on others, Belli often quoted a California Court of Appeals decision rendered in one of his cases. The court wrote, "The trial of a lawsuit is not a game where the spoils of victory go to the clever and technical regardless of the merits, but a method devised by a civilized society to settle peaceably and justly disputes between litigants. The rules of the contest are not an end in themselves. Unless the rules tend to accomplish justice, strict compliance is not always required."

THE IMPORTANCE OF the notoriety was not lost on the barrister. "Fame, I discovered," he said, "is a grass that grows in any dirt when no one's looking. And fame had it's advantages: it would bring in cash by bringing in more cases."

Belli's knack for shameless self-promotion was well known. Attorney Bob Lieff, a colleague of Belli's, said his first duty when they arrived at

Caesar's Palace or the Riveria in Las Vegas was to locate the house telephone so he could tell the operator to say "MELVIN BELLI, PAGING
MR. BELLI, MELVIN BELLI, PAGING MR. BELLI" over the inter-
com. Belli also pulled that stunt once himself at the Orly Airport in Paris.
"He simply loved to hear his name," Lieff recalled with a laugh.

Reporters flocked to him, he knew, because the phrase "no comment"
was not in his vocabulary. He was always ready to entertain the press with
an anecdote for a story in the morning newspaper. Belli was what
reporters termed "good copy." George Safford, an associate, said, "He
owned the press. They loved him because he was so irreverent, ready to
take on anyone." Seymour Ellison echoed Safford's thoughts, saying,
"Mel loved the media and the media loved him."

Belli said, "I always liked talking to guys from the press. They were
bright and they did not have time for too much bullshit." When he
returned from his lecture tour, reporters met him at the San Francisco
airport, armed with questions.

Asked if he was angry about being portrayed as "flamboyant," Belli
answered, "I'm not flamboyant in court. On trial I've always contributed
to the dignity of the courtroom."

"What about when you're not on trial?" a reporter asked.

Before Belli answered that question, he asked for a specific example.
The reporter was ready.

"Well [how about], the one about your sending thirty-five hundred
dollars to your ex-wife's attorney in two sacks of small change—with
some stinking fish inside?"

Belli paused before he replied, "There were not fish in the sacks. Lou
Ashe made me take [them] out."

The quote would be prominently featured in newspapers the next
morning.

Belli's favorite media outlet was legendary *San Francisco Chronicle*
columnist Herb Caen. Through the years, the barrister made certain he
was mentioned in Caen's must-read column on a regular basis. When he
believed he had achieved something newsworthy, he'd say, "Call Herb, he
needs to know about this." If his name wasn't featured at least three or
four times a week, he called his buddy to see if he had offended him.

If Caen embellished Belli's celebrity, the headline-making lawyer
returned the favor. Many of Caen's more than sixteen-thousand columns

were enhanced with tales of "The King of Torts" as he galloped across the national and international scene.

Ever the publicity seeker, Belli agreed to a stunt that amazed even Caen. In his quest for notoriety, the barrister agreed to have his white locks "permed." When it was over, he was featured in the Pink Section of the *Chronicle*. Secretary Joyce Revilla said he looked like a "kinky little poodle." Belli didn't care. The next day he wore the "do" to court.

Belli found his next wife care of the media. While he was recounting details of his whirlwind speaking tour around the country, he noticed a lovely photographer snapping photographs of him. Instantly, Belli was smitten, but the woman resisted his advances, telling him, "Your reputation got to me before you did, Mr. Belli."

Despite her initial mind-set, the *Life* magazine photographer finally succumbed to Belli's charm. On November 27, 1951, Toni Nichols became Toni Belli after a wedding ceremony near Mexico City. He called her "Rover."

5

MODERN TRIALS

BELLI'S LOVE FOR "ladies of the night" was well known. On a Thanksgiving weekend while he was writing *Modern Trials*, Belli accepted an invitation to visit the California Street "cat house" owned by a client, the prosperous madam Lorraine Fontaine. Belli enjoyed turkey with all the trimmings, and the company of seven of Lorraine's most beautiful girls. After he had eaten and downed several glasses of cabernet, Lorraine made her lawyer an offer he couldn't refuse.

"Mel Belli," she said, as he looked on, glassy-eyed, "I want to give you your Christmas present right now."

Lorraine then ordered, "Girls, introduce yourself to Melvin Belli." The girls did so, and Lorraine continued: "Mel, as my Christmas present to you, I want to present you with these seven: one for Friday, one for Saturday, one for Sunday, and so on, if you want. Or if you prefer, take one of them home for a week."

Choosing was difficult for the inebriated Belli, but he was up to the task. "I circled the group, came back to the table, poured myself another cognac and pointed to a tall redhead (Melody) who couldn't have been more than nineteen and a callipygous brunette (Mary) with a turned-up nose. 'I'll take these two,' I said, 'for the weekend.'"

Representing madams became a Belli specialty. When madam Molly Regan was subpoenaed to testify before a grand jury, she contacted

Belli. He told her to keep her mouth shut, and to make sure she did, he sent her to court with a copy of the Declaration of Independence, the Constitution, and "for good measure," he said, the Gettysburg Address. She showed them to a perplexed judge who simply shook his head.

Belli represented a Broadway Street madam named Gertrude Jenkins after she was arrested for encouraging one of her girls to have an abortion. When the case was tried, Belli knew that Jenkins would make a questionable witness on her own behalf. Determined not to have her testify, he came up with a brilliant, if somewhat unethical, idea.

After Belli rested his case, he stood and announced in a loud voice, "Your honor, Mrs. Jenkins will not take the stand." The judge began to speak, but was abruptly interrupted by Gertrude. She stood, waved her hands in the air, and exclaimed, "Wait a minute, wait a minute, I do want to take the stand. I'm innocent." Quick to react, Belli said, "Gert, we *know* you're innocent. You don't *have* to testify."

Though the prosecutor objected, the damage was done. Predictably the jury returned with a verdict of not guilty, never realizing that Belli and Gert had rehearsed the ruse the night before.

BELLI'S CLOSE ASSOCIATION with various madams was of great help when it came time to throw a party. In 1951, Melvin Belli imported twenty "actresses" and "models" from Los Angeles for the National Association of Claimants' Compensation Attorneys (NACCA) convention. Belli observed, "They weren't hookers, just young women a little bit ahead of their time that didn't mind going to parties and getting laid if they chanced to meet the right guy." "Wrong," alleged several associates, "they *were* hookers." Famous madam Sally Stanford, who later became mayor of Sausolito, came along to keep her employees in check.

Using contacts he had made with various madams through the years, Belli not only invited the NACCA lawyers to his "party," but also local attorneys, firemen, police, bookies, and judges. Errol Flynn, who had asked Belli to show him the "real San Francisco," also attended.

Belli enjoyed playing host to his NACCA cronies at the Mark Hopkins Hotel in San Francisco. Not only did he decorate the convention with his hired beauties, but he entertained his honored guests on his new toy, the *Warwine*. The yacht was a fifty-one-foot beauty that had belonged to actor Warner Baxter. It slept ten, sported twin Chrysler engines, and cost Belli $7,500.

When he wasn't on the yacht, Belli lived in a Vallejo Street apartment, where a back view captured the romanticism of both the Golden Gate and Bay Bridges. It was rented for $500-a-month from Mrs. Ambrose Dieht, a San Francisco socialite. Here, Belli hosted some of the greatest parties ever thrown in San Francisco. "There is only one thing I like better than a good party," Melvin Belli once said, "And that is several good parties."

Despite his affinity for wild times, Belli, in the early 1950s, was introspective, concerned with what was expected of him as a prominent lawyer. More than anything he hated hypocrites, phonies, and those who were judgmental.

"There's a little bit of Pharisee in all of us," he said. "We like to think that someone can keep all of the Commandments all the time in order to preserve our sense of law and order and the fitness of things. We need heroes and saints and impeccable public servants, need someone to take up the slack in what we supposed to be that tug-of-war called life, and we deride the hero or saint, priest, or president who turns human on us."

Belli reflected on his psyche and his sins. "But life isn't a tug-of-war or a battle or a forced march," he said. "It's more like a dance: sometimes wild, sometimes gentle, often exhilarating. During a dance, of course, people can stumble every so often. No big deal. The dance goes on. The beat goes on."

Those were brave words from a man who many people believed had had his heart cut out when Betty gained custody of their children. "The biggest blasphemy of all," he said, "is to say to life, I won't join in. I had stumbled and fallen pretty hard and lost my kids. But, for me, life went on."

Belli received mixed reactions from fellow lawyers in the 1950s. Many respected his talents and truly believed that he was a one-man crusade for legal reform. Others deplored his self-promotion and tendency to be a know-it-all.

NACCA attorneys looked to him for leadership. After emceeing a full-blown debate over significant developments in the various avenues of personal injury law, Belli hatched an idea. Each year at the NACCA convention, Belli led a discussion with the finest legal minds in the country. At the urging of Sam Horovitz, the conferences became known as "The Belli Seminar." The session notes were printed and bound into several volumes. They became a chief resource for lawyers around the world.

But Belli soured on the NACCA, and at the next American Bar Association (ABA) convention in St. Louis, he set up a new version of his seminar. When the ABA attempted to stop the seminar. Belli convinced a *St. Louis Post-Dispatch* reporter to write an article bearing the banner, "Maverick of Bar Conducting Own Seminar Here for Bored Lawyers."

Unable to secure what he considered proper space, Belli rented Keil Auditorium, a sporting venue. After the seminar, the *St. Louis Globe-Democrat* reported his exploits under the headline, "Belli's 17-hour ABA Show Beats Three-Ring Circus." The reporter wrote, "Dressed in his usual black cowboy boots (highly polished but run over at the heels), Mr. Belli pushed and prodded his cast of characters through lively demonstrations of hypnosis, 'demonstrative' evidence techniques, trial tactics, medicine, and mechanics."

To promote interest in the art of hypnosis, Belli featured Hollywood physician Dr. William J. Bryan Jr. To convince skeptics, the doctor hypnotized six lawyers, then stuck five of them in the hand with needles. There was no pain or bleeding.

The *Globe-Democrat* reporter covering the event was obviously impressed, writing, "A seventeen-hour session of hypnosis, hoopla, and horse sense which topped the best of Barnum & Bailey shook the dignity of Kiel Auditorium Saturday under the skilled guidance of a flamboyant but friendly enemy of the ABA."

Belli continued to be a thorn in the side of the legal establishment with his bold assertions about the law. To organize his thoughts, Belli decided to write a book he intended to call *Modern Trials*. It was June in San Francisco, but crisp temperatures confirmed the famous quote attributed to Mark Twain, "The coldest winter I ever spent was a summer in San Francisco."

Despite the brisk weather, Belli wrote feverishly. His office personnel had never seen him so dedicated, so focused. He and Lou Ashe had several young lawyers working in the office, and that summer, Belli handed off most of his cases to them. *Modern Trials* was his first priority.

"I dictated into [a] damn machine every weekend," he recalled. "The secretaries would type it out during the week and I'd polish it up a bit, and then by Thursday night, I'd be ready to plunge ahead with more dictation. It was an exhausting time for me, and I kept myself going on cigarettes, Dexedrine, and gin." Belli was especially gratified when Roscoe

Pound agreed to write the book's introduction. Pound labeled the work "an indispensable book for the trial lawyer in personal-injury cases."

Belli's obsession with the manuscript caused friction with his new wife, Toni. She had two children by a previous marriage and had expected her new husband to spend time with them. He didn't, often not even returning on weekends.

After six months, Toni had had enough. The two separated. Belli was single once again.

When it was finished, the manuscript totaled more than three thousand pages. Instead of writing one book, Belli had written three. When his editor at publisher Bobbs-Merrill looked at the six-foot high stack of material, he nearly fainted. Closer inspection indicated that while much of it had been typed, several pages were handwritten in both pencil and pen. There were also side notes, additions, and corrections clipped or taped to the manuscript.

Working with Belli to finalize the book was an exercise in patience for the staff at Bobbs-Merrill. Publisher and author had to agree on illustrations, photographs, the cover, and so forth. Bobbs-Merrill and Belli disagreed with regard to the cover photograph. "I didn't want your standard stuffed shirt of a legal portrait," he recalled. "I wanted an X-ray of my head and neck." The publisher prevailed.

Belli flew to their home offices where he was provided with an Audograph Dictaphone. Belli called his own "a damn, fucking thing," and the new one was no better. Upset with a malfunction, he tossed it over a partition and down a flight of stairs, where it nearly hit the repairman who had been called to fix it. Belli vowed never to return, but Bobbs-Merrill placated him by buying a brand new Dictaphone.

Modern Trials became one of the biggest sellers in the history of their company. It sold more than six thousand copies within a month and earned Belli more than $75,000 in royalties. By the end of Belli's life, the figure had reached more than a million. Reprints continue to sell six decades later and are still valued in law school libraries. Professors often quote Belli on courtroom tactics.

Attorney John O'Connor once listened to phonograph records accompanying the books volumes. "They were full of legal revolution," the lawyer recalled. "And a newspaper review of them stated the obvious. Listen to them once, to one of his final arguments, and you weren't impressed. But then the second time, it became clear and you realized what he was doing, that he was connecting with a jury by tying in affiliations with the Elks Club, or a church group, or with some way of attaching himself to the jury. It was brilliant."

Besides the three-volume set, Belli wrote the abridged *Student's Edition of Modern Trials*. In the introduction, Belli writes, "Of course one should begin his active learning in the law early and once having achieved his beginning proficiency, as witness his license, he should never stop his study—if he is to be a true lawyer." He maintains that every lawyer must possess "imagination, second only to integrity." He writes, "And with the teaching of the law given to me by my law school, I learned to discipline this imagination, to view my client's case in perspective, indeed as a layman would view it, unlettered in the law, as well as to understand how my associate lawyers and those judges on the appellate court would view it. . . . There were complaints that my imagination was too vivid and, indeed, I have on occasion been accused by opposing counsel in trial court of being too demonstrative."

Belli adds, "It was said that Shakespeare must have been a trial lawyer because he knew so much about everything. The trial lawyer's pursuit of facts and man's activity in a long professional career will take him from a study of submarines, to airplanes, to poliomyelitis drugs, to ballistics, to the identification of a the head of a cricket, to problems of homosexuality in prison, to counterfeiting of old masters: indeed to very ultimate of the philosopher's question 'what is life itself,' in some breach of warranty case where the question is (and this one I had), 'Is there *'living'* virus in this vaccine?'"

To the students, Belli expounds on the "Black Book" he had kept since law school graduation. Packed with practical information regarding trial tactics, lessons on presentation of evidence, and valuable insight into all facets of trial practice, the book was Belli's constant resource prior to trial.

An adjoining photograph of the book shows "Melvin M. Belli" embossed above "San Francisco." The caption reads, "This is the 'Black Book.' It is indexed, has a large ring binder, and contains about three hundred loose-leaf pages. The practice is never to take a page from the book except to replace it then and there. Pages taken out are pages lost. This book is taken to court every time you go to trial."

On the subject of curiosity, Belli writes, "*Curiosity* is sibling to *imagination*. Before one soars, he must examine, test, prod, burrow and *inquis-*

itively inspect. I like to think of the trial lawyer as the one who, when flying, asks to go up to the flight deck, when on the ocean liner asks to see the engine room, and the navigation equipment on the bridge. I hope he's the one who dares (and here we come to another commodity—courage) to visit the bottom-most level of the mine in the rapidly falling skiff; who asks to 'ride in the cab of the engine' on the train. . . . He's the one I as a trial lawyer would expect to meet in unusual places, detailedly examining unusual clues while looking for unexpected results."

Belli concludes his introduction by saying, "I should say that lawyers never stop talking and writing and thinking about this great thing, the law, once they get the call and hear 'the whirring of the wings'."

In a chapter on witness examination, Belli writes, "How does one become a good 'cross-examiner?' The answer to this lies not in one's ability to memorize various procedures of the great artists but rather to becoming a raconteur of the club or bar. Putting it simply—one who is able to interest another human being can interest a witness and a jury." He adds, "We search for truth in cross-examination as we do in everyday life, so that which portrays or signifies the 'lie' in daily conversation, too will portray it in the formal cross-examination. The art of cross-examination does not require a course in formal psychoanalysis. It does necessitate a knowledge and appreciation of human behavior and its manifestations, only to be acquired by observation and reflection in daily contact with men."

While *Modern Trials* was an unqualified success, Belli's relationship with Toni continued to be stormy. Though they had reconciled, she complained that their marriage in Mexico wasn't legal, so he officially married her in Nevada. Belli later said he and Toni were "separated" eighteen times during their marriage

The episode caused the overworked attorney to assess his feelings toward his profession. "[Toni] didn't feel married, because I was really married to the law," he said. "Most trial lawyers are. . . . They work under a lot of stress, and strain, they put in impossible hours, usually with a secretary who's always there and ready to go out with them for drinks and a late supper and some kind of release. Pretty soon, they're having a romance with their secretary."

He had advice for the love interest of a trial lawyer: "They need a release, and if their wives aren't there when they come down, they'll find it elsewhere. If a trial lawyer's wife wants her marriage to last, she has to be there when her husband needs her."

Belli believed the psychological aspects of being a lawyer created the need for an outlet. "Trial lawyers are hard drinkers, and most, on the defendant's or plaintiff's side," he said, " are pretty damn good guys. But no matter how hard they prepare, there's always the unexpected in that courtroom; that, and the tensions of the battle keep them on a high wire."

Toni convinced Belli to see a psychiatrist. He talked with one, then was referred to another with disastrous results—for the psychiatrist.

"I ended up converting *him*," Belli said. "I recounted my escapades, and he got so fascinated and horny that he decided to go out and start chasing too. His marriage ended up in a divorce."

Bob Lieff recalled the tumultuous relationship. "At one point," he said, "I understand Mel got a gun and threatened to shoot her. Lou Ashe, a partner of Mel's, apparently stopped him before he committed murder." Belli said, "[She] didn't know what to do with me." Later, in *Divorcing*, Belli wrote of the marriage, "It was one of those cases of 'marry in haste, repent at leisure.' After their breakup, he told reporters, "You can say I am through with women from here on out."

His second marriage doomed, Belli amused himself with other interests. Even though high overhead and "miscellaneous" expenses were draining revenue from his law practice, he purchased an expensive apartment building on scenic Telegraph Hill. It faced Coit Tower, the San Francisco landmark named after colorful 1870s heiress Lillie Coit.

Never one to do things halfway, Belli commissioned four architects to make improvements to the penthouse. After visiting the apartment, journalist and author Robert Wallace said, "His personal quarters are a mixture of Early American, Victorian, and high class Swedish massage-parlor, the dream home of a Mother-Lode man who has struck it rich." He added, "There is a graceful niche in one of the brick walls, housing a lovely weather-beaten wooden Madonna bought in Italy. He is not, despite the Madonna and the silver-dollar-sized St. Christopher medal he wears, a Catholic. He is not sure what he is."

Belli's description of the abode differed a bit from Wallace's. "I did it in Mother Lode, whorehouse Victorian," he said proudly, "with velvet drapes, cut-glass chandeliers and a white carpet that was ankle-deep. I had two bedrooms enclosed in floor-to-ceiling picture windows overlooking the City and the Bay and a large open kitchen done in copper and sandstone. I filled the terrace with flowers of every kind I could grow in the city: camellias, begonias, and roses and Burmese honeysuckle and orange trees that gave off ambrosial perfumes through much of the year."

No expense was spared. "In one of the bathrooms, I installed a sunken marble tub for two and a sauna bath. Over the john, I hung a colorful framed poster I had picked up in Germany, advertising something called the 'Circus Belli.' I had a fireplace built with bricks from the White House [which I bought when Harry S. Truman remodeled]."

Wallace observed that Belli's bathroom was fascinating. "The floor is covered with mosaic tile," he said, "in which are worked various Latin inscriptions familiar in the law, [such] as *'De minimis non curat lex,'* 'the law does not concern itself with trifles.'"

Belli had a pine-paneled steam room, useful for curing hangovers. Wallace said that Belli, while on the road, normally "shut himself in the bathroom, plugged up the cracks around the doors with towels, turned on the hot water in the washbasin, tub, and shower, and sat steaming until the condensation was an inch or two deep on the floor."

The bedroom added to the apartment's elegance. "Up above the fireplace on a jutting platform, I installed a full-size bed with a coverlet made with the fur of Alaskan wolves. Up there on that bed, a cunning bit of engineering surrounded on three sides by plate glass, I could show any visiting young lady the most romantic city on earth." An office employee said, "What a place to screw," and associate attorney John O'Connor dubbed the bed, "A great place to get laid." Belli offered his own view. He said it was a place where "you could screw with the whole world watching."

When New York Mayor John Lindsey visited Belli for a fund-raiser, his comment about the penthouse was, "If I lived here, I could get in a lot of trouble."

Constant nightmares caused Belli trouble in the bedroom. "It's like Rin Tin Tin," one wife reported. "He howls in his sleep, starting with a low, small noise, and continuing louder and louder until he wakes." To combat his headaches and prevent the howling, Belli swallowed Benzedrine tablets. He called them "Crispy Crunchies."

THE REVERED DEAN William Prosser of Boalt Law School provided an apt description of Melvin Belli. He wrote, "Every good trial lawyer is to some extent an actor, be he artist or ham, and he is also a playwright and a director, who prepares the script, sets the scene and stage-manages the evidence. Mr. Belli is all of that, and more. He is a Hollywood producer, and his trial is an epic of the supercolossal."

Prosser's words proved prophetic when *Life* magazine profiled Belli and christened him with a title that would forever distinguish him from all others who practiced law.

The cover of the October 1954 issue depicts a politician riding in a convertible along crowded streets during a campaign stop in Tacoma, Washington. The headline reads, "Tacoma Congressional Campaign."

The issue chronicles the latest exploits of Franklin D. Roosevelt Jr. and Jacob Javits, both running for the Senate in New York. It features behind-the-scenes details on why baseball great Joe DiMaggio and heartthrob actress Marilyn Monroe had split up. Sultry actress Ava Gardner was also spotlighted. Photographs capture her singing and mooning for the camera wearing expensive gowns and women's suits.

Written by journalist Robert Wallace, the article on Belli is aptly titled, "King of Torts." This would be Belli's label for the rest of his life.

Surprisingly Belli wasn't sure he liked the article. Though Wallace lauds *Modern Trials* as "the Bible of personal injury lawyers," he goes on to ask his readers, "How can this clown have such a national influence?"

Wallace, who wrote one book about Belli and collaborated on another, begins the article by outlining Bell's famous "butcher paper" case. After detailing the facts and recalling the spilling of the artificial leg on a juror's lap, he asks, "What kind of lawyer is this? Is he a deliverer of the oppressed—or an unscrupulous, melodramatic spellbinder. Your sense of human values as well as your wallet are involved in the answer."

Defending Belli's reputation, Wallace later wrote, "Belli's enemies incessantly accuse him of being a 'chaser,' but no one has ever observed him in *flagrante delicto* at full gallop down Market Street at noon with a contract in his hand and a pen in his teeth."

Quoted sources heap praise on Belli. Paul Dana, whom Wallace refers to as "a brilliant attorney of the august law firm of Dana and Smith," said, "Belli is a magnificent trial lawyer. I know. He once beat me in a $225,000 verdict." Judge Meikle of the San Francisco Superior Court added, "He is the best trial lawyer I have ever seen."

Wallace notes the changes in personal injury law and the mounting damages being awarded to victims in the 1950s. He compares two cases to show the difference. Belli won a $100,000 verdict for Katherine Jeffers. At the turn of the century, a thirty-year-old stevedore suffered a similar injury. The U.S. Circuit judge awarded the man 98 cents a week and $500 for pain and suffering.

To demonstrate Belli's affinity for the bizarre, *Life* included several photographs of the lawyer. In one, he sits with wife Joy in their Telegraph Hill home. In another, he is driving his Rolls-Royce convertible with Elmer, his famous one-legged courtroom skeleton, sitting in the passenger seat.

A third photograph shows Belli, along with a nurse and another lawyer, staring down at Belli's 682-pound client. The title of the photograph is "The Fat Man."

Many in the legal establishment were quick to label Belli a showboat, a quack, and a shyster. Wallace wrote, "In some circles, Belli is regarded as a genius, a true friend of the downtrodden. Elsewhere there are people who claim that is merely an ambulance chaser, but they insist that at the first sound of an emergency vehicle [Belli] picks up his ears, breaks out all over in large black spots and barks." Belli, according to Wallace, replied, "That's ridiculous. Ambulances can do up to eighty or ninety mph. I can scarcely do five." On another occasion, asked about the same subject, he said, "I am not an ambulance chaser, I'm usually there before the ambulance."

This did not stop the State of Texas from passing what investigator Jasper Watts called the "Belli Rule." This occurred after Watts appeared on a Texas airport runway to interview potential clients before, as he described it, "the flames of the burning plane had been put out." Based on objections to the way Belli's employees were "ambulance chasing," a ten-day waiting period was enacted to prevent contact with those associated with an accident.

Never afraid to characterize himself, Belli later told *Playboy* magazine, "God knows I've endured more than my share of slings and arrows. 'Belli's a nut, a charlatan, a publicity seeker, an egomaniac.' Sure, I'm flamboyant. I can afford to be because I'm a damn good lawyer. You've got to ring the bell to get the people into the temple. But my brand of nonconformist is so offbeat they don't know what to label me. About the only thing they haven't tagged me is a communist."

6

A DAY IN THE LIFE

"HISTORICALLY, THE AMERICAN Bar Association has been anti-Catholic and anti-Semitic."

This summed up Belli's contempt for the ABA. He believed the organization was composed of bigots, bought and paid for by insurance companies and big corporations, who inhibited the freedom of practicing lawyers. In his mind they were the enemy of every self-respecting attorney. Later he hung his ABA plaque upside down in his office bathroom in protest.

In *My Life on Trial*, Belli made it clear that his contempt extended beyond the American Bar Association. "Today, the legal establishment is not there to serve the people, but to serve itself," he wrote. "I blame all lawyers for this. They've abdicated their responsibilities to their local bar associations and let mediocre lawyers from the big firms come in to fill the vacuum, politicking and going through the chairs."

The ABA began attacking Belli in the mid-1950s, calling him unethical and immoral. They believed he was a self-promoting ambulance chaser who gave their profession a bad name.

Belli claimed he unsuspectingly fell into a trap the ABA had set for him. Eager to discipline him for his stinging criticisms, ABA officials asked him to visit the organization's Chicago headquarters. They wanted to discuss his perspective on personal injury tactics. He accepted the invitation, expecting an afternoon filled with stories about his legal conquests. Instead, the discussion turned to his contempt for the organization and their policies.

To his astonishment, a few weeks later he received a pointed letter informing him that the ABA was suspending his membership for six months. Worse, they had contacted the California Bar Association and suggested that further disciplinary action be taken.

Belli first laughed, then became incensed at the ABA's attempt to sanction him. He hired his own lawyer, and the ABA retreated.

He was ready for the next ABA convention in Miami. During his "Belli Seminar," he introduced Professor Julian O'Brien, a tax expert from Harvard University. The professor proceeded to lecture the attendees with what Belli described as "an amusing pastiche which ended with altogether fitting proportion, 'My advice to you guys is, pay your taxes.'"

Duly impressed, the delegates to the convention began to discuss Professor O'Brien's speech. They were shocked when they discovered that it wasn't a Harvard professor who had spoken to them but Belli's friend Meyer "Mickey" Cohen, a Los Angeles mobster.

The ABA promptly issued a rebuke, but Belli defended himself, saying "I always present odd and interesting guests." This was true. During one seminar, he paraded twenty-five-year-old former schoolteacher Patti White in front of the gawking lawyers. Her theme was "What Legal Education Really Needs." To emphasize her message, Patti slipped off her cap and gown, seductively removed her red satin slip, and told the attentive audience, "From this point there can be no reasonable doubt."

Nor was there any doubt that Professor O'Brien was Cohen. Told that the local police knew in advance of his appearance in Miami, Cohen said, "That's nothing unusual, they know I'm coming a lot of times before I know I'm going."

In the foreword of *Belli Looks at Life and Law in Japan*, Errol Flynn gave another version of the incident. He wrote, "[Belli] announced that he had persuaded none other than the famous European jurist, Sir Julian O'Brien, to address them. Sir Julian was a sensation, to put it mildly. At one point, he electrified his stunned audience by thundering, 'Youse guys wouldn't know how to spring a hood even if the bum wasn't guilty. I'll lay odds I know more about the inside of prisons than alla ya put together.'" Flynn added, "This was no idle boast. Sir Julian happened to be Mickey Cohen, that picturesque man of the world from Los Angeles."

The *New York Times* chronicled the story under the headline, "Mobster's Lecture Embarrasses Bar." After detailing Cohen's appearance to discuss "tax evasion and other criminal cases," the reporter wrote that immediately after speaking Cohen was questioned by detectives regarding the murder of Chicago gangster Fred Evans.

Belli never hid the fact that Cohen was a friend and client. Cohen, a Los Angeles cult hero in the 1940s and 1950s, was formerly a bodyguard to Benjamin "Bugsy" Seigel. He rose to power after members of the Dragna mob family made an unsuccessful attempt on his life and the media dubbed him "Public Enemy #1."

According to former FBI Agent Bill Turner, coauthor of *Deadly Secrets: The CIA-Mafia War against Castro and the Assassination of JFK*, consensus was that Cohen was the "front man" for Los Angeles Mafia chief Meyer Lansky. "We wiretapped Cohen's telephones," Turner said.

Cohen was a bandit from birth. The would-be mobster was first arrested at age nine, for bootlegging. An amateur prizefighter, he was a bulldog of a man, with a receding hairline, large, sloping nose, and deep-set eyes. Like Belli, he was a lady-killer, and nearly married an exotic dancer named Miss Beverly Hills. He thought enough of her to include her photograph in his autobiography, *Mickey Cohen, in My Words*. She provocatively posed wearing lingerie that barely covered her ample breasts. The caption read, "Miss Beverley Hills was a nice piece of real estate."

Cohen had faced income tax evasion charges when he didn't heed, as he stated in his book, "[Melvin] Belli's advice that certain gifts I'd received had to be reported as income." Though it is unclear when their friendship began, Belli first represented the mobster in the late 1950s, after Cohen cold-cocked a federal narcotics officer who claimed that the gangster was dealing drugs. When an inmate named Estes McDonald bludgeoned Cohen with a steal pipe, Belli was summoned. He represented his friend in a lawsuit against the federal government, winning a $110,000 judgment that tax authorities promptly confiscated, including, Belli complained, his fee.

In *My Life on Trial*, Belli wrote, "Was Cohen a crook? On many counts. I'd put Cohen up against the high priests and hypocrites in the ABA or some of the fixers in certain Washington law firms who never go to court. . . . I would have put Cohen up against J. Edgar Hoover himself. And certainly Richard Nixon."

Even though Cohen was a convicted felon and widely considered one of the most dangerous men in the world, Belli had a soft spot for him. "To me," he wrote, "Cohen wasn't a 'pug ugly.' He was a gentleman of great courtliness and charm who was doing the best he could with the lot he had been given in life. . . . The press suggested Cohen had rubbed out Bugsy Seigel as part of the gang war stretching all the way from Las Vegas to Los Angeles." In his autobiography, Cohen wrote, "Attorney Melvin Belli and I were very good friends."

Belli and wife Joy let the gangster babysit for their six-year-old son Caesar. Guests, including newspaper tycoon Randolph Hearst, were visiting their home when suddenly Cohen appeared at the top of the stairs with little Caesar behind him. As Caesar made sounds mimicking gunfire and stuck a banana in the mobster's back, Cohen yelled, "Don't shoot, don't shoot!" Belli started laughing, but several guests quickly darted out the door at the sight of the dangerous underworld figure.

WHILE BELLI CONTINUED his legal career, wife Toni filed divorce papers. She solemnly told *Chronicle* columnist Herb Caen, "You can say I was overmatched." She was awarded a settlement of $27,500.

Belli told friends that he was divorcing his second wife because she had been unfaithful. He had hired a private detective who photographed Toni in a compromising situation with a naval officer. When snapshots of the two embracing landed on Belli's desk, he ended the marriage. She disputed that allegation.

To keep his mind off the divorce, Belli began to write a "general-public" version of *Modern Trials*. The result of his considerable labors was *Ready for the Plaintiff*. A reviewer for The *New York Times* wrote, "Mr. Belli is brash, aggressive, unpleasant, but not entirely wrong."

As with *Modern Trials,* Roscoe Pound found much to praise in *Ready for the Plaintiff.* Belli's friendship with Pound was a delight for both men. When the professor visited San Francisco, Belli entertained him as if he were a sitting president. On one occasion, he stayed at his host's home. Late in the evening, a lovely young woman knocked at the door looking for Belli. Pound, in robe and slippers, answered. When Belli heard whispers in the bedroom, he checked and there was the woman sitting on the floor at the base of the bed. "He was discoursing on Henry VIII," Belli recalled, "and the laws of Edward II and the Boston Red Sox's chances of winning the pennant the success of the Marshall Plan in Europe, and she was absolutely fascinated."

Belli described seeing Pound during his later years at the gifted scholar's home in Cambridge. "A ray of light fell across his snow-white hair, and there was a long ash lying on his vest," Belli wrote. "It took a while for him to wake up. Like a 1917 Ford on a frosty 1957 morning. You could hear the nuts and bolts, kind of rusty, and the gears grinding. But once the engine got going, it was as smooth as a Rolls-Royce."

IN THE MID-1950s, Belli was called upon to represent a Flying Tiger stewardess. She had lost a leg and an arm in a boating accident on Lake Arrowhead, east of Los Angeles. Famous hotel baron Conrad Hilton owned the speedboat. As part of his argument that Hilton was liable for the accident, Belli had several other stewardesses sit behind his counsel table to emphasize the extent of the injuries. One was Joy Turney.

Belli convinced the jury that the wealthy entrepreneur was liable, resulting in a $265,000 verdict. Besides winning a courtroom victory, Belli captured Joy's heart. Milton Hunt, Belli's friend and chauffeur, said Joy's mother "thought that Belli was a good catch." She convinced Joy to marry the older man even though Joy admitted "she was a little afraid of him." They were soon married at the Lutheran Church in San Francisco. Joy was nineteen, Belli two years shy of fifty.

Joy had striking facial features and golden-blond hair. Already pregnant when she married Belli, she soon gave birth to son Melvin Caesar, named after his father and grandfather. He would be called Caesar. Caesar's birth, Belli said, "made me feel young at fifty."

A married man for the third time, Belli began to ply his trade in order to support his family. He and partner Bill Choulos attempted to free two individuals from Mexican prisons.

Dyke Simmons was imprisoned at Monterrey Penitentiary: wrongly accused, Belli believed, of murder. When Belli suggested that his client go to a nearby town to be examined for brain damage, the prison's warden granted the request with one caveat: "One of the you better come back and I don't care which one." Belli nervously remained at the prison the entire time his client was free. He was understandably relieved when Simmons returned to the compound.

In the end there was nothing Belli could do for his client. But Simmons helped himself. He dressed as a woman, hid in the trunk of a car leaving the prison yard, and escaped to Fort Worth, Texas. Unfortunately a wayward motorist ran over him a few months after his escape.

The second Mexican captive, Joel Kaplan, was also charged with murder, though Belli was never told whom Kaplan had murdered. For months Belli and Choulos tried every legal strategy they knew to secure Kaplan's release. The Mexican courts refused to let him go.

Discouraged, Belli met with Kaplan. The discussion, according to *Time* magazine, turned to escape. Belli denied the allegation, saying, "The only legal advice we gave Joel was that in Mexico it's not a crime to escape from jail provided no force or violence or deadly weapons are used."

A short time later, Joel Kaplan stood in the prison yard and watched as a helicopter, painted with the insignia of the Mexican attorney general's office, landed on the prison's grounds. While the guards were attempting to figure out what to do, Kaplan and a fellow inmate jumped aboard. The helicopter flew them to freedom as other inmates cheered below.

Kaplan wrote a book, *Ten-Second Jailbreak*. Actor Charles Bronson starred in the film version, *Breakout*.

IN 1955, BELLI had faced a difficult tort case. At issue was whether or not a new wonder drug, intended to immunize those who were susceptible to infantile paralysis, had been responsible for paralyzing nearly eighty people.

Manufactured by Cutter Laboratories, the vaccine was intended to prevent polio. More than 400,000 people had been successfully injected with the drug. Belli was representing young children from San Francisco's East Bay who had taken the drug, but had still been stricken with polio. Some would never crawl or walk again.

Belli believed Jonas Salk, who developed the vaccine, was not at fault; Cutter was the culprit. They had circulated the polio vaccine prematurely, before final government approvals. All the paralyzed victims had received their vaccine from Cutter, the only one of five manufacturers whose vaccine had caused paralysis.

Belli planned to use strategies he had developed during one of his most famous cases, *Escola v. Coca-Cola*. Prior to the case, personal injury lawyers had been unsuccessful at pinning liability on major corporations. From the moment the case was decided in 1944, it became a legal precedent and the panorama of consumer rights expanded considerably.

Belli's client, Gladys Escola, had picked up a bottle of Coke and attempted to place it in a restaurant refrigerator. Somehow, the bottle exploded and injured her hand so badly that it was virtually useless.

Belli pondered the case for many days. He could certainly sue, but would he have to prove the specifics by which the Coca-Cola Bottling Company was negligent? Was he required to show exactly why the bottle exploded?

The more Belli thought about the case, the more he knew the answers were "no." Instead, he realized, the fact that the bottle had blown up was itself evidence of negligence.

This prompted the lawyer to recall the age-old doctrine of *res ipsa loquitur*—"the thing speaks for itself." "[It was] a doctrine that hadn't been overly used in the law since medieval times," Belli explained, "when they cut the swordmaker's hand off with his own sword if the blade wasn't any good."

After using this principle to reassess his case, Belli turned to his next obstacle. Precedent required a connection between the victim and the perpetrator of the negligence. Without this connection, called privity, there could be no recovery for damages.

Belli set about to making new law. "I argued that the time had come to change all that. Manufacturers—even Coca-Cola Bottlers—ought to stand behind their products. They had a general duty. If those products didn't do what their makers said they would do, or if they injured us during normal use, then the manufacturers should pay."

To the shock of companies around the globe, California's Supreme Court justices agreed with the lawyer's proposition. Justice Roger Traynor stretched accountability even further, stating that there was "absolute liability" on the part of those responsible for the product in question.

Belli was ecstatic with the decision, saying, "Traynor's opinion was a decision for the little people, entirely in accord with the winds of change that were blowing in the country—and the world. It was a time when people were becoming increasingly conscious that we were all brothers and sisters, that no one need be alone, that, acting in convert and in justice, we could all make life more worth living."

Now Belli wondered if he could apply the same principles to the Cutter Laboratory case. The answer, Belli believed, lay in the hands of a legal principle called "warranty." It had been the focus of Justice Traynor's concurring opinion in *Escola v. Coca-Cola*. He set out to make it work for his young clients, Anne Gottsdanker and Randy Phipps. On their behalf, Belli alleged breach of warranty and negligence on Cutter's part.

Belli felt strongly that the pharmaceutical industry, intent on preserving their right to produce experimental drugs, did everything possible to thwart his efforts in the cases against Cutter.

Dr. Jonas Salk helped Belli combat what he believed was a conspiracy to hide the facts. When Belli interviewed Salk, the doctor explained the precise manner by which the vaccine was manufactured. He surmised that Cutter had not followed the correct procedures. He also advised Belli to check government records, since federal regulators had tested various companies' vaccines when the paralysis cases were reported. After the tests Cutter was the only company denied permission to continue manufacturing.

Armed with Salk's suggestions, Belli subpoenaed Cutter records. The company's lawyers refused to provide them, until the presiding judge boldly ordered, "Have the records here at nine-thirty in the morning."

The records clearly indicated that technicians at Cutter had not followed Dr. Salk's procedure. Ten of their twenty-eight batches were contaminated.

Belli called to the stand Dr. Walter Ward, Cutter's medical director. Little by little, Belli prodded the doctor into admitting inconsistencies in the production of vaccine, especially Lot Number 19764, which had been injected into the arms of Belli's clients.

For days, Belli squared off against Ward and other Cutter employees. Realizing they were in trouble, Cutter subpoenaed Nobel Prize winner Dr. Wendell Stanley. He scoffed at Belli's notions that Cutter was responsible for the faulty vaccine.

The night after Stanley testified, a colleague in Washington told Belli that the doctor had previously testified at a congressional hearing. When asked a question about vaccines, Stanley said, "I know very little about polio." When Belli confronted him the next day, Stanley slouched in the witness chair and admitted to making the statement.

The jury awarded Gottsdanker $131,500 and Phipps $15,800. Both verdicts were based on breach of warranty, signaling a new national precedent that sent a chill through manufacturers and their law firms.

Belli's latest contribution to the law did not go unnoticed. *Time* magazine lauded his efforts as "Herculean" and said the case was "the most potent new weapon aimed at making business safeguard consumers." David Casey, president of the California Bar Association, agreed. In a letter to Belli, he wrote, "To my mind, this is the greatest single blow for justice that has ever been struck by any lawyer and to you must go the satisfaction of having almost single-handedly produced some relief for these poor unfortunates who ten years ago would have received no compensation."

Brimming with confidence, Belli represented another polio vaccine victim, and in doing so, took his demonstrative evidence concept to another level. Eleven-year-old Brian May was trapped in an iron lung as a result of Cutter vaccine. To provide the jury with a glimpse into his client's diminished existence, Belli produced "A Day in the Life of Brian May." After the film was shown, there wasn't a dry eye on the jury.

This was the first such film to be used in a trial, but a witness for Cutter disputed whether Brian even had polio. Belli erupted, later recalling that as he rose to cross-examine, "I was Clarence Darrow, Louis Pasteur and Albert Einstein all wrapped into one."

Belli's performance would have earned him an Oscar. Instead, he had to be satisfied with the knowledge that those who witnessed it called it his finest hour. The jury agreed, awarding Brian's mother $75,000 and Brian $600,000, the highest personal injury sum ever.

BOOK II

7

JACK RUBY

ON NOVEMBER 22, 1963, President John F. Kennedy was assassinated. Police soon arrested Lee Harvey Oswald as his killer.

Before Oswald could stand trial, Dallas nightclub owner Jack Ruby shot him in the basement of the Dallas Police Department. Melvin Belli was contacted and soon agreed to act as Ruby's defense attorney.

Belli summarized his reasons for defending Ruby in *My Life on Trial*. "This was a big trial that could focus world-wide attention on mental health, and its unsatisfactory, archaic relationship to the law," he wrote. "Primarily I thought I could do some good for Jack. A lawyer who takes causes instead of clients is in the dangerous position of the surgeon who operates on a disease instead of a single patient. Law and medicine are professions in which you must deal with people one by one; there were many causes in my mind in accepting the Ruby case, but the main cause was the attempt to save the life of this lonely man."

Belli was less clear on how and why he was retained. He gave two accounts, both of which appeared in conflict with the facts. In one version Earl Ruby appeared in a courtroom in Los Angeles where Belli was trying a murder case and asked him to represent his brother. In the other he was brought into the case because he was "famous" and would add to the amount of money syndicators could charge for Jack Ruby's life story.

"Mel told me that the family was going to sell foreign rights to Jack's story," cocounsel Joe Tonahil recalled. "They'd raise $100,000 and that would be the fee. He [Belli] only got about $15,000 and I never got anything."

Tonahill said he warned Belli "that Oswald and Ruby might be part of a conspiracy and if they were, we don't want any part of that." He and Belli then met in Dallas, and after Belli assured him that there was no connection between the two killers, Tonahill agreed to participate in Ruby's defense. Tonahill said his decision was also based on his realization that Oswald and Ruby were simply "two nuts."

Earl Ruby told the Warren Commission he had never heard of Belli until he met Los Angeles journalist Billy Woodfield. Earl had telephoned Reprise Records executive Michael Shore at his brother's behest. He gave this account of the conversation: "Well, I mentioned that Jack had said people were interested in a story on Jack and Jack had said to contact [Shore], [and] ask his advice. And so [Shore] says, 'Gee, isn't that a coincidence,' he says, 'because I've got somebody sitting right here in my office that would be the perfect man to do a story on Jack if one is going to be done.' And he says, 'his name is Billy Woodfield. . . . ' So he says, 'I think you ought to come out here,' the conversation got to that, 'so we can talk it over.' So I flew out there a day or two later."

Earl Ruby reported that Shore and Woodfield met him at the Los Angeles airport. "The first thing they say," Earl said, "'Have you got a lawyer yet?' I says, No . . . I tell them what is going on, so I am not sure yet. So they start talking about Melvin Belli. I have never heard of him. . . . And they say, 'By coincidence he is in town. He is in L.A.'"

Earl also told author Gerald Posner that Belli agreed to take the case for nothing since the publicity and the book that would result would be payment enough.

Belli's colleague Seymour Ellison remembered speaking to Belli on the telephone about the Ruby matter. "He told me, 'Hey, Sy, I'm really into this case. Can you handle it? Tell them I'll get back to them tomorrow.'" The case Belli was trying was, in Ellison's opinion, a loser. "It was a twenty-eight cent case," he said. "A client was charged with lewd conduct in connection with having oral sex with a client on his desk. I think Mel liked the facts more than what the case was worth."

Ellison carried out his orders. He was told that Belli had to call by 10:00 am the following day if he wanted to be retained as Ruby's attorney. Three hours before the deadline, Belli telephoned and asked, "Did you call me last night and say something about the Oswald case?'" Ellison said he told his colleague "that I understood from the Vegas people that Jack Ruby's brother Earl wanted to talk to him. Mel finally figured it all out and called Vegas and then talked to Earl and the two made a deal. I always was amazed because Mel almost missed out on the case of his life due to the piece of shit, worthless case he was trying."

Ellison couldn't recall who the Vegas caller was. "It wasn't Earl Ruby," he said, "And not a lawyer. It was someone connected with what I called the 'gaming industry.' The name was on a memorandum in the Ruby files that Mel brought back from the trial. There were five or six boxes stuffed with them." In 1981, Ellison told author Robert Blakey that the person was "a Las Vegas attorney who said, 'Sy, one of our guys just bumped off the son of a bitch that gunned down the President. We can't move in to handle it, but there's a million bucks net for Mel if he'll take the case.'"

WHEN MELVIN BELLI stepped out of a fancy automobile in front of the Dallas County Courthouse on the chilly morning of February 18, 1964, flashbulbs popped, frenzied reporters shouted questions, and police manhandled the boisterous crowd. Belli, briefcase in one hand, his trademark black Homburg in the other, stepped lively up the steps. Inside, Judge Joseph Brantley Brown prepared to convene what the media dubbed "The Trial of the Century."

The trial would decide the fate of Jacob Rubenstein. Known widely as Jack Ruby, the snaky strip-club owner was charged with gunning down suspected presidential assassin Lee Harvey Oswald. A jury of Ruby's peers would decide if he was guilty of first-degree murder or not guilty by reason of insanity. If found guilty, Ruby would face death by electrocution.

Belli's appearance on the scene added to the Hollywood atmosphere surrounding the trial. Several publications were more interested in Belli's fashion statements than his prowess as an attorney. *Time* magazine applauded his "Chesterfield overcoat with fur collar." *The Saturday Evening Post* described his tailor as having "added certain nonconformist modifications. The jacket and matching vest are lined with bright red silk, and the pockets of the sharply creased trousers are cut parallel to the waist, frontier style."

Washington Post reporter Bill Flynn focused on the overall "Belli look." He described the lawyer's fondness for "Saville Row suits, hand-made shirts with diamond studs, flowing Byronesque ties, starched cuffs, and polished high-heeled black boots." New York reporter Dorothy Kilgallen, Belli's steady lunch partner during the trial, observed, "The Carl Sandburgs of the future will spend whole lifetimes trying to analyze the drama of this week and this scene." She described Belli's demeanor as "Chesterfieldian."

Al Maddox, who booked Jack Ruby into jail following his arrest, remembers that Belli was "very gracious, had a lot of class. He was ooz-ing with intelligence and knowledge. I'd put him and Jack in a room and let them talk."

As Belli stood beside Jack Ruby, court observers noted the physical dif-ferences between them. Belli, shorter in stature, was a commanding fig-ure with noticeable bulk. Bushy eyebrows and a furrowed brow crowned black horned-rimmed glasses, perched on an oversized nose and square set jaw. When he made a point, he thrust his glasses forward as if to say, "Now, listen closely or you'll miss something important."

In contrast, fifty-one-year-old Jack Ruby's small frame seemed to have gotten even smaller since his arrest eighty-six days earlier. His face was nondescript and expressionless, his hairline, receded. He spoke in a high-pitched voice with a slight lisp, a trait that caused some to dub him a "sissy."

If Lee Harvey Oswald's killer possessed any distinguishing character-istic, it was his eyes. Belli said, "There was something about [Ruby's] eyes. They shone like a beagle's."

BELLI AND RUBY were highlighted in the February 21, 1964, issue of *Life* magazine. Featuring the controversial photograph of Lee Harvey Oswald brandishing his rifle on the cover, the magazine's headline read, "Exclusive—Oswald Armed for Murder, in Full and Extra Ordinary Detail, the Life of the Assassin." Below the caption, a blurb read, "As Jack Ruby Goes to Trial, Cast of Characters: How the Law Applies."

If Belli wanted the world to believe Ruby was insane, the two-page vertical photograph of Jack on pages twenty-six and twenty-seven must have pleased him. Ruby, in a dark suit, white shirt, and tie, stood hand-cuffed, blankly staring out of the page. To Belli's delight, the photograph's caption read, "As Ruby goes to trial, the question before the court: Was This Man Sane?" Readers were informed "that this extraordinary picture of Jack Ruby was taken as he was leaving jail for pretrial tests by doctors to examine the physical and mental condition of the man who shot Lee Harvey Oswald." When asked about the insanity defense, DA Henry Wade stated, "We think it is a case of cold-blooded, calculated murder."

The article featured photographs of Ruby at various stages of his life. He was shown in Army uniform holding hands with a woman friend, as a "song and dance man" tapping his feet with a young dancer named Sugar Daddy, alongside sister Eva, and at the moment when he approached Oswald, gun at ready. The final photograph featured a smiling Ruby, dapperly dressed in a black suit and white tie, with two of his Carousel Nightclub strippers. A portion of the caption said that Ruby was "basking in the attention of two of his strippers."

The story described Belli as "a Californian with a fantastic record of courtroom victories." On pages thirty-two and thirty-three, the "Cast of the Courtroom Drama" was presented. In a photograph, Belli stands in his office, flanked by law books and a brick wall peppered with memorabilia. Pictured in smaller photographs are chief prosecutor Henry Wade, Assistant DA Bill Alexander, and presiding Judge Joe Brown.

Wade, wearing black horn-rimmed glasses, is pictured chatting on the telephone, tugging at a cigar stuffed into the right corner of his mouth. The caption mentions that Wade's office had won 189 felony trials and lost only thirteen that year.

Left out of the photographs was Belli's three-hundred-pound cocounsel, Joe Tonahill. A native of Hot Springs, Texas, Tonahill, like Belli, was more experienced in personal injury law than criminal law. "Tonahill did not belong in the case," attorney Bill Alexander said. "He was a big, bullfrog of a guy, a bullshit artist who liked to overpower people with his size and his voice. I guess he was chosen since he a personal injury lawyer buddy of Belli's and because he was from Texas. But he was from the southeast part, not Dallas and that didn't help the defense any."

As jury selection approached, Belli and Tonahill knew they faced an uphill battle. Their client had committed murder in front of millions. Viewers who sought a glimpse of Lee Harvey Oswald instead watched in horror as the Dallas strip-club owner shot and killed the alleged presidential assassin.

Ruby's case offered Belli few options. He could attempt to strike a plea bargain with the prosecution, plead his client guilty, and throw Ruby on the mercy of the court. Later Bill Alexander would express shock that Belli had not chosen this line of defense.

But DA Wade, who would later become famous as "Wade" in the momentous *Roe v. Wade* case, decided that Ruby would be prosecuted to the full extent of the law. No plea bargain would be made.

Belli's second option was to plead Ruby guilty but argue special circumstances. This way Belli hoped to convince the jury that Ruby should be spared the death penalty. Though his legal colleagues urged him to take that line of defense, Belli ignored it.

Instead Belli chose to plead his client "not guilty by reason of insanity." He was determined to base his defense on "psychomotor epilepsy," a condition that could excuse Ruby's actions.

It was risky. Belli knew that although it was a recognized excuse for criminal conduct, most juries disliked the plea since it freed a guilty man based on a "technicality." Every member of the defense team and his legal colleagues in San Francisco discouraged the often-unsuccessful strategy, but Belli was stubborn.

"I ask Mel what he was doing," Seymour Ellison said, "and he told me, 'Cy, what greater accomplishment could there be in law than to have a man found not guilty when so many millions of people saw him do it? If I can walk the guy out, I'd be bigger than Clarence Darrow ever was.'"

From that moment on, Ellison believed his partner was on a mission. "It was his new Holy Grail," the lawyer said, "to get Ruby off."

Ruby's defense team believed that no jury in Dallas, or even the whole state of Texas, could give their client a fair trial. The city had watched Ruby shoot Oswald. Furthermore Belli felt the citizens of Dallas had been embarrassed over Kennedy's assassination. To that end he argued that it was impossible for any juror to be impartial. Sending Ruby to the electric chair would provide closure and show the world that there was justice in the Lone Star State.

The city of Dallas concerned Belli. Never one to hold back his feelings, he described Dallas as "a city of hate, a city where Adlai Stevenson was spat upon and hit on the head with a picket sign and where the American flag was hung upside-down by General Edwin Walker, a man relieved of his command in Germany for indoctrinating his troopers in the right-wing extremism of the John Birch Society." He added "[Dallas] was a city where the 'Minutewoman' would get on the telephone and call all over with such messages as 'Mental health is Communistic' and

'Fluoridation is a Communist plot.' And this was not just a lunatic fringe, this was the prevailing mood of the Dallas oligarchy who ran the town and told it what to think."

Later, Federal Judge Sarah Hughes agreed with Belli's assessment. She called Dallas "The only American city in which the President could have been shot." Reporters called Dallas "Murder capital of the world," a "sick city," a "festering sore," and a "city of shame and hate."

If lack of a viable defense for Ruby and Dallas's prevailing mood of hatred toward him weren't enough, Belli believed Judge Brown was bent on executing his client. Belli would later say, "He was weak and he let the District Attorney make his decisions for him, because he knew he was too ignorant of the law to make many decisions on his own."

In asserting Judge Brown's lack of competence, Belli pointed out that the judge had never graduated from high school, that he attended what the barrister called "a third-rate law school, practiced law for one year, became a justice of the peace, and two decades later was appointed to the criminal court."

An early ruling called for the judge to check case law and the application of a basic legal term, *res gestae*. Belli swore that Judge Brown summoned him to the bench and said, "Mel, I wish you'd lay off that pig Latin."

In later articles Belli accused Judge Brown of racism. He claimed that when he mentioned several cases supporting his plea that Ruby be released on bail, Judge Brown whispered, "Mel, them's nigger cases. Don't cite 'em."

JFK assassination expert Mary Farrell defended Brown. "In Texas in the 1960s," Farrell said, "judges were not noted for being PhDs on the bench. They were ordinary people but that was okay. Not Harvard or Yale, but smart men with good common sense."

Though Judge Brown was concerned with the safety of those involved in the trial, Belli admitted he was apprehensive about his own welfare. He was advised to keep out of sight, but in pure Belli style, he and Tonahill paraded down Dallas's main streets like they were tourists.

Belli refused the county sheriff's offer to provide security, but told *Playboy* magazine, "I'm going to tell you the truth. I was scared shitless. I used to say, despite all my enemies, that no one would ever actually want to shoot me. But after walking down the street and seeing the hate in the eyes of everyone who watched, I never would say that again."

During his first press conference in Dallas, Belli swore that Jack Ruby would be afforded his every Constitutional right. When Judge Brown pounded his gavel to quiet noisy spectators and begin "The Trial of the Century," Belli was determined that justice would prevail. Twenty-five days later, he would scream that it had not.

8

INSANITY

"**OUR OBLIGATIONS IN** the Jack Ruby case were multiple," Melvin Belli stated. "To [our client] we owed a defense waged sincerely and strongly. To the community . . . we owed a disciplined, sober, complete presentation, to bare the facts, to lay to rest the rumors, and, not incidentally, to show the watching world how a defendant's rights were protected under the American legal system."

With this in mind, Belli set out to disprove the district attorney's assertion that Jack Ruby was sane and accountable for his actions when he shot Lee Harvey Oswald. Determined to push forward with the insanity defense, he rounded up an all-star cast of psychiatrists. Thirty years of practice had brought him into contact with science's finest minds. He intended to use the best of the best to defend Jack Ruby.

Belli's psychomotor epilepsy theory was based on a medical paper written by Cyril Courville, a noted neuropathologist at the University of Southern California. Dr. Courville was generally recognized as the country's leading authority on head injuries. After studying the paper, Belli asked the doctor if an epileptic "fit" might have caused Ruby's behavior. Courville said that this was possible and referred Belli to Dr. Manfred Guttmacher, heralded as the most distinguished forensic psychiatrist of the time.

Building on Courville's assessment, Belli secured court permission to have his client examined by doctors. First up was Dr. Roy Schafer, a renowned Yale University psychologist. He spent three days with the accused, peering through thick-lensed spectacles while speaking to Ruby in a soft, fatherly voice. Dr. Schafer performed more than a dozen tests on Ruby. Belli was impressed with the results, observing, "It is fascinating how the clinical psychologist, through the accretion of piece after piece of response, of evasion, of mannerism, is able to fit together a picture of a man's mind."

Belli discovered that Dr. Schafer utilized multiple avenues to dissect Ruby's psyche. After pegging Ruby's IQ at 109, Schafer surmised, "Of special interest are indications of disruption and confusion in Mr. Ruby's experience of his own body. He feels generally damaged, impaired, and impulsive. . . . He is likely to be abrupt and explosive in his actions, and particularly so in his aggressive reactions."

Dr. Schafer then added, "[Ruby's] poor judgment and his feeling that he is not fully in possession of his body and its actions, and mistrustful and grandiose tendencies all point to the likelihood of his committing irrational acts of violence."

To conclude, Dr. Schafer said, "On the whole, the test results indicate the presence of brain dysfunction on a physical basis." The physician believed further tests, including electroencephalographic and physical neurological examinations, should be conducted. Belli immediately appealed to the court for permission to conduct the tests. Without them he believed a jury would find his arguments unconvincing.

While Belli appreciated the first medical report, he was overjoyed when two other experts, Dr. Walter Blomberg and Dr. Manfred Guttmacher, confirmed Schafer's analysis. Even the court's independent expert, Dr. Martin Towler, concurred. "It is my opinion that the subject [Ruby] is suffering from a seizure disorder." Henry Wade dismissed the report as inconsequential.

ARMED WITH PSYCHIATRIC reports that Ruby should not be held legally responsible for his behavior, Belli's outlook on the case vastly improved. He knew gaining a jury's support would be an uphill climb, but he was confident that he was building a convincing case.

The task was more difficult than it first seemed. There was bad blood between Belli and Judge Brown. The two had met once before, when Belli joined a Texas appeal case involving a stripper named Candy Barr.

Candy, one-time girlfriend of Belli's friend Mickey Cohen, started her career as a dancer at Barney Weinstein's Theatre Lounge. She was well known not only for her striptease, in which she let a Stetson dangle from her left breast, but for having shot a former husband.

Narcotics officers decided she was too popular, and a "Get Candy" order was issued. During a raid on her apartment two days later, Candy reluctantly pulled an Alka-Seltzer bottle full of marijuana from inside her blouse. She was convicted of a narcotics violation and sentenced to fifteen years in prison.

Belli appealed the decision, but a sidebar issue got his attention. In a sworn affidavit, Candy alleged that during a break in her trial, Judge Brown had ordered her to his chambers. There, he asked her to pose for photographs. She acquiesced in the interest of justice.

Judge Brown disputed the stripper's story. Belli believed his client. He wrote Judge Brown a scathing letter condemning the unprofessional conduct.

When they first met regarding the Ruby case, the judge greeted Belli by saying, "I remember you. You sent me the telegram."

BELLI DESCRIBED JUDGE Brown as "chunkily constructed, white-haired, and handsome in bulldog-faced fashion."

The judge's chief characteristic was his folksy charm. During the Ruby case, he knew that the world was watching, especially the voters in his Dallas precinct. In a special pretrial report delivered to the defense by R. B. Denson, a Dallas investigator, Brown was described as being, "extremely sensitive to political pressures, especially from wealthy and influential persons." Ironically they also knew that Brown had solicited Jack Ruby when he applied for membership to the Dallas Chamber of Commerce in 1959. The judge, who earned a lifetime membership by signing up one hundred new members, said that "he hadn't really known him [Ruby] then."

Judge Brown toyed with Belli throughout the trial. In chambers between court sessions, he told the barrister, "Mel, you've got the case beat right now" and "You're the best lawyer who has ever appeared before me."

BELLI BELIEVED BAIL was chief among Jack Ruby's rights. The attorney insisted release prior to trial was appropriate, despite the capital charge against his client.

This was a strategic decision. Belli intended to use the bail hearing to question witnesses and discover what evidence the prosecution had amassed against his client. While there was no doubt of Ruby's "moral" guilt, the "not guilty by reason of insanity" defense could eliminate his legal guilt. Belli wanted to know how the prosecution would refute his claim.

The day after Christmas, 1963, Judge Brown called to order the first of Ruby's two bail hearings. San Francisco Attorney Nathan Cohn warned Belli of the outcome. "I told Mel that Judges in Texas only permitted bail in one type of case," Cohn said. "That was when a white man shot a black man."

When Ruby, described by Belli as "an intense, emotional man," noticed photographers ready to pop their flashbulbs, he quickly removed his glasses and told a journalist, "I feel wonderful." Enjoying his celebrity status, he had donned a dark blue suit and swept back his thinning hair. Sheriff Bill Decker hovered nearby, hoping against hope nobody would shoot his captive.

Interestingly enough, for one of the few times in his life, the famous San Francisco attorney intended to play down the rhetoric. "My own press notices had been bad," he said. "A lawyer should be something of a showman, and I confess readily to a certain affection for the dramatic. . . . My use of such devices had earned me adjectives in the press like 'showy' and 'flamboyant' . . . I was determined . . . that the defense presentation would be pointedly sober and serious."

When he stood to begin questioning Captain Will Fritz, Belli learned of Texas courtroom custom. Henry Wade objected—not to the question, but to Belli's having risen from his seat. Apparently Judge Brown preferred lawyers to sit while speaking. Belli recalled other judicial idiosyncrasies he had witnessed. "I have been told to stand in Maine," he told a reporter, "[to] be seated in California, argue from a lectern in Florida, argue from counsel table in Spokane."

Belli, though uncomfortable in his seat, questioned Captain Fritz and Detective James Leavelle, and George Senator. He also questioned a stripper named Little Lynn, who was Ruby's roommate, and Doyle Lane, the manager of a Western Union outlet where Ruby purchased a money order shortly before shooting Oswald. The latter three were called to establish that there was no "malice aforethought."

Little Lynn's appearance in the courtroom ironically triggered *her* arrest. Court matron Nell Taylor patted down the stripper as she marched past reporters to gain entry to the proceedings. The security check included a search of the witness' purse. Inside, Taylor found a 6.35 caliber Italian-model gun with a blue steel barrel and mother-of-pearl handle.

Sheriff's deputies, in tandem with the prosecution, seized the opportunity to discredit one of Belli's main witnesses. Little Lynn was charged with carrying a weapon without a permit. FBI agents questioned her in Judge Brown's chamber. She cried, swearing she had no intent to cause harm, and was released on $1,000 bail. Lynn had broken the law despite the fact that the weapon was unloaded and had no firing pin.

Once she composed herself, Little Lynn testified on Ruby's behalf. "Jack is a most wonderful fellow," she said. She went on to describe how methodical Ruby had been on the telephone prior to the shooting. The Western Union manager testified that although there was someone in line ahead of him, Ruby seemed in no hurry.

Belli believed he had proven that Ruby was calm just minutes before the shooting. He turned his attention to expert testimony. Dr. Blomberg and Dr. Schafer recounted their findings for the court.

Belli had Dr. Blomberg explain "confabulation." Dr. Blomberg told the court it was "a process by which those mentally ill who go through amnesiac periods fill in the details subsequently, to keep their listeners—and themselves—from realizing that they cannot remember what happened." Blomberg explained that this was why he felt Ruby had "made up" much of what he told the police.

AS THE TRIAL date drew near, Belli told colleagues he might still save Ruby's life. A judge he knew warned, "Don't let it [Dallas] fool you, they'll make it look good, but you haven't got a chance in this hanging town." Belli continued his efforts to give his client a fair trial. On February 10, the court held a hearing for a motion for change of venue.

To support his contention that Jack Ruby could not have a fair trial in Dallas, Belli interviewed more than 150 city residents. From the outset, Belli believed that *Dallas Times Herald* columnist A. C. Green was correct when he had written "we are on trial." Based on that assertion, he now set out to prove that the citizens of Dallas felt they must "convict

Ruby to acquit the city."

Belli and Tonahill found an unlikely ally when they sauntered into the Neiman-Marcus store that JFK's motorcade had passed before his assassination.

As the lawyers browsed the store during a sightseeing tour, a short, jovial man approached them. "I'm Stanley Marcus," he said. For nearly an hour, the three men chatted about the store, Jack Ruby, and the city of Dallas.

When the question of fair trial came up, Belli noted Marcus's skepticism. "I have grave reservations whether the defense or the prosecution can get a fair trial in Dallas," he explained. The lawyers asked him to testify.

During the hearing Marcus repeated his viewpoint. Belli believed his testimony and that of others who felt likewise produced a strong case for change of venue.

Judge Brown considered several alternative sites, including San Antonio, Midland-Odessa, Beaumont, El Paso, and Waco. The latter was dismissed because of its "Bible-Belt" population.

Journalists reported Judge Brown's decision, verbatim. "The true test," he said on Valentine's Day, 1964, "of determining whether or not the state and defense can receive a fair and impartial trial in this case rests upon the actual examination of the prospective jurors."

Joe Tonahill said Judge Brown "didn't have the courage to grant the motion to move the trial." To Belli, the decision meant Jack Ruby would be tried for murder in Dallas. Few jurors, he believed, were ever going to admit that, like Assistant District Attorney Bill Alexander, they wanted to "fry him."

AFTER A LUNCH at Joe Bank's Chili Parlor near the Dallas courthouse, Belli stopped in a barbershop for a trim. As he adjusted to the chair and the barber placed a warm towel around his neck, the attorney heard an onlooker comment, "And they got Jew psychiatrists out of Maryland."

As his blood pressure began to rise, he heard another patron say, "Yeah. Those slick Jew psychiatrists with their slick Jew lawyers."

Belli, whom no one had recognized, had heard enough. He tossed the towel aside, leapt up, and stared straight at the barber. While pressing his hand in the air, he shouted, "*Achtung. Achtung. Heil* Hitler!"

"I goose-stepped out of the place while the barber stood there open-mouthed," Belli recalled. "And no one had the balls to follow me."

9

RUBY ON TRIAL

A DETERMINED MELVIN Belli pushed past reporters shortly after 8:00 am on February 18, 1964—day one of Ruby's trial. Dallas's honor was at stake, and the city was intent on reclaiming its dignity.

To that end Judge Brown and public relations expert Sam Bloom decided what media would be allowed in the courtroom. "Liberal" newspapers such as the *Chicago Tribune, San Francisco Chronicle*, and *New York Herald Tribune* were not permitted courtroom entry and were forced to be part of a "coverage pool." Seats were given to *The National Observer, Life, Time* magazine, and the *Saturday Evening Post*. The *Post* had printed a scathing article about Belli.

The decor of the second-floor courtroom was outdated and fading. The pale green walls needed a fresh coat of paint, and the high ceiling, with a dozen slow-moving fans, was a dirty white. Green-tinted Venetian blinds hung on the windows. Judge Brown's wooden bench sat in front of the flags of the United States and Texas. Belli wondered which weighed more heavily in the courtroom.

The judge sat in a high-backed leather chair with a spitoon positioned nearby. Spectators were forced to sit on uncomfortable wooden benches. The lawyers sat behind huge wooden counsel tables squarely in front of the judge, with the prosecution positioned nearest the jury. This disturbed Belli, but he had no choice in the matter.

To Belli, jury selection was an art. Time and time again he had proven his knack at selecting jurors who supported his clients. On occasion there was no valid reason for his choices. His "gut hunches" had proven correct.

Several times during his career, Belli was asked to describe the perfect jury. He said, "I think a jury is created to reflect the mores, the temper, the feeling, the economic, social, and political interpretations of a particular community at a particular time. We do not need a collection of eggheads in a jury box." He added, "Jurors should mirror the community foibles and prejudices; they should be the community in a looking glass."

Asked to comment on the likelihood of finding an open-minded panel in Dallas, Belli said, "I believed quite simply that the community was so self-conscious, so inflamed with shame, and with the need to find a scapegoat that it was impossible to find a fair jury there." Colleagues back in San Francisco wondered why Belli kept criticizing Dallas and its citizenry when he needed the city on his side.

When the first of nine hundred potential jurors stepped into the courtroom, Belli's face froze. "We're going to get a good belting," Belli whispered to Joe Tonahill. "We've had it. . . . There's not a union man on this list, not a Jew or a Catholic." The panel in front of him was Anglo-Saxon-Protestant. Many cast a baleful eye at Ruby, Belli said, as if *he* had killed JFK.

Both sides had fifteen "peremptory" challenges at their disposal. Regardless, Belli was certain that Jack Ruby's jury, supposedly a jury of his peers, would be anything but. His initial horror was cushioned somewhat as new jurors replaced ones dismissed. He eyed several promising jurors, distinguished by their black, Jewish, and Catholic status.

Hilliard Stone was a calm, middle-age man whom Belli immediately spotted as a defense attorney's worst nightmare: someone who craved a spot on the jury. They would avoid answering any question that might disqualify them. A lawyer had to decipher not what they said, but what they didn't say. Mr. Stone was a perfect example.

Prosecutor Wade asked Stone how he felt about the death penalty. Stone, a red-haired gentleman with a pleasant smile, replied, "I would never restrict society so that it could not rid itself of its undesirable elements." To Belli the answer meant, "Yes, I can fry him if necessary."

While Stone spoke, Belli watched him closely. "[It] was a rather chilling, unctuous way of putting it," he explained. "[And I could tell] he meant it. His hands lay calm and steady in his lap. A juror who says he can vote death and keep his hands steady when he says it is a juror who can honestly make such a vote. If he twists his hands, that means he won't vote death."

When Belli began questioning Stone, he focused on Stone's ability to be fair based on the potential juror's pretrial knowledge of the case. Based on that prior knowledge, Belli theorized that every person who had "viewed Ruby shooting Oswald was a 'witness.'" If he could prove this, Stone and others like him would be disqualified. Texas law dismissed any potential juror who was a witness to the alleged crime. Hilliard Stone was the perfect example: He had viewed Ruby's killing on television and read about it in the newspapers.

After coaxing Stone into describing the exact images he had seen on television, Belli asked him, "[So], I'd have a difficult time then if I tried to produce evidence that no man came out of the crowd and shot Oswald?" Stone's answered, "I've seen this."

Belli submitted a motion to Judge Brown asking that Stone be excused from the case on the grounds that he was a witness to the crime. The judge listened to the argument, heard Henry Wade's counter, and ruled against Belli. Round one to the prosecution.

Undeterred, Belli proceeded to question Stone regarding insanity pleas, his knowledge of the Dallas Citizen's Council, and whether he believed the Dallas police department was Ruby's coconspirator. Stone provided predictable answers, but Belli knew this was not a juror he wanted to keep. "Stone's eager-to-please, eager-to-say-the-safe-thing manner had turned into clipped-voice iciness," the attorney noted. Belli was forced to use one of his fifteen precious peremptory challenges to dismiss him.

As BELLI LAY awake at night during the trial, he said the image of Jack Ruby shooting Lee Harvey Oswald flashed through his mind. How, he wondered, was he going to expect any juror who witnessed what he had to forget that image? The moment was indelibly branded in people's minds. History had been made.

Convinced that "jurors were witnesses and thus disqualified to serve," Belli cranked-up his argument with a courtroom antic that infuriated Henry Wade and Judge Brown.

Texas-native Joe Tonahill questioned a potential juror, a nervous Southwestern Bell Telephone employee. Having established that the man saw Ruby kill Oswald on television, the attorney briskly stepped toward the jury box to serve him with a properly documented subpoena as a witness.

Rising from counsel table, assistant DA Jim Bowie shouted, "Don't take it . . . don't take it." Tonahill could have simply handed it to the juror, but contact without judicial permission was prohibited. Instead the intimidating Tonahill turned toward Judge Brown and said, "You're not going to let me serve it?"

The judge, face flushed, quickly answered, "No, I'm not." Tonahill noted the ruling for the record and believing he had prejudiced the juror with his actions, promptly excused him.

AS JURY SELECTION continued, the cry of the day was, "Of course, I can be fair." No juror, Belli believed, wanted to admit they couldn't. All they knew, or cared to know, was that Ruby's lawyers were attempting to get him out of something he had obviously done, using a technicality meant for sick people. Based on what they had witnessed on television, Ruby wasn't a sick person; he was an assassin.

Midway through the laborious process, Belli was distraught. "Our task was not," he said later, "to pick a good jury; that was impossible. Rather it was our task to head off the dedicated hangman, those whose minds were completely closed against us."

Belli added, "The whole jury [pool] looked like they came out of insurance companies. I decided if I couldn't get warm people— waitresses, etc.—and I had to have cold fish, at least I wanted to have intelligent cold fish."

One hundred sixty-two jurors were examined—125 were dismissed: fifty-eight by the defense, sixty-eight by Henry Wade, and one due to illness. The judge gave Belli three extra peremptory challenges. Belli used all eighteen. The prosecution used eleven. When the jury was finally sworn in, the mix was fascinating: an administrative engineer, a mother of six, a Braniff Airline mechanic, a U.S. postal worker, a chemical company vice president who swore he didn't view the Oswald killing on television, and a bookkeeper whose hero was television series lawyer Perry Mason.

Max Causey was selected jury foreman. Later, he wrote, "In my thirty-five years on the planet I had never been exposed to a more devastating shock than at that moment. I suddenly felt as though the ceiling and all the upper seven floors of the building had collapsed on my head."

Jurors stayed in sleeping quarters near the jury room. Windowless, they were the size of a spare bedroom. They contained a bunk bed, lavatory and commode, with a mirror over the sink. A bare lightbulb hung from the ceiling. Juror Rose, who later turned down $25,000 from *Life* magazine for his account of the trial and jury deliberations, said, "We were in jail too."

At long last Jack Ruby had a jury of his peers, one that would decide whether he lived or died. Could they debate his fate without bias? Belli wondered. Would Ruby truly be given a fair trial?

ON MARCH 4, 1964, Belli sat at his counsel table ready to hear Henry Wade outline the evidence against Jack Ruby. In Texas the defense was not permitted to present an opening statement. This meant the prosecution began full force, with no chance for the defense to tell its side of the story.

When Ruby entered the courtroom, his face was sullen, his fright apparent. Sheriff Bill Decker, aware of the circumstances surrounding the trial, bunched five armed, burly officers around him.

Belli learned that not only was he not permitted an opening statement, but also the prosecution was allowed to open its case by reading the full indictment against the accused. Standing directly in front of Ruby, Henry Wade adjusted his black horned-rim glasses and read out the charges. Ruby's face reddened as the charges were presented, but otherwise he appeared to be oblivious to his surroundings. To ensure that the public and the jury knew that Oswald's killer was a Jew, the indictment read, *State of Texas v. Jack Rubenstein a/k/a Jack Ruby*. This was later perceived as an act of anti-Semitism.

Belli edged closer to his client. Regardless of other emotions, admitted or perceived, the attorney truly believed Ruby was a sick man who required treatment, not death.

When Henry Wade completed his reading, Judge Brown asked for Ruby's plea. The accused said in a soft tone, "Not guilty, your Honor." Belli quickly added, "By reason of insanity."

The best lawyers, Belli knew, were those who truly bonded with their clients. "When I try a case," he wrote, "I suffer all of the ailments, pains and agony, all the ridicule, humiliation and embarrassment of my client. I have been a sick pregnant woman, a man with one leg, a blind man, a woman about to be committed to Bedlam, a man with a burst appendix, a woman with quadriplegia, [and] a chorus girl with diarrhea."

Belli's dedication to a case was profound. "I'm working my cases in the shower," he later told *Playboy* magazine, "when I'm trying to sleep and can't, when I'm on the john, when I'm driving my car, when I'm sitting in those late-night planes." Ruby's case was no exception.

WITNESS CROSS-EXAMINATION WAS Belli at his best. He wrote, "[It] searches the innermost recesses of the closet of the mind, selects, and sweeps it clean. And everybody has some sort of skeleton in his own personal closet. That's why he's afraid of cross-examination."

Belli's skill in this area was tested, since he knew it was critical to Ruby's defense that he had acted without premeditation. To this end, Belli carefully cross-examined the manager of a Western Union office who had sold Ruby a $25 money order for Little Lynn. When the man stated that Ruby seemed "calm" at the time, Belli utilized his trademark "show not tell" tactics to support his position.

He presented the manager with a copy of the telegram sent to Lynn, with the time, 11:17, clearly imprinted on the back. After the manager admitted that the stamp could have indicated as late as 11:17:59, Belli knew he established the exact time when Ruby was "calm." The evidence indicated that less than four minutes later, he shot and killed Lee Harvey Oswald.

Belli watched nervously as Detective James Leavelle testified that as he was being led away after the shooting, Ruby remarked, "I hope the son of a bitch dies." Belli's cross-examination produced a bit of uncertainty as to the exact words Ruby used, but they established for the jury the fact that Oswald's killer had no remorse for his actions.

The next prosecution witness established Ruby's feelings toward John F. Kennedy. Wes Wise, a television commentator, testified that when he showed Ruby photographs of two western saddles to be given to JFK and Jackie, "He [Ruby] had tears in his eyes." This testimony confounded JFK research expert Martha Moyer. "If Ruby loved the President so much," she stated, "why wasn't he in Dealey Plaza or along the motorcade route welcoming his hero instead of at the *Dallas Morning News*?"

The murder weapon, confiscated within seconds of the shooting, was produced in court. It was a .38 caliber Colt Cobra. Ruby had purchased the gun in Chicago three years earlier. The Brantley's Hardware store owner who sold it to Ruby in 1960 displayed it proudly. The gun dealer was asked pull the trigger, and the "click-click-click" resounded eerily in the hushed courtroom.

All the while Ruby sat stone-faced, doodling on a tablet. His expression rarely changed. When the snub-nosed revolver was being mock-fired, jurors flashed a look at him, but he never met their stares.

Ruby's defense was damaged considerably by the testimonies of Dallas policemen Thomas McMillion and D. R. Archer. Belli believed Archer's testimony was more damaging, as it described Ruby's anger prior to commission of the crime.

Archer testified that he was standing nearby when Ruby reached out toward the manacled Presidential assassin. "I saw his face momentarily. . . ." the officer said. "A split second before the shot was fired . . . I did make out the words . . . 'son of a bitch.'"

Worse, Archer recalled that Ruby, while being escorted away, said, "I hope the son of a bitch dies." He also testified that he exchanged words with Ruby in the elevator shortly after the shooting: "I said, 'I think you killed him.' And he replied, 'I intended to shoot him three times.'"

McMillon embellished on Archer's statement, saying that while Ruby approached Oswald, he muttered, "You rat son of a bitch, you shot the President." Belli knew McMillon's testimony was being imprinted into the jurors' minds. If they believed it, Ruby was a dead man.

Ruby's shoulders slumped at the sound of those words. Belli believed that as time passed, his client was becoming more removed from the proceedings that would decide his fate. On several occasions the attorney had to remind Ruby of certain testimony that he had obviously blocked out.

Hearst reporter Bob Considine vividly described Ruby's courtroom demeanor, "All through the day," he wrote, "Ruby sat nervously. He fidgeted, rubbed his jowls, blinked his eyes, and engaged in intense whispered conversation. . . . He is a shadow of the man who poked a gun into the side of Oswald . . . and fired a single lethal bullet."

Sergeant Patrick Dean was head of security for the transfer of Oswald from police headquarters to the courthouse. Along with the television tape of the shooting, Dean's testimony was the state's most effective weapon. In rapid staccato, Dean revealed that Ruby told him he first considered shooting JFK's killer "when he saw Lee Harvey Oswald on the 'show-up stand.'" This referred to the midnight news conference during which Oswald was presented for the world to see. If Dean's testimony were true, then Ruby had formed his intent to kill two days prior to the illegal act.

Dean said, "He [Ruby] believed in due process of law, but he was so torn up—he and his sister—this man had not only killed the President but also Officer Tippit—that he didn't see any sense for a long and lengthy trial that Mrs. Kennedy might be brought down for." Ruby then told him, "That when he noticed the sarcastic sneer on Oswald's face [the night after the shooting], that's the first time [he] thought he would kill him." He added that Ruby said he decided to kill Oswald, "because he wanted the world to know that Jews do have guts."

Dean, Belli said later, "was the man the prosecution needed, the man who would testify to premeditation, who would take the edge off the overwhelming weight of testimony that showed the act itself to have been the spur-of-the-moment culmination of a series of unique circumstances."

10

ON BEHALF OF RUBY

.

TO COMBAT THE mounting evidence presented by the district attorney of Dallas County, Melvin Belli believed he needed a miracle.

Sergeant Patrick Dean alleged that Ruby's crime was premeditated. During cross-examination, Belli continually attempted to trip Dean up and discredit his testimony. Belli was especially tough when pointing out that Dean had not told authorities the salient points of his conversation with Ruby right after it occurred. He also claimed that words Dean attributed to Ruby were not in his client's normal vocabulary.

No matter how much doubt Belli cast on Patrick Dean, he knew the sergeant had been a pivotal witness. So important was his testimony that after he left the witness stand, DA Henry Wade rested the state's case.

On March 6, 1964, Belli implemented his strategy, designed to circumvent the prosecution's accusation that Ruby had planned to assassinate Oswald.

First up was Little Lynn Bennett. Belli's described his witness as "a striptease dancer, an object of a certain sort of celebrity interest. She was a plump and pretty little girl with a demure, round, white collar on her pale maternity suit; she looked more like the girl next door than the girl you'd see on the Carousel Club stage."

After carefully leading her along with easy questions designed to relax her, the attorney finally centered upon the reason for her testimony.

"Lynn, did you speak to Mr. Ruby on Sunday, the twenty-fourth of November?" he asked.

After stating that she chatted with Ruby between 10:00 and 10:30 am, Lynn said, "He sounded like he had been crying." Belli hesitated a moment before proceeding. Ever one for the dramatic, he wanted those seven words to seep into the jury's minds. He believed they accurately depicted Ruby's emotion regarding Kennedy's assassination.

Little Lynn next testified about Jack Ruby's normal demeanor. "He had a very quick temper," she recalled. "He'd fly off the handle. But then it was over."

THE TRIAL RECESSED for the weekend and resumed on Monday, March 9. Up to this point, jurors had only seen one side of Jack Ruby—the side presented by the prosecution. Belli was determined to show them the other side.

Chief among the witnesses was a brunette stripper named Patricia Ann Kohs, aka Penny Dollar, one of Ruby's employees. She told the jury that she witnessed her boss shove an unruly patron down a flight of stairs. "Then we came down," she explained, "[and] Jack was beating [the guy's] head on the sidewalk. Then he stopped all of a sudden and said, 'Did I do that?'"

Kohs's testimony was Belli's attempt to establish that Ruby had a tendency to "black out." The attorney hoped the jury would decide that such a black out had occurred when Ruby shot Oswald.

WNEW radio reporter Ike Pappas cast considerable doubt on prosecution testimony. Pappas, later to enjoy a successful twenty-five-year career as a CBS correspondent, had been standing close to Ruby during the shooting, holding his expensive Swiss tape recorder.

"At the time of the shooting," Pappas recalled, "I was holding what we call a pencil microphone. My proximity to the shooting was . . . five or six feet."

When the tape recording was played, Pappas was heard to ask Oswald, "Lee, do you have anything to say in your defense?" Instantaneously the "pop" sound of Ruby's pistol interrupted. Then confusion reigned.

Belli was quick to point out in no uncertain terms that the recording did not contain any statement by Ruby, contrary to prosecution testimony. To solidify the point, Belli asked Pappas, "What did you hear?" to which the newsman replied, "I heard nothing before the shot."

★ ★ ★

AT 3:39 PM ON March 9, Belli summoned Dr. Roy Schafer to the stand. Without hesitating, he asked Dr. Schafer's opinion of Jack Ruby's mental state.

"I determined that he did have organic brain damage," Dr. Schafer reported.

Satisfied with the impact of the answer, Belli asked what caused Ruby's fury toward Oswald. Schafer paused, then said calmly, "The most likely specific nature of it was psychomotor epilepsy."

Belli intended to establish the trigger that caused Jack Ruby to have an epileptic episode. He asked, "What sort of stimulus might set [Ruby] off?" Dr. Schafer responded, "Very strong emotional stimulation . . . states of fatigue . . . certain kinds of light stimulation, a certain kind of flickering light." When Belli asked Dr. Shafer if he believed Ruby possessed a deranged mind, he answered, "I do."

Certain that he had provided the jury with a bona fide reason for the shooting, Belli excused Dr. Schafer.

When flaxen-haired Dr. Martin Towler took the stand the next morning, the jury was attentive. They wanted to hear what their home-state psychiatrist had to say.

Dr. Towler swore that Jack Ruby had serious mental deficiencies. His diagnosis stemmed from EEG tracings of Ruby's brain. His analysis indicated, "What we refer to as paroxysmal discharges . . . in both temple areas" and that such was "an abnormal finding." He added that Ruby experienced "prickling sensations to the head . . . pressure feelings."

With the wave of a hand, Belli led Dr. Towler to the jury box. As the back row of jurors stood to peer over their colleagues, Belli positioned himself on one side of Dr. Towler while Joe Tonahill stood on the other. Unfolded was more than five hundred feet of the charts, each imprinted with spidery lines representing Ruby's brainwaves.

"The EEGs were the most important single piece of evidence we would have," Belli later said. "And I wanted those intent jurors to understand fully what they told us."

Certainly no one could argue the brilliance Belli displayed when Dr. Manfred Guttmacher was sworn in as a witness. "Do you have an opinion as to Ruby's mental condition at the time Oswald was shot?" Belli began.

The doctor's answer was based on his examination of Jack Ruby on December 21 and 22. A cautious man prone to considerable thought before testifying, Dr. Guttmacher had searched for cause and effect regarding Ruby's conduct. In his report, he stated, "The patient has all of his life exhibited extreme emotional instability and episodic outbursts of aggression. . . . That there is persistently a high degree of impulsively in his behavior cannot be denied."

Dr. Guttmacher was prepared to answer Belli's question regarding the accused state of mind when he shot Oswald. The doctor's response was, "I don't think he was capable of knowing right from wrong or understood the nature and consequences of his act." As Belli knew, this was the precise language contained in the McNaughton Rule, one used as a standard regarding proof of insanity. If the jury believed that Dr. Guttmacher was correct in his diagnosis, then Jack Ruby was not guilty by reason of insanity.

THE CLOCK READ 3:40 pm when cross-examination of Dr. Guttmacher began. The jury shifted in their seats. Belli later said, "[Bill] Alexander had done his homework . . . his was not the blustering, countrified style of his boss."

One particular exchange was noteworthy. Alexander asked when Ruby's seizure state began. Dr. Guttmacher emphasized his previous point, saying, "In my opinion, when he walked down the ramp there and saw all the people, the bright lights." Alexander then asked, "Did he know what he was doing?" to which Dr. Guttmacher replied, "He was very much like a sleepwalker."

Moments later, when asked for his opinion, Dr. Guttmacher stated, "[He was] a mental cripple, carrying an unbearable load, who cracked."

AT 9:21 AM ON March 11, Belli startled the courtroom by announcing, "The defense rests." That meant that Jack Ruby would not testify.

According to jury foreman Max Causey, Belli's decision caught him and the rest of the jury off guard. "The biggest shock of the trial," he wrote, "came . . . when Mr. Belli rose to his feet and told the court, 'The defense rests' . . . I don't think we were any more surprised than the prosecution. I looked over [at them] to see what they were going to do now, and I noticed that they appeared to be taken completely by surprise."

After presenting several doctors who believed Ruby sane, Henry Wade said loudly, "The state rests." Despite his opinion that his office had presented a formidable case against Ruby, Wade believed he would be found not guilty. Describing the scene in Judge Brown's office, Belli recalled, "There was Henry Wade, impatient and angry with the edginess of a man who thought he had lost his case."

Judge Brown was adamant about the final argument. "This case will go to the jury tonight and I don't give a damn what time you finish arguing it. You take as long as you want, but if we run until nine o'clock tomorrow morning, we are going to have the arguments tonight."

The judge, whom Belli alleged read comic books during the final arguments, set down specific rules and regulations regarding courtroom conduct. During summation there would be no radio broadcasts. When the verdict was announced, both radio and live television cameras would relay Jack Ruby's fate to the world.

Belli's description of the courtroom after he returned was vivid. "The high-ceilinged old courtroom was bathed in an unnatural shimmering glare, and there was a circus-like odor of orange peels and tobacco, of packed humanity. For the first time, the ban on standees was relaxed, and all the benches were filled, the walls were lined, and a crowd bellied out around the bailiff's desk near the door to the judge's right."

At 8:04 pm, the jury was led into the courtroom. Judge Brown, enjoying his celebrity, first read the "charge" to the jury. Belli noted their reactions: "Carefully, I watched their expressions. They lit up cigarettes, then sat blank-faced through his [Judge Brown] recitation of legal definitions of murder, insanity, proof, evidence."

The first to rise and make final argument was Assistant DA Bill Alexander, whom Judge Brown had disarmed, at Tonahill's request, of his loaded .44 Magnum. Alexander spoke with the eloquence of a high-school debater attempting to win first prize in the state competition. "I'm not going to defend Oswald to you," he said, "but American justice is on trial. American justice had Oswald in its possession. Oswald was entitled to the protection of the law. Oswald was a living, breathing American citizen."

The moment those words were spoken, Alexander, in the first of many theatrical moments to come, quickly turned to the defendant, who had showed no emotion as the prosecutor mentioned his name, and said in a strong, accusatory tone, "Just like *you*, Jack Ruby, who were judge, jury, and executioner."

Ruby flinched when the prosecutor blasted him, but Alexander wasn't through. He called Ruby "nothing but a thrill killer, seeking notoriety," and said, "Don't tell me it takes guts to shoot a man who is manacled. This is a wanton killing." He then summed up by urging that the jury inflict the death penalty since "he [Ruby] has mocked American justice while the spotlight of the world was on us."

Belli was impressed with co-counsel Joe Tonahill's final argument. As he sauntered across the courtroom, the commanding Texan hammered the prosecution's case. "Scorn dripped from his voice," Belli recalled, "as he roared that the prosecution was vindictively trying to kill Ruby because they had to "get somebody as a substitute for Lee Harvey Oswald."

Regarding the few seconds that caused Ruby and Oswald to meet, Tonahill said, "[It was] probably the greatest coincidence in the history of the world." He exclaimed, "DA Wade is politically ambitious" and sought "another scalp for his belt." He also believed that Alexander, a man he described as having "tarantula-like eyes," was gleefully awaiting the day when he could visit the Huntsville prison and witness Ruby's electrocution.

After a break at half past eleven, the tired-eyed jurors returned. All appeared nervous as they anticipated Belli's final argument.

Regarding the moment, he later said, "When I arose from the counsel table in the dead silence of the expectant courtroom, the fetid odors striking from nostrils, the lights over head glaring down on the haze from cigarette and cigar smoke, I caught a curious look of anticipation in Judge Brown's eye."

Belli added, "I walked the five miles from counsel table to jury rail. It took me several hours. I felt like Alice in Wonderland falling down the hole. My feet didn't seem to touch the floor. I was about to make my plea for Jack Ruby's life."

Some later questioned Belli's motives in representing Ruby, but experts agreed his final argument was a command performance. When the barrister finally sat down, no one could say that he hadn't delivered anything but a sterling performance.

For fifty-eight minutes, Belli was evangelical, the conductor of a symphony, the king of the courtroom. Majestically, he cast his vote in favor of reason, of sympathy, for a client he believed was truly mentally ill.

Reporter Harold Scarlett of the *Houston Post* wrote, "Belli was gifted by nature with a velvety, hypnotic voice that could charm cobras out of their baskets." Whether he could "charm" twelve jurors into supporting his call for a verdict of not guilty by reason of insanity remained to be seen.

Belli, his voice wavering with emotion, surprisingly began by prais-
ing Dallas. "My mother always told me," he said, "that when I came to a
strange place, if I was treated graciously, to thank my hosts. And that I do
here and now first. I have been treated graciously here from the high to
the low, from the taxicab driver to the waitress, from the millionaire to
the pauper, the Rabbi and the Reverend; all individually have treated me
graciously."

The hour was 11:52 pm. Belli reminded the jurors, most of whom
appeared more interested in a good night's sleep, to keep alert. "Let us now
see in these beginning small hours of this morning," he pleaded, "early
morning hours when great discoveries in the history of the world have
been made in garrets and attics and basements and even caves, if here in
your own temple of justice in Dallas we can't rediscover something that
has never really been lost in your great city of Dallas; that we may rediscover justice!"

To do so, Belli said, required paying close attention to the evidence.
"You've heard," he said, "everyone from the 'Weird Beard' [a disc jockey
who described Ruby's potential to shoot Oswald at a press conference]
to the great Dr. Gibbs. How shall you know whom to believe? Whom
shall you cast aside, and in whom shall you find the truth? . . . Well, here
is one infallible test that I give you at the start: If there were someone near
and dear to you, a mother who was sick, if a little one at home in the crib
was convulsing, and you called your doctor in, you'd called someone in
and talked to him and asked him, 'Who shall we send our child to? Who
may we call that we may honestly know before operating on his brain?'
I think then you will get your answer."

This said, Belli lavished praise on Dr. Gibbs, whom he touted as "the
man whom doctors around the world send their electroencephalo-
grams." He added, "When I tell you here is the justice that you can now
discover this waking morning in Dallas, the justice of science and law;
the science of a great doctor whom we brought to your city. . . . If you
believe this great man, Dr. Frederic Gibbs, the man to whom I would say,
'Send your child, your patient,' then this man has given you your answer
for Jack Ruby: Jack Ruby has rage states."

He then lauded both Dr. Schafer and Dr. Guttmacher, and reminded the
jury that Dr. Schafer had said of Ruby, "He has organic brain damage."

Belli also quoted Dr. Walter Bromberg. "[He] told you the same thing
[as Dr. Schafer], organic brain damage that manifests itself functionally or

clinically in the psychomotor variant type of epilepsy which accounts for the 'blackouts' or the 'rage states.'"

Summing up the physician's findings, Belli said, "So we have our diagnosis from our doctors; we have our prognosis. We know why Jack Ruby shot Lee Harvey Oswald, and we know he wasn't responsible at the time."

Belli reminded the jurors that the Ruby case was simple one. He said, "We are not here to try the shooting. We are here to look into this mind with the help of our doctors."

If Belli's preliminary remarks were grandiose, his next statements were a masterpiece of argument. He began by informing the jury that there were multiple questions to be answered before a verdict could be rendered. "Now, let us talk," he began in a fatherly tone, "if I may, about the three lawsuits were are trying. We are not trying one man, one Jack Ruby, we are trying three human beings at one time—take your choice which of the three."

Regarding the first, he said, "That is the law for the ordinary human being in normal mind who under the stress of a tragic event, such as these tragic three days, did what Jack Ruby did. That would be one man we are trying. Your law says you could give him a suspended sentence if you felt the stress, the object of his passion, was too heavy a burden."

Elaborating, Belli told the jurors, "Let us stay with the first man we are trying here. The normal individual who had the 'normal breaking point'—and when I say normal man and normal breaking point, it must run through your minds, the mind of each of you, how you felt on that tragic day when our President was shot. . . . What was your breaking point, you normal people, what were your feelings toward the assassin?"

Regarding President Kennedy, Belli said, "I remember him standing in front of the Berlin Wall saying, 'I am a Berliner,' his hair flying in the wind and the roar of a million German people filling the air to echo far into East Germany."

Returning to his client, his voice booming across the courtroom as reporters noted his every word, Belli said, "So here is the one man I am defending. A normal Texan, a Dallasite who had shot the assassin of the President. I stand in front of you and say, because of these terrible circumstances, the assassination of our President, I cannot advocate lynch law, but our legislature of the great Lone Star State has said that where there is great stress . . . there is an excuse for murder to be committed."

Turning to another line of thinking, Belli offered, "But this first man isn't the case that we have here. We have much more. We have a second man, and a third man."

His voice never wavering, Belli continued: "Let's take this second man, the man who has just the unstable personality, him with his breaking point, the unstable human being, not the ordinarily intelligent or ordinarily emotional human being. This is the man who runs onto the football field to tackle a man on the opposing team, or the man who runs the wrong way, or the man who phones the radio station when the Orson Welles spectacular invasion by the Martians is broadcast. . . ."

To describe the "second man's" psyche, Belli quoted Dr. Holbrook who said, "Jack Ruby has an unstable mind," and Dr. Guttmacher, who opined, "He, Jack Ruby, has more than plain emotionalism, he has a psychotic personality."

Belli was attempting to humanize Ruby, to encourage jurors to compare him to someone they might have known. He said, "Ah, what great sport to have in our community 'the character.' In the old days, we used to call him the village clown, the village idiot. There's a chained wolf to be tormented, there's the hunchback of Notre Dame, there's our own Emperor Norton in San Francisco, the old Humpty-Dumpty who bent over and allowed people to hit him on his backsides with a board for fifty cents."

Concerning the "character," Belli then said, "Ah, what great sport for this troubled human being we're trying, until something goes wrong. Then the cry goes out, 'Whom do you suspect the most, who would do an unusual thing like that?'"

"The answer," Belli said, "the village idiot. You substituted the village clown, the village idiot, Jack Ruby. The man who is always around the police station bringing the coffee, the man who brings the doughnuts, the sandwiches, who can be sent out rousting for the cold beer. He's not the first-class citizen in emotions, or he wouldn't be doing this. He's the second class of man that we are trying here, much more to extenuate him than the first man we could be trying."

Belli then launched into prose that was simple, but eloquent. He said, "But what will you say of the second-class citizen? Publicity he wants, publicity he seeks? Ah, ladies and gentleman of the jury, I supposed before that handful of dust that is each of us settles down on the plain to be scratched by the dancing tumbleweed, that we'd all like to engrave our initials in some big oak tree, that we'd like maybe to be in Bob Considine's or Inez Robb's or Dorothy Kilgallen's column." He added, "There are some of us even who have our faces immortalized at Mt. Rushmore. There are some others of us who do the immortal Shakespeare, Gray's 'Elegy' in the churchyard. There are others who seek more humble forms of immortality. There's this lonely craving that we all have, whether we are the first-class citizen or this now second-class citizen."

Addressing his client, Belli said, "Jack Ruby: This poor sick fellow—and sick he is, and you know he's sick, every one of you in your heart, every one of the twelve of you know he is sick. He is of this second-class for the moment now. There cannot be any doubt that there is something wrong with Jack Ruby."

Belli addressed motive with a rhetorical question. "He did it for money, for glory, for heroism, for a messianic purpose?" Answering it, he alluded to testimony from Penny Dollar, Rabbi Silverman, and Captain Fritz. All, he alleged, had described Ruby as a man who was "staring, staring," one who, after he committed an act of violence, asked, "What did I do, what did I do?"

The wall clock ticked to half past twelve. Belli contrasted Archer's testimony with that of others who heard nothing. Belli asked, "Now, ladies and gentlemen of the jury, even if Jack did say what Officer Archer claims, aren't you satisfied that the mental process of Jack Ruby was confabulation? These big psychiatric terms don't bother us anymore. We're intelligent. We're sophisticated.

"You know what confabulation is. We are psychiatrically oriented: the mind abhors a vacuum. It abhors the insult to the ego of not being able to remember everything that went on. . . . So thoughts, suggestive thoughts, pop back into the human mind as soon as consciousness is regained, and these thoughts are substituted for one's own. It's like water rushing into a dry well."

Belli told the jury that his client did not remember the facts regarding the moment he shot Oswald. He had simply invented a version based on what he was told by others. Truly, Belli said, Ruby was simply filling in the holes since his mind was unwilling to accept his inability to recall details.

Having described the first and second persons that could have stood before the jury for judgment, Belli now allocated time to the third. "The third-category man is a person who not only is the unstable personality who comes—and we didn't ask to come into this troubled world, so that I can say this in good grace—from bad stock."

Belli was referring to accounts that Ruby's mother was mentally ill and his father a drunkard. Certainly, Ruby's stock was questionable.

If the jury agreed with his analysis, Belli believed that he could show that Ruby was indeed the "third man" standing before the jury, and should be evaluated based on the history of mental deficiencies in the family and his own incidents of unstable behavior.

He went on to describe the moments leading up to Oswald's assassination. Belli said, "He walks down the ramp, here this lid that had been on him, and on so *many of us*, not only here in Dallas, but all over the United States—myself—blows off." He surmised that Ruby's feelings were exacerbated by the media frenzy surrounding Kennedy's assassin and the smirk on Oswald's face. Belli said, "This man does not belong in prison. Acquit him—not guilty by reason of insanity." He then added, "He is sick. Give a just and fair verdict compatible with modern science. That's what the world wants to see in justice from this community."

Reporter Harold Scarlett of the *Houston Post* was impressed. He wrote the next day, "Clarence Darrow, the great defender, would have liked it. . . . In less than an hour, [Belli] had ranged over a lifetime of learning. Like a mountain goat, he leaped unerringly from Pasteur to the hunchback of Notre Dame, to Anatole France and 'Penguin Island,' to Humpty Dumpty, to President Kennedy.

"Arguing before the jury," the journalist wrote, "he played that voice [of his] like a symphony. It was by turns a Stradivarius, a bugle, an oboe, a snare drum racing at breakneck speed through key pages of trial testimony."

When Belli concluded at 12:50 am, not a sound was heard in the courtroom. The jurors stared at Belli, and at Jack Ruby. Had they agreed that the accused was a sick man who should be acquitted because of his inability to tell right from wrong?

Prosecuting attorney Henry Wade's retort was short and to the point. For sixteen minutes, he chastised Belli's attempts to confuse jurors with words like "conflabberation," then belittled Ruby, calling him a man who "wanted to go down in the history books."

Challenging the jurors, Wade asked, "What do you want the history books to say about you?" and "Our laws are no stronger than the weakest heart on this jury." He added, "If you turn this man loose, you'd set civilization back a century. You'd set civilization back to barbarism. You'd set civilization back to the lynch laws. I ask you to show Jack Ruby the same mercy, compassion, and sympathy that he showed Lee Harvey

Oswald." He ended his appeal by stating, "Let Communism know that we believe in the right of the law here."

Moments after Wade sat down, the jurors were excused. They retired to their living quarters. While they began to consider the case, Belli chatted with Ruby for a minute, then ambled out of the courthouse.

"I walked uptown," he recalled. "The dark streets were deserted. Sybille Bedford, the English journalist, and I had a chicken sandwich in an all-night lunch counter that reeked of rancid deep-fry oil, and then I walked to my hotel room and tried to go to sleep. The jurors went to bed in their monastic little courthouse cells, preparing their consciences, every thought, for long, careful deliberation on one of the biggest decisions of their lives."

11

THE VERDICT

THE JURY ROOM where Jack Ruby's fate would be decided was unremarkable. "The jurors got there," Belli recalled, "by walking up a curving flight of twenty metal stairs behind the judge's bench. The room was a cheerless, windowless place, about twenty by thirty feet. It had black and tan linoleum on the floor, air ducts and pipes crisscrossing beneath the low, acoustic-tile ceiling. A dozen tan plastic chairs, the kind that come with a kitchen set, lined the oblong ten-foot table."

After an abbreviated night of sleep, the twelve jurors ate breakfast at the Dallas-Jefferson Hotel, then climbed the twenty steps to enter the jury room at 9:15 am. The date was March 14, 1964.

First priority was the selection of a jury foreman. Max Causey had decided on a bathroom break. In his absence, he was elected foreman. He made them repeat the election upon his return.

Causey said his first order of business was to remind his fellow jurors of the "importance and solemnity of the task" at hand. "I then ask for a couple of minutes of silence so that each juror could search his or her mind," he said, "and ask divine direction in arriving at a decision."

To organize the deliberations, Causey said he jotted down the important issues the jury needed to consider. The first was a given: Did Jack Ruby shoot Lee Harvey Oswald as charged? The second: Was Jack Ruby legally sane at the time of the shooting? The third, Causey said, was: Is

Jack Ruby legally sane at the present time? The fourth could only be answered if he was determined to be sane at the time of the shooting; Was there malice aforethought on Ruby's mind at the time of the shooting?

Causey told the jurors that after debate of those issues, then and only then could they discuss the alternative punishments, from suspended sentence to death. This said, the jurors were set to discuss the pertinent issues.

But they didn't, at least not for very long. Apparently, two jurors had slept through important medical testimony and asked that it be reread. It wasn't. Then, after minimal discussion, an initial ballot was taken as to each of the initial issues. The votes came in: twelve to zero in favor of yes, Ruby shot Oswald; no, he was not insane when he did so; no, he was not insane now; yes, he had shot Oswald with malice aforethought. It was game, set, and match for the prosecution.

Causey said, "I asked each juror to write down the sentence that he or she felt should be assessed Ruby based on the evidence that we had heard. I asked them to take their time and not to make a hasty decision since a man's life was at stake." Sitting at the north end of the conference table, Causey tallied the votes. Nine called for the death penalty, two for life imprisonment, one for sixty years.

Admitting he was one who had voted for life imprisonment, Causey then told the jury why. In his journal, he later wrote, "I had felt from the early stages of the trial that Ruby was most probably a mentally unstable individual, a social deviant, a personality obsessed with notoriety who with certain stimuli might become violent."

When he expressed this view, Causey said, other jurors reminded him that he had "not hesitated or wavered" in his vote for guilty. He said he agreed that they were right, but added in the journal, "I felt that there should have been more latitude within the law as it would apply to an unstable personality that was within McNaughton Rule. . . . To me, it looked as thought we, the jury, were on a tightrope with no place to go but to the death sentence for Ruby."

A second vote was taken as the minutes ticked away. This time ten voted for death. Causey said he was one of the dissenters: "I was deliberately attempting to slow down what I felt was to be the ultimate sentence of death."

The third vote was twelve to zero for death. Jack Ruby would be electrocuted.

Two hours and nineteen minutes after Max Causey was elected foreman, the verdict was sealed. Causey climbed down the metal steps and startled bailiff Bo Mabra when he announced proudly, "We have a verdict." A nearby clock read 11:34 am.

At that very moment, Belli was en route to the courthouse, accompanied by film producer Sam Gallu. He was compiling a documentary about the case. Offhand, Belli predicted the outcome of the case by saying, "I wouldn't be surprised if we had a guilty verdict by noon."

Even though it was still three days before St. Patrick's Day, Dallas citizens were celebrating, and Belli and Gallu encountered revelers on their way to the courthouse. "The streets were full," Belli recalled, "of tootling high school bands, girls on prancing horses, officials running around with mimeographed charts."

When Belli approached the courthouse steps, a court worker said, "Hey, they were looking for you. The jury has a verdict."

Belli simply nodded at the news. "I can remember a feeling of elation for the first time in the trial," he later said. "No civilized community, I told myself, could vote death that quickly. It would be hard for them to even find him guilty."

When Belli entered the courtroom, his hopes were heightened considerably. Henry Wade, sitting at counsel table, appeared morose. Bill Alexander didn't agree, spitefully yanking his tie around his neck to indicate his belief the jury was going to hang Ruby.

Two members of the Ruby clan were in the courtroom when the verdict was announced. As reporters bustled about, and spectators captured the available seats, Ruby's sister Eileen and his brother Earl showed their support. Eva, the sister Ruby had called after receiving news of JFK's death, was absent.

Meanwhile, the jurors waited to be called into the courtroom. Max Causey said several paced anxiously around the jury room. One matter brought up was Causey's wish that every juror face Ruby when the verdict was read. All agreed.

Belli recalled the moment. "At 12:20, the judge stepped to the bench, and Ruby was led to my side. He bit his lip, and the loose flesh below his chin quivered, but he seemed more tense than apprehensive."

Like all attorneys, Belli feared what was known as a "weekend verdict." Anytime a case was submitted to a jury either on a Friday night, or Saturday morning, they were inclined to deliberate for a short time so they could spend the weekend at home or at play. Whether this played a part in the Ruby jury's final decision, Belli could not be certain, but the short deliberation made him believe it did.

As the jury filed in, they were somber. Each took their seat, Belli said, without glancing in his direction. To Belli, this meant the worst, and he turned to Ruby, put his hand on his shoulder, and whispered, "It's bad. Take it easy. We expected it all along and we tried this case for an appeal court. We'll make it there. I'll stick with you."

Causey, as foreman, handed the verdict form to bailiff Bo Mabra, who in turn handed it to Judge Brown. After reading it, he did not hesitate, and for the world to hear live on television and radio, said loudly, hurriedly, in a bold voice, "We the jury find the defendant guilty of murder with malice, as charged in the indictment, and affix his punishment at death." The judge then quickly asked, "Is this unanimous. So say you all? Please hold up your right hands." Twelve hands instantly stretched to the sky.

The crowd appeared dazed, confused as to how to react. There was no eruption of cheering, no sobbing. Reporters scurried to write their stories, but even they were staid.

Eileen, tears welling in her eyes, and Earl Ruby bowed their heads. Eileen's comment was, "He didn't get a fair trial." Jack Ruby appeared nonchalant. He was encircled by sheriff's deputies and hurried out of the courtroom. This didn't quiet Belli, who stood, his face pulsating with anger, and screamed, "May I thank the jury for a victory for bigotry and injustice."

Causey wrote of Belli's comments, "I felt at the time that Mr. Belli's conduct was most unethical and below the dignity of a professional man of his esteem." He would incur the wrath of those who disagreed with the verdict. Moments after it was announced, his wife had picked up their house telephone to hear an unidentified caller scream, "Your son-of-a-bitch husband should be shot right between the eyes."

Henry Wade told reporters, "I thanked the jury for what I thought was a fair and impartial verdict."

Belli, anxious reporters at his side, dabbed his moist eyes and brushed a hand through his silver strings of hair. Later, he recalled, "I said that Ruby had been 'railroaded,' that this had been a 'kangaroo court,' that the jurors had made Dallas 'a city of shame forever more.' My words were bitter, contemptuous of court and city."

Upon reflection, Belli said, "I stand by everyone of them. American justice had been raped. I was outraged, and shouting, and in tears. I was its spokesman there."

Belli later attacked Dallas even more strongly for the verdict. "The Ruby trial," he explained, "was an opportunity for Dallas, as it was opportunity for all of us. It could have helped bring the law into happier conformity with the discoveries of science. It could have provided Dallas, a wounded city, with an avenue to intellectual adjustment, to mercy and understanding that would help cleanse the city and the nation after the awful events of November." He added, "But the trial left Dallas worse. Now this self-conscious city had taken still another step in upon itself, had still another act of brutality and anti-intellectual defensiveness to add to its municipal sins."

BELLI TOLD *Playboy* magazine, "It was a spontaneous outburst of horror at the callous death sentence from a jury that had taken actually less than one hour to consider all of the complex scientific testimony of that pitiful, afflicted little man." Summing up his feelings, he was quoted as saying, "Too often have our courts of law shown us that vindictive streak, that drive to heap society's sins upon an individual, that hypocritical refusal to face facts inherent in which are unpleasant untruths about ourselves."

Belli, who appeared to blame everyone but himself for the crushing defeat, chastised the city of Dallas further on ABC Radio: "I've reassessed my feelings about Dallas. I think that it's sicker than I originally felt when I came here—those horrible, bigoted, little, narrow nasty people that sat in judgment of this 'Jew boy.' I hope to get back to New York, and stand on Times Square and see some free Jews, and niggers, if you will, and some Puerto Ricans, and some dagos, and Chinese, some free Americans walk by and take 'em by the hand and say, 'Thank God, I'm back in America and out of Dallas.'"

Belli continued to berate Dallas's justice system whenever and wherever he could. Speaking at Yale, he told the audience "the only time that Judge Joe Brown leaned over backwards was when he was aiming at the spittoon behind the bench." To the delight of the students gathered, he added, "If his aim at the law had been as good as his aim at that spittoon, I wouldn't have been in any trouble."

Henry Wade commented that Belli had "slipped into a fugue state of mind himself," a snide reference to a term used by the defense during trial.

If one moment signaled Belli's outrage at the verdict, it was when he and Judge Brown met on the courthouse steps as reporters surrounded them. When the judge extended his hand, Belli refused to take it. Concerning the encounter, Belli wrote, "There were tears in my eyes, some of them for this fundamentally humane and decent man who had been a prisoner of his community's prejudices. 'I can't shake hands with you, Judge, You've got blood on your hands.'" Judge Brown, his eyes on fire, replied, "I'm sorry you feel that way about it, Mel. Come back and see us again."

Belli's conference with his client in Ruby's cell was short and sorrowful, though the attorney later wondered whether Ruby had fully understood the verdict. According to Belli, Ruby praised the lawyer who had lost the biggest case of his life. "'That's all right, Mel,'" Belli recalled him saying, "'Next time you try it the same way. You're the one I've always had the most confidence in.'"

Juror J. Waymon Rose said of Ruby's chief attorney. "I thought he was an extraordinary man. He was flamboyant, well-educated, and well-informed on what he was doing . . . I thought he did a very good job, and I was really sorry to see him lose."

Juror Glenn Holton recalled Belli with fondness. He said, "I thought he was a real good lawyer and everything, colorful . . . he stood out like a star." Asked his opinion of Henry Wade, Holton said, "He kind of reminded me of a Baptist preacher, when he gets up there and starts ranting and raving."

Belli and Ruby met one more time. It was in boiling hot August, months after the verdict. "Jack's skin was flabby," Belli said. "It no longer had the taut tone that his constant calisthenics had maintained even during the long imprisonment leading up to the trial. His hair was wispy and there were sores on his scalp; he had been pulling hair from his head."

After the perfunctory exchange of pleasantries, Ruby startled his former lawyer with a question. "Mel," he asked, "Do you think I'm crazy?"

Belli paused before answering. "What could I say to this poor shrunken man," he recalled later. "I lied. 'Jack, I don't know,' I said. 'I do know you need some treatment.'"

When it was time for Belli to leave, "Jack stepped forward and gave me a strange handshake, a sort of secret grip of some sort I assumed. That pathetic gesture was his last that night. He was led away, back to his flood-lit mattress in the metal corridor of the brutally hot jail with the guards to watch him."

Belli later told *Playboy* that the Ruby case produced instant repercussions. "By the time I got back [to San Francisco] . . . I found that insur-ance policies had been canceled without explanation; a book publisher had backed out on publishing *Black Date; Dallas*, the title I had planned for; mortgages had been foreclosed; my name had been withdrawn from the official list of lawyers; my mail was frozen; some TV appearances and lectures were canceled. I'm not being paranoid when I say that those bas-tards from Texas were behind the whole thing." He added, "Why you wouldn't believe some of the mail I got postmarked Texas. Imagine opening a letter addressed to you as 'Dear Rectum.' Heartwarming."

In the fall of 1964, Belli discussed the Ruby case in his new book, *Dal-las Justice, the Real Story of Jack Ruby and His Trial*. Reviewers were criti-cal. Thomas Szasz of the *New Republic* dubbed it "a highly slanted, propagandistic account." George Fuermann of the *New York Times Book Review,* while calling the effort "one-sided" and "dogmatic," nevertheless believed Belli made his case that the Ruby trial should not have been held in Dallas.

In *My Life on Trial*, he wrote further of Jack Ruby, "The trial had been too much for him. Showing the nature of his peculiar insanity in public as we did provided the last disintegrating blows to a personality that had been held together with bubble gum and bailing wire for years before Ruby ever saw Oswald." He also noted that *Saturday Evening Post* jour-nalist Edward Linn was correct when he surmised, "It would have been kinder to have stoned [Ruby] to death."

Ruby's belief in Belli apparently waned and he fired him, though Belli said he simply withdrew from the case. With the appeal pending, Belli, who filed a friend-of-the-court brief on Ruby's behalf, told *Playboy* mag-azine, "I pray for the sake of that sick, pathetic little man, Jack Ruby, whose already paranoid schizophrenic condition has deteriorated shockingly during his long imprisonment without psychiatric care."

Belli's concern for the "pathetic little man" was reflected in a prophetic letter he penned to Judge Brown. "What I write about now," he said, "is the condition we both know Jack Ruby is presently in. He is psychotic . . . I know that if this boy isn't given some medical attention directly we're not going to have this tragic figure alive by the time his case gets through the appellate court."

Ultimately Ruby was vindicated when the jury verdict was overturned on October 5, 1966. The Texas Court of Criminal Appeals ruled, among other things, that the judge's denial of the change of venue motion was reversible error. They ordered a new trial be held and not in Dallas. Judge W. T. McDonald, after discussing the machinations of emotion seething in Dallas after Kennedy's murder, wrote, "Against such a background of unusual and extraordinary invasions of the expected neutral mental processes of a citizenry from which a jury is to be chosen, the Dallas County climate was one of such strong feeling that it was not humanly possible to give Ruby a fair and impartial trial which is the hallmark of American due process of law."

The Supreme Court was critical of Sergeant Patrick Dean's testimony. The justices condemned Judge Brown's decision to permit his recollection of what Ruby told him fifteen minutes after the shooting. That length of time, they said, did not bring the utterance within the *res gestae* rule.

If the Texas justices were critical of Judge Brown, Elmer Gertz, one of Ruby's appellate lawyers, was even tougher on the judge. He denounced Brown for "his bumbling ineptitude, his inexcusable haste, and his lack of judicial decorum and wisdom."

Ruby's first suicide attempt occurred when the glassy-eyed convicted killer stood twenty feet from a concrete wall. His face soaked with perspiration, he ran as fast as he could head first into the wall, hoping to crack open his skull. He didn't, merely getting what attorney Tonahill described as "a knock as round as a silver dollar" on his head.

Ruby's second attempt involved use of an electric light socket, resulting in a few burns on his hands. On his third attempt, he tried to hang himself using his pants legs. The knot he devised was not sturdy and a guard, always on watch, stopped him.

Ruby turned to the Bible, a leather-bound version given as a gift by an admirer, as he awaited results of his appeal. The friend did not include an inscription so Ruby wrote, "Presented to Jack Ruby by the will of God, April 15, 1964." Guards said he read incessantly about persecution of the Jews.

Ruby's death occurred in January 1967, before a new trial, the defense hoped, could be held in Wichita Falls. Cause of death was listed as cancer. Joe Tonahill said the autopsy confirmed Ruby's diseased mental state. "Ruby had fifteen brain tumors," Tonahill recalled.

Ironically Ruby died at Parkland Hospital, the same one where both John F. Kennedy and Lee Harvey Oswald had been declared dead. Ruby would thus never have his true day in court. Technically he died innocent of the crime with which he was charged.

Ruby was buried at West Lawn Cemetery in Chicago. Belli did not attend the funeral. William Kunstler, who had been asked by the American Civil Liberties Union (ACLU) to fly to Dallas to protect the rights of Lee Harvey Oswald, and Phil Burleson were among the pallbearers.

Television cameras recorded Rabbi David Graubart's final words. He stated, "Jack Ruby linked himself with one of most tragic moments in American history. He acted as a patriot, but as a misguided patriot and avenger."

The fate of the principles involved in the Jack Ruby case was most revealing. Judge Brown died in March 1968, his fifteen minutes of fame tainted by the Appeals Court. Assistant DA Jim Bowie also died in 1968.

Deputy DA Bill Alexander left Henry Wades's office after fifteen years. He allegedly stated that instead of impeaching U.S. Supreme Court Chief Justice Earl Warren, they should "hang him." Wade continued in office until 1986. He then practiced law with the firm of Geary, Porter, and Donovan before entering private practice.

Asked about his impressions of Belli, Alexander said, "He was a damn good lawyer in his field; personal injury, medical cases. He made a good presentation, but he didn't have a style Texas juries were used to. He walked in wearing a cummerbund and carrying a velvet briefcase. He talked down to people, the California style, rather overpowering, like a salesman."

Regarding Belli's prowess as a criminal defense attorney, Alexander said, "Belli didn't know what game he was in, even what ballpark he was in." Asked whether others attempted to explain the nuances of Texas justice, the veteran prosecutor said, "How could anyone tell Belli anything? He wasn't much of a listener."

"We teased him and he teased us," Alexander said. "He told others and they told us that he said, 'If you want to hide anything from the prosecution, put it in between the pages of a lawbook.'"

Alexander said, "It was easy to get under Belli's skin. I sat three feet away from him. During one exchange with the judge, he was waxing eloquent and after he was done, I said, 'Show him your muscle, Mel,' and he went ballistic."

Concerning Belli's ability, Alexander said, "his command of the English language was unique. He had such a knowledge of the vocabulary and loved to use big words. He'd needle me by translating words down 'for Mr. Alexander's benefit,' he'd say." Asked whether they became friends during the trial, Alexander said, "No. He didn't like us, particularly me. And everybody loved me. They should, but I was the hatchet man, the bad guy in the DA's office. That made a difference."

After chuckling at his own words, Alexander recalled, "My first impression when I learned that Mel was going to be Jack's lawyer was 'That's interesting.'" He added, "Mel wasn't familiar with Texas law and it has a lot of peculiarities. And there is only one law, one set of facts and evidence, and lawyers can't change the facts. I had tried a lot of cases, death penalty cases, and been exposed to the best of the best. Belli wasn't going to intimidate me."

Belli's propensity for media attention didn't bother Alexander. "Practicing law is a business," he stated. "People with the big egos get publicity, but frankly practicing law beats chopping cotton, but not by much. I had already gotten my name in the newspaper a lot. I didn't have anything to prove."

Henry Wade died in March 2001, at the age of eighty-six. The Henry Wade Juvenile Justice Center on Lone Star Drive in Dallas was named after him. Joe Tonahill and Phil Burleson continued to practice law in Dallas. Burleson died of a heart attack in 1995, Tonahill in 2005.

Melvin Belli's final thoughts about the case were reflective. He wrote, "In 1963, I had reached a pinnacle in the law. Then, all of a sudden, I was plunged into a whirlpool of hatred from which I have never completely emerged. My crime was daring to defend Jack Ruby, killer of the man still officially designated as the assassin of President John F. Kennedy. In the public's mind, I might just as well have been defending Lee Harvey Oswald."

BOOK III

12

722 MONTGOMERY STREET

BELLI'S FIRST SAN Francisco office was located in the TWA Building across from Union Square. It housed a plethora of items even Goodwill would have rejected: piles of yellowed newspapers, shirts and pants that needed mending or laundering, postcards where writing had faded due to exposure to sunlight, and airline tickets, some used, some not. It was a packrat's paradise. Amid ancient magazines and tattered law books, the legal magician hatched cockeyed ideas that drove his opponents crazy.

Belli's waiting room was chaotic. On any given day, a heavily bandaged soul whimpering in pain might occupy the couch, while a scantily dressed lady-of-the-night wearing inch-thick rouge stood against the wall puffing on a Camel.

A trail of framed checks garnered from successful cases greeted visitors. Several were positioned on paint-starved walls adjacent to the office door. They revealed a history of Belli's triumphs; the amounts of the checks increased from ten and fifteen thousand to fifty, to seventy, to one hundred. The final check was written for $187,000—comparable to more than a million modern-day dollars.

Near the window sat a chipped whiskey box full of pigeon food. Belli put the box on the windowsill when the landlord refused to wash the windows. The pigeons arrived on cue. The window washers appeared the next day.

One bright day a fellow TWA building tenant peered out his eleventh-floor window. He saw Belli, an odd-looking hat covering his head, perched on the window ledge of the floor below. He called the police, assuming that a crazed man was about to commit suicide. It turned out that Belli was simply experimenting with an "imitation tropical sun helmet containing a crystal radio set." Upset with transmission static in his office, he had purchased the hat to improve reception. It didn't. Belli then marched down Market Street, located the vendor, and demanded his money back.

The storeroom adjacent to the office was home to Belli's trusty court-room allies: a plastic human skeleton, a mutilated plaster woman with colorful organs, a skull with a massive hole in it. All had been court exhibits.

Photographs hung at odd angles in every room. Belli was featured posing as a seaman, holding court to a group of reporters, speaking at banquets, and studying at Cal/Berkeley. His favorite poster, depicting several comic book–like characters in a traveling Italian road show, adorned one wall. The poster was appropriately titled "The Circus Belli."

Ever conscious of appearances, Belli purchased a six-foot-long aquarium bursting with tropical delights. Secretaries were warned that if one of the tiny creatures died for lack of food, they were finished. Legal briefs as well as scrapbooks mentioning Belli in the media surrounded the aquarium.

Belli often slept on an office couch and bathed in a basin in the storage room. One day, a young associate walked into the office to retrieve a brief and found Belli standing proudly in his pajamas and slippers. "Attention, space cadet!" he ordered. The startled associate obeyed, as Belli, laughing, retreated into the storage room.

The "space cadet" incident occurred when Belli was, as an associate put it, "going through his space phase." He wore a "cadet button" on his lapel, and flashed it at unsuspecting people as they strolled down the street.

During one of these "phases," Belli had the brilliant idea to hire an actor and dress him up like a Martian, complete with goldfish bowl helmet. He said he then intended to drive the "alien" to government space headquarters at the nearby Palomar Observatory where he would stand at the door and say, "Any mail for me?" to startled scientists.

IN 1958, BELLI purchased properties at 722 and 728 Montgomery Street, then known as the Langerman Building and the Genela Building.

The Langerman Building had been a tobacco warehouse, Melodean Theatre, and Turkish bath. Belli would tell guests, "Exquisite Lotta Crabtree, a chanteuse celebrated in more than one tale of San Francisco's Gold Rush days, sang there."

The Genella Building had been home to French mural artist Jules Tavernier and author Bret Harte, who wrote *The Luck of the Roaring Camp* while in residence. The building had housed Joseph Genella's china and glass operation, the first Masonic Lodge in California, a mining company, and a Spanish newspaper. Appropriately enough, the building was the meeting place for an organization called the Odd Fellows.

Belli purchased the building from ten Chinese businessmen and spent more than $450,000 restoring it. Outside, he proudly hung his shingle: "Melvin Belli, Lawyer." Renamed the Belli Building and Caesar's Annex, 722 and 728 Montgomery Street were located just a few blocks from San Francisco Bay. Richly Victorian, both had colorful histories.

In the brochure prepared for visitors, Belli wrote, "You are standing in Jackson Square, in historic Barbary Coast, half a block away from 'Murderer's Corner' on one side, and about as far the old gold weighing station on the other, you are two doors from Hotaling's old distillery. . . . Under you is an ancient secret tunnel and you are in a building which is floating on a raft." Soon after he moved in, Melvin Belli's office on Montgomery Street became a regular stop on the Grayline Bus Tour. For out-of-towners visiting San Francisco, the prime sights to see were the Golden Gate Bridge, Alcatraz, Fisherman's Wharf, Coit Tower, and, for many, Belli's headquarters.

Tours weren't restricted to official visits. At one point, attorney John O'Connor recalled Belli giving a cab driver permission to lead groups through the office. "I'd be researching a brief in the library," O'Connor said laughing, "and in came the cabbie with his tour group."

When tourists gazed through the windows, they witnessed a scene, as one writer suggested, "out of the lair of Dickens, a gallimaufry of exotica." The office featured an enormous Bengal tiger skin rug purchased from Elizabeth Taylor, Nepalese tapestries, a case of aged burgundy, a huge fireplace, quill pens, antimacassars, oil paintings, and an array of apothecary jars. Thousands of rare books were encased in mahogany bookshelves that stood floor to ceiling. The office also housed a huge bar with a significant history. "[That bar] served the thirsty citizens of Sonora [including my father] at Ellsbee's Saloon," Belli boasted, "until I brought it to San Francisco."

Many of the antiques were the result of barter in Europe. When Belli handled a European case and his clients couldn't pay in cash, he gladly accepted their family heirlooms and had them shipped back to his office.

Belli purchased two eighteenth-century gas Copenhagen street lamps that illuminated the sidewalks in front of the buildings. It took eighteen months of legal wrangling with city officials before he could install the twelve-foot cast iron lamps.

Other distinguishing features of the office included high white ceilings trimmed in gold. A wooden fan whirled between crystal chandeliers. The office featured pinball machines, ceremonial hats, menus from every restaurant known to man, a 1910 Copenhagen telephone, hundreds of pipes, and various clocks, bottles, and books.

Belli had also collected a Swiss Madonna statue wearing an ostrich plume from South Africa, a photograph of Queen Victoria on the label of a bottle of Bombay gin, and a huge armadillo. A favorite of his was an apothecary jar labeled, "The Great Gonorrhea and Gleet Remedy, Prepared Only by Penn Drug Co., Inc. of San Francisco. Price: $1.50."

The prized possession and master of the office was Elmer, a life-sized, labeled, movable skeleton that became Belli's constant courtroom companion. He was the standard-bearer for Belli's coat of arms, which featured "the words REX TORTIUS (King of Torts) over a shield and scroll, a crutch in one quadrant of the shield, an ambulance in another, a dollar sign in a third, and a corkscrew in the fourth." The scroll read, "The Holy Grail Insurance Company."

Over time, the office walls featured autographed photographs of many of the most famous celebrities in the world. They included Presidents Harry S. Truman, Herbert Hoover, and Hubert Humphrey, Mae West, Johnny Carson, Flip Wilson, Rosanno Brazzi, Lenny Bruce, Mike Douglas, Marlene Dietrich, Frank Sinatra, Joe DiMaggio, and Merv Griffin. Later framed photographs of President Bill Clinton, Belli with the Pope in Rome, and Giants' baseball star Barry Bonds would be added to the collection.

During the famous Patty Hearst trial, Hearst's attorney F. Lee Bailey used Belli's offices as his home camp. When Belli criticized his handling of the case, Bailey called secretary Maggie Quinn, screaming that he wanted his files out of the office by noon. The rift between Belli and Bailey remained in place for years, though they eventually reconciled.

A giant oil portrait of Belli in a three-piece suit—complete with old-fashioned gold pocket watch and chain—hung on the wall. Painted by Frank Ashley, it had a "Napoleonic" aura about it.

Belli's friend J. Kelly Farris commissioned the portrait. In 1960, he contacted Ashley, best known for his paintings of horses, who agreed to paint the portrait for $2,500. Farris wrote five hundred members of NACCA requesting a ten-dollar donation from those who wanted to be signatories on a gift card that would be presented to Belli along with the painting.

Farris estimated that at least half of them would donate. To his surprise, the response was overwhelming. "Mel was immensely respected by the lawyers," Farris recalled. "I was oversubscribed to the tune of a thousand dollars." At first, Belli had been disappointed at the portrait, believing it didn't present him as being manly enough. "The artist made me look more like Dorian Gray than Melvin Belli," he laughed. He grew to love it.

The sea of red velvet used to decorate the office gave it the feel of an old-time whorehouse. The comparison didn't offend Belli in the least. More than once, he recounted that when Hastings Law School Dean Robert E. Snodgrass took one look at the audacious furnishing, he quipped, "Mel, I'll take my champagne down here in the reception room. I'm a little too old to go upstairs to visit the girls."

When East Coast attorney William Sweeney visited the office, he gawked at the outlandish décor. But when he noticed the brass pole upon which one could slide down to the basement, he walked out onto Montgomery Street shaking his head. "If this was Philadelphia," he proclaimed, "Belli would be disbarred."

Visitors could take the pole or a winding black metal staircase to get to the basement. There, they would find a shower, sink, and a steam room, with a wall-tile mosaic depicting Belli riding a stallion named Blackstone. Appropriately titled "Belli on Blackstone," it had been commissioned from a local tile maker whom Belli admired.

At the foot of the staircase in the basement was a worn couch. Maggie Quinn called it the "sperm sofa." Belli, his associates, partners, and good friends took advantage of the privacy. Sharron Long said that every day there was close inspection to see if "pecker tracks" were visible.

Nailed to the wall adjacent to the steam room was an unusual collection. More than a thousand stolen hotel keys, many stamped with tags that read, "Drop in Nearest Mailbox," were displayed. Keys from such intriguing locales as The Fountainbleu in Miami Beach, the Hotel

Reformer in Acapulco, the Hotel La Paz, Cocos, Baja, California, the Hotel Normandie in Trinidad, the Ritz in Paris, The Plaza in New York City, the Hotel Victoria Plaza, Montevideo, South America, the Lord Nelson in Nova Scotia, and the Plaza Hotel in Buenos Aires adorned the wall. "If only those keys could talk," one secretary wondered.

TO THE DISGUST of the entire office, Belli covered the walls with photographs of car crashes and victims with their heads chopped off. They were constant reminders, he said, of what personal injury was all about. His employees thought they were morbid.

Since the wall nearest Montgomery Street had several large windows, onlookers were given a full view of the sunken office. "I'd sit there taking shorthand," secretary Joyce Revilla said. "All of these tourists would gaze in wonderment. People were constantly gawking at Mr. Belli. Once in a while, he'd yell, 'Hello, you assholes,' but no one could hear him." On another occasion, Belli stood gawking at pretty young college girls with their noses against the window. He smiled and waved—then blurted out, "Boy, would I love to pork the one in the blue dress."

Even the office bathroom was audacious. Ingrained into the tile was the Latin phrase *Re Ipsa Loquiter*, "the thing speaks for itself."

The waiting room, with its large Victorian table and giant grandfather clock, was particularly compelling. On any given day, it was full of police, firemen, lawyers from as far away as Burma, prison officials, court bailiffs, judges, card sharks and gamblers of all types, athletes of prominence, and national political figures. "It was an exciting place," attorney John Hill recalled. "The courtyard fountain, the festive atmosphere, TV crews always wandering around looking for a good quote."

Associate John O'Connor recalled shoving his way through a group of waiting people, all wearing cervical collars. "They were on the steps, everywhere," he said. "The crazy chiropractor in the valley that knew Mel had sent them up. They came from Fresno on a bus so we could sign them up as clients." This type of scene caused partner Seymour Ellison to exclaim, "the waiting room looked like San Francisco General."

The office had been featured in an issue of *Time* magazine. The author wrote, "The handsome, gregarious 'King of Torts' smiled benignly at the one-legged skeleton beside him and explained the secrets of his success. 'The ingredients of a trial lawyer,' said Melvin Belli (rhymes with Dwell-I) in San Francisco last week, 'are imagination and initiative. You

Belli, right, and co-counsel Joe Tonahill flank their client, Jack Ruby. (*Author's collection*)

The famous San Francisco office of Melvin Belli, a must-see tourist stop. (*Courtesy of Nancy Belli*)

Forty-seven-year-old Melvin Belli (bottom row, second from right) appears bored during the first meeting of the International Academy of Trial Lawyers. (*Courtesy of Nancy Belli*)

A messy desk was a Belli trademark. (*Courtesy of Nancy Belli*)

Fellow lawyers listen intently as the legal legend educates them about tort reform. (*Courtesy of Nancy Belli*)

Belli, left, enjoys a laugh with future California governor Pat Brown and other lawyers. (*Courtesy of Nancy Belli*)

Belli dictates the text for his classic book, *Modern Trials*, on an Audiophone machine. (*Courtesy of Nancy Belli*)

Everybody's Guide to the Law is still popular ten years after Belli's death. (*Courtesy of Nancy Belli*)

Belli surrounded by family and friends. (*Courtesy of Nancy Belli*)

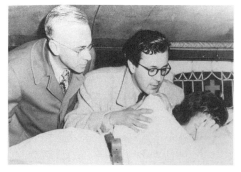

Defender of the downtrodden, Belli comforts an accident victim and future client. (*Courtesy of Nancy Belli*)

Belli with the "Belli Belles," secretaries and other office workers who worshipped their boss. (*Courtesy of Nancy Belli*)

Belli consoles famed actor Errol Flynn's sixteen-year-old girlfriend after Flynn's death. (*Courtesy of Nancy Belli*)

A stripper shows her love for Belli during his 85th birthday celebration. (*Courtesy of Nancy Belli*)

Wearing his trademark black Homburg, Belli steps into a car on the way to a trial. (*Courtesy of Nancy Belli*)

Belli strikes an intimidating pose. (*Courtesy of Nancy Belli*)

A playful Belli dons a firefighter's hat during a festive evening at the office. (*Courtesy of Nancy Belli*)

Melvin Belli celebrates his 2nd birthday, July 29, 1909. (*Courtesy of Nancy Belli*)

Dear Melvin

This is the Zodiac speaking I wish you a happy Christmass. The one thing I ask of you is this, please help me. I cannot reach out for help because of this thing in me wont let me. I am finding it extreamly dificult to hold it in check I am afraid I will loose control again and take my nineth & posibly tenth victom. Please help me I am drownding, At the moment the children are safe from the bomb because it is so massive to dig in & the triger mech requires much wonk to get it adjusted just right. But if I hold back too long from no nine I will loose complet all controol of my self & set the bomb up. Please help me I can not remain in control for much longer.

A letter from the Zodiac killer, who picked Belli to plead his case on the radio. (*Courtesy of Nancy Belli*)

Belli with his beloved dogs.
(*Courtesy of Nancy Belli*)

Sixth wife Nancy Ho cared for Belli during his waning years. (*Courtesy of Nancy Belli*)

Belli and daughter Melia get ready to meet Pope John Paul II. (*Courtesy of Nancy Belli*)

Belli stares at one of the hundreds of keys he stole from prestigious hotels all over the world. (*Courtesy of Nancy Belli*)

Belli's fifth wife, Lia, with Henry Kissinger and an unidentified friend. (*Courtesy of Nancy Belli*)

Caesar, Melia, Lia, and Melvin help Lia with her political campaign, during happier times. (*Courtesy of Nancy Belli*)

Belli and son Caesar. The two were close during Caesar's early years but the relationship soured as time passed. (*Courtesy of Nancy Belli*)

need to have a feeling for the plaintiff, the desire to do him some good, and to stick with him through thick and thin, and the guts to do just that while everyone is criticizing you.'"

The journalist pointed out that in the previous ten years, personal injury awards had skyrocketed 266 percent. He noted that Belli had won over one hundred cases whose awards exceeded $100,000, and that his fee was 33 1/3 percent of any funds garnered.

The article also quoted Belli on his favorite subject: himself. "I believe that we must do something for those who have been injured," he said, "but I am not sure Belli is the man to do it. I am regarded as either a shyster or savant. There is no middle road for me."

BELLI'S DOGS WERE constant office residents. Welldone Rumproasts I, II, III, and IV, tan Italian greyhounds, inhabited Belli's office as he conducted business. One of them drew secretary Maggie Quinn's ire since "the dog would burp and the most nauseous, gaseous, odiferous odor came bellowing out. It scattered people for fifty feet."

Quinn called her boss' dedication to them "anal." Seymour Ellison said the dogs were all right, but "Belli didn't believe in training them. They shit in the car, in the office, in his bed, everywhere." Secretary Joyce Revilla recalled that the dogs "left little presents by my desk." She also said the dogs chewed Belli's hearing aids until they were unusable.

Alessandro Bicarri knew Belli loved his animals more than people. "He didn't care if they shit or pissed all over the office," he said. "He'd say 'Clean it up but don't frighten the dogs, don't traumatize them.' That was most important."

Bob Lieff recalled that the dogs literally destroyed one of Belli's expensive Rolls-Royces. "They chewed it up, the seats, everything," he said. "It couldn't have been worth $500 when they were through with it."

Ever the softy with animals, Belli took in a mixed Lab named Ozzie. When she escaped, the good Samaritan who brought her back came into the courtyard and said, "Did Mr. Belli lose a pregnant Chihuahua?" Joyce Revilla said it was no wonder the man thought the dog was pregnant. "He and another Italian Greyhound named Azrielle ate everything in sight," she recalled. "They'd steal sandwiches, eat garbage, anything."

Jeanne Belli called the dogs "disgusting." "I knew they were dad's way of keeping people away from him," she recalled. "Because in truth, he was a very insecure man. But those dogs, well, they crapped everywhere. It was awful."

At one point, Belli felt mediation was needed between some of the dogs. "He called in a doggy psychiatrist," Jeanne Belli said laughing. "She advised about who should be top dog, how to feed them, and so forth. Of course, dad never did anything she said. When he got the bill, which was thousands of dollars, he went crazy."

Belli also owned a pet parrot, one that had peculiar tastes. "Captain John Silver," as Belli dubbed him, became famous. A gift from Bob Callahan, he may have been the only parrot to regularly drink Kentucky bourbon.

Columnist Jack Rosenbaum wrote, "Captain John Silver, the drinkingest bird in town, is also the fussiest. His keeper, Barrister Melvin Belli, insists that the only thing he'll drink is Jim Beam, Black Label."

Owning a Beam-drinking bird paid off for Belli. The president of the Jim Beam company learned of the bird's taste for their product and invited them to a board of director's meeting. "When Captain John and I refused," Belli recalled, "He sent us a free case of Jim anyway." Law partner Lou Ashe didn't care much for the fowl, asking, "Have you ever smelled the breath of a drunken parrot?" Captain John died during a trip to Europe when Belli's secretary cut his whiskey supply off.

Another bothersome office pet was Bill Choulos's white cockatoo. "He made the most awful noise," Maggie Quinn recalled. "Squawking all the time. And there was bird seed all over Choulos' office." Bird food was stored in the office kitchen. When the food disappeared, a sign was posted promising severe repercussions for the perpetrator.

One birthday, Belli received an iguana as a gift. Unfortunately, while he was away a short time later, the lizard died. Office workers, afraid of their boss' rage when he returned, scampered around to find a substitute. They did, but the markings were different. To their delight, Belli didn't notice.

Though Belli liked his other pets, his dogs were his passion. His housekeeper and cook, Curt and Erma, gave their boss a Weimaraner. He became just as fond of the dog as he was of Curt and Erma.

Belli brought the dogs on annual trips to Sonora with the office staff. When the entourage went to fancy restaurants, the dogs did, too. "If the dogs couldn't eat," Joyce Revilla said, "the boss didn't eat." According to Milton Hunt, Belli loved to sneak the canines under the table where he fed them from his plate. People were understandably offended, but Belli didn't care.

Joyce Revilla organized many of the trips to Sonora. "We either rented a mini-bus that held eighteen," she recalled, "or a full-size one that carried forty-two. Members of Mr. Belli's family, office workers, the dogs, other lawyers, all went along. We even picked up a channel four television reporter once who covered the escapade."

MELVIN BELLI NORMALLY had three secretaries working for him: two to handle his legal work and one who functioned as a "social secretary." He expected them to keep up with his fast-paced lifestyle. "At one point," Revilla said, "The boss decided all the secretaries needed to enroll in Evelyn Wood speed-reading classes. I declined, but others took them."

Belli also wanted his secretaries, many of whom were paid more than junior attorneys, educated about the human body, to give them a better idea as to what personal injury was all about. "He told us," Sharron Long recalled, "that everyone had to attend an autopsy. I went to Doro's and got drunk before I went to look at the dead body."

Working at Belli's office caused many secretaries to become near-alcoholics. "Some days we couldn't stand it anymore," said Revilla, "and so we'd dash into the back door of Doro's next door, where Belli once escorted Sophia Loren, and Jay the bartender would serve us. That might be at 2:00 in the afternoon." Carol Lind said, "It was the longest year and eight months of my life. You had to be pickled to work there."

Revilla once drank so heavily in a restaurant at the TWA building that she became disoriented. "I started to go up the stairs to find my hotel room," she recalled. "A security guard stopped me and said, 'Ma'am, this is a bank. You can't go up there.'"

Sharron Long recalled that Belli escorted her to the opera. "But I was so exhausted from work that I slept through it," she recalled. Long also said that "'No' was not a word that he understood. He'd say 'Bring the Bunny,' and I was supposed to be ready to go." Belli called Sharron "Bunny" because she had worked for *Playboy*.

Carol Lind said, "Belli was basically a lonely man. He always wanted people around him. He hated to be alone." She called him "a funny guy when he wasn't yelling, screaming, and making life miserable for everyone."

Revilla pointed out that the "first order of the day" in Belli's office was for fresh flowers to be positioned on his desk, the back bar in his office, the receptionist's desk, and in the waiting room. "Heaven forbid if that wasn't done," she said. Boxes of seasonal flowers lined the walls in the courtyard. Belli's first order of business when he returned from a trip was to stick his fingers in the soil to check whether proper watering had taken place in his absence. If it hadn't, he stormed toward the secretaries and boomed, "Where the hell is the gardener? Fire him."

Anyone accepting a call at the office, no matter night or day, was required to record it in a red logbook. Failure to do so was mutiny or "bad news" as secretary Suzanne Ellison put it. "Even the kook calls, every-thing," she said, "went into the book."

Handling the mail at the offices was a gargantuan task. "Mr. Belli emphasized that any good lawyer returned all calls and answered every letter," Joyce Revilla said. "So we took every single call and read every crazy letter. At one point, we sorted out the junk mail, but then he said one day, 'Is this all the mail?' so we put the junk mail back in."

Belli had a standard return letter for the crank ones he received. Instead of acknowledging their complaint or reacting to the ridicule, he wrote, "Dear Sir or Ma'am, Please send me twelve custom shirts, in assorted col-ors, and several neckties. Thanks, Sincerely, Melvin Belli." Secretaries also kept on file a multitude of letters from women "madly in love with Belli."

Lawyers and secretaries spent time dealing with what were called "spec" clients. That meant checking out any potential case to see if it was worthy of follow up. Failure to follow up was also considered mutinous.

The eccentric barrister would "strongly urge" his secretaries to "date" potential or current clients and "do what you gotta do" to keep the client happy. When they acquiesced to Belli's wishes, they received envelopes of money. Milton Hunt said many of the secretaries' husbands weren't too pleased with Belli's practices.

Belli's schedule was kept in a red ledger. Failure to keep that in tow and up to date, according to Joyce Revilla, was "the kiss of death." Dur-ing a trip to court in England, Belli noticed that the barristers kept dic-tation and other papers in red velveteen boxes. Soon, his office was filled with them. Belli had several, and expected them to be checked at all times for work needing completion.

Secretaries were constantly bombarded by Belli's temper tantrums. Suzanne Ellison had a broken pencil thrown at her when the boss was upset that his Italian boots couldn't be fixed. "He was very intimidating," Suzanne recalled. "But later he said 'I'm sorry dear,' and I was touched because I knew he didn't apologize much."

Jeanne Belli said, "I hated the way he treated people at times. He just lost it and I had to watch. He was just into himself, so narcissistic. But dad didn't get to where he was by being a nice guy."

Sharron Long learned how to deal with the anger. "Mr. Belli didn't like to be bullshitted," she said. "If you screwed up, then you better admit it because he was psychic and knew when someone was camouflaging something. One time, I sent out all the invitations to the ATLA convention from A to L twice and forgot the last half of the alphabet. When I told him over the phone, he said, 'Well, why don't you just burn my building down!' Unfortunately, I had to pick him up at the airport. When he saw me, he said, 'Well, if it isn't my little fuck up.' But he didn't go crazy or anything because I leveled with him and admitted my mistake."

BELLI FIRED HIS secretaries on a whim. Lawyer Tim Palm said Belli went through secretaries "like dirty socks." This didn't deter Kent Russell from accepting a job as an associate. "There were beautiful women all around," he said. "There was a gorgeous one named Tammy who looked like a Hollywood movie star. I took one look at her and said, 'This is the place for me.'"

"He was always 'between' secretaries," Joyce Revilla said. "Being fired was more like a recommendation than a black mark. Some never made it through the lunch hour." One secretary, nicknamed "Hanna Banana," was hired and fired three times in one day. She finally left, completely disoriented.

Maggie Quinn, like Revilla and Long, was a member of the "Belli Bells," an exclusive "club" of Belli secretaries who had lasted more than a week. The Bells even had a theme song whose first chorus was, "Of all the Bells I've loved before." Their fame was chronicled in a *California Living Magazine* article titled, "Tales from the Court of the King of Torts." An accompanying photograph depicted more than thirty women sharing stories about their days in Belli's offices.

The author of the article, a former secretary named Rosemary Nightingale, said the qualifications to be a member of Belli's court were "the stamina of an athlete, the memory of an elephant, the charm of an angel, and the stubbornness of an ox." Nightingale said, "One moment I'd be chatting with a deputation from the Hell's Angels, and the next tripping over the fringes of Sacheen Littlefeather."

Regarding her boss, Nightingale wrote that he was a man "whose charisma seemed to permeate the walls." Agatha Fey said, "The Belli office was like a kaleidoscope, the patterns forever changing." Another secretary, Karin Weishaar, said, "He's the most fascinating, brilliant man I have ever known, but there were times when I could have cheerfully put poison in his coffee without blinking an eye." She recalled that Belli once invited all of his former girlfriends to a party at the Telegraph Hill penthouse.

Belli once organized the secretaries to protest a new fad of which he disapproved. "One night at dinner," Sharron Long recalled, "Mr. Belli said, 'We should have a parade to protest *midi*-skirts.' The next day, after he had alerted the media, a band played as we paraded down Montgomery wearing *mini*-shirts for all to see. Some girls rode on a fire truck and our banners read, 'Ban Midi-Skirts.'" They carried signs, including one that read "Liberate and Elevate!" More important to Belli was a headline in the *Chronicle* that read, "Belli Girls March on Montgomery Street."

Many of those who worked in the offices ended up as Belli's sexual conquests. Belli's favorite trick while traveling was to telephone a good-looking secretary and tell her, "I'm simply swamped, overloaded, lots of mail here, and so forth. I really need you." He then strongly suggested that she fly to wherever he was on the pretense of working. The girl would join him, enjoy dinner and drink, perhaps sleep with Belli, and return to the office questioning her morals. Belli would then ease her out of the firm if he didn't care for her lovemaking skills.

Belli once asked Joyce Revilla, "Joyce, how come we never made it?" She answered, "Because I can run faster than you can." Belli simply smiled.

A secretary who quit later sent a letter to a friend. It called the Belli office a "den of inequity." "The bookkeeper is sleeping with the attorney," she wrote.

One young woman, faced with "sex with Belli or else," was warned that if she went to Alaska, where Belli was trying a case, she was expected to put out. Against better advice, she traveled to Belli's location, but refused his amorous advances. The woman was promptly fired, much to the chagrin of those who worked for the barrister. Thankfully, she did not file a lawsuit—at one time, there were at least twelve on file with the labor board over Belli's misconduct.

In 1956, two secretaries, Beatrice Davis and Arlye Fast, actually had their ex-boss arrested. They charged he had failed to pay them overtime wages. Fast alleged Belli owed her $81.15; Davis, $95.76. Belli claimed,

"The girls were paid more than they were worth anyway." Judge Charles Peery agreed and the case was dropped.

Sharron Long had wandered into the offices one day. "I interviewed Sharron," Revilla recalled laughing. "And I couldn't figure out if she wanted a job or got lost and came into our offices instead of the Playboy Club, which was next door. I didn't have a clue as to what to do so I had some of the attorneys interview her. They hired her on the spot." Long knew why. After asking about her secretarial skills, she recalled, "the next question was, 'How short do you wear your skirts?'" When she explained that she had just shortened all her skirts, the job was hers.

George Safford, an associate, witnessed a bizarre incident when Belli mistook one of his clients for a secretary and the dire consequences that ensued.

"I brought into the office a lovely woman named Bobbie Sue Counts," he recalled. "She was the poor widow of a pilot who was the victim on an aircraft carrier of a faulty cold catapult shot. His plane veered off into the ocean, but the 'ear burner' on the back of his seat ejected him perfectly. The problem occurred when the seat's rocket didn't fire and he didn't separate and fell into the water still bound to the seat and drowned."

"I was standing in Mel's office talking to him at about fifteen minutes after nine," Safford said. "I notice he kept looking at the courtyard and when Bobbie Sue walked through, he began screaming, 'You're late, God-damn it. That's it. You're fired. Get your ass out of here.'"

Belli's tirade was the result of a scathing memo he'd circulated warning secretaries not to be late. When he spied Counts, he'd assumed she was a violator and had acted accordingly, much to Safford's chagrin. He raced over to Belli and tugged at his coat sleeve. Safford recalled, "I said 'Mel, you just fired my client.' He looked at me in amazement, and then just as quick as could be extended his hand to her and said 'I'm Melvin Belli, nice to meet you' and went on as if nothing had happened."

Confusion was commonplace at the Belli offices. When Bob Ingram appeared for an interview, he found himself being asked questions as if he were a prospective client. "I wanted to be hired as a lawyer," he said, "And the person was questioning me about my injuries."

Belli hired an attorney named John on a Friday. John then sped down to Los Angeles with his wife to pick up their belongings. He assumed he was to start the following Monday. When he didn't appear at the next day's Saturday meeting, Belli was furious.

Belli ordered secretaries to find "the son of a bitch," but they could not. When John showed up on Monday, wearing a new suit and ready to work, he was promptly fired. Belli explained, "I can't use someone as irresponsible as you." John retreated out of the office, a beaten man who lost a job he never started.

Realizing John wasn't at fault, associates in the firm took pity on him and stashed him in the basement doing research. Four or five months later, Belli called the basement looking for some documents. John was the only one there, and despite reservations, delivered the material to Belli. He took one look at it, dismissed John, and promptly barged into partner Bob Lieff's office. "Bob," Belli began, "that John is pretty damn sharp. What the hell is he doing in the basement?"

BELLI WAS CONTINUALLY soliciting clients in a way that potentially violated State Bar ethics. When a plane crash occurred, killing several Cal-Poly University basketball team members, the barrister sent copies of *Ready for the Plaintiff* to the victims. The California Bar investigated, but one judge saved Belli when he said, "Well, [Belli] sends me copies of all his books, too."

Chauffeur Milton Hunt recalled that Belli solicited policemen to follow accidents and then funnel the victims to him. He gave them kickbacks and invited them to his coveted parties. "I was a runner who tracked down cases," Hunt said. "I carried a stack of Belli business cards and if I saw an accident, and we got the case, I'd get a share. Of the little cases, I'd get six percent, of the big ones ten to twelve percent."

Hunt, an African American, also helped the office bring in minority cases. "Sometimes blacks or Hispanics were afraid to talk to the white attorneys," Hunt said. "So I would help to calm their fears."

Belli's reception room manner was legendary. He'd waltz out into the bevy of waiting clients and say, "Okay, now what can I do for you. Is it murder, rape, divorce, personal injury? When the answer was given, Belli would summon an associate and say, "Now you talk to him." To the attorney, Belli said, "And you report back to me before they leave." This made the client feel important even though they weren't seeing the famous lawyer.

For all the modern equipment that the office purchased, Belli was incompetent when it came to anything technical. He once told daughter Jeanne, "Honey, I've got to learn computers but I just don't understand them." Instead, he utilized an old blue audophone recording device that recorded on records. The ancient machine often disobeyed his commands. On one occasion, a client was entering his office when the machine came flying through the door as Belli yelled, "You fucker." The client gawked at the receptionist, retreated to his seat in the waiting room and said, "I don't think he is ready to see me yet."

Attorney John Hill said Belli never could figure out how the speakerphone, which he constantly used, really worked. "With the old ones," Hill said, "the other person couldn't hear when Mel was talking while that person was talking and vice-versa. So Mel would be chatting away, and when there was no response, he'd just keep going on and then to chastise the other person he'd go 'woof, woof, woof' like a dog and say fuck 'em. He never could get that process right."

Many of Belli's favorite employees lunched with him and enjoyed a drink (or several) after work. "A favorite hang-out was Tommy Toys at 655 Montgomery Street," Joyce Revilla recalled, "that featured French-Chinese cuisine. . . . Mr. Belli would have a glass of port with lunch. I didn't like it at first, but the boss would holler, 'Bring my aunt here a port.' After a while, I started to drink with him."

Another drink of choice for the jolly giant was an Italian martini called a Negroni, a drink consisting of equal parts of Campari, gin, and sweet vermouth with a twist of lemon. Joyce Revilla said. "Three of those and wow, they were something."

Belli's other favorites included sidecars, cognac, and something called a Zabaglione. It contained whipped eggs and liqueur. Carol Anna Lind said it was a "frothing drink that almost gave you a heart attack."

Belli's appetite was gargantuan. "His favorite foods were Italian and French," Maggie Quinn said, "But he was a huge eater. I couldn't believe how much food he went through. And he loved wine, really good wine." He was especially fond of Oysters Rockefeller. Joyce Revilla almost gagged when she ate the dish the first time.

Belli had a penchant for pepper. During a phase where he felt it was good for his heart, he doused everything in sight with the stuff. On many occasions, he screwed off the top, and simply dumped it onto his food. Those nearby sneezed uncontrollably.

Belli's passion for garlic disgusted everyone around him. He had read an article touting it as a cleanse-all for the digestive system. After that, he began chewing several cloves of garlic at lunch or dinner's end. Most times he ate it raw, but the chef at Tommy Toy's restaurant would roast it for him. Longtime friend Alessandro Baccari said Belli's passion for garlic was "dilusionary." "He ate garlic as if it was candy," Baccari recalled. "It was like Ronald Reagan ate jelly beans."

"He just reeked of garlic, it emanated from his body," Maggie Quinn recalled with a laugh. He hung several cloves on the bookshelves to the right of and behind his desk. Joyce Revilla said that when Belli passed by her desk, she had to hold her nose. "It smelled just like he had B.O.," Revilla explained. "I told one of the investigators he needed a bath."

Friend J. Kelly Farris recalled a garlic-eating spree in Montana or Idaho that nearly cost them their airline seats. "We were at a bar eating garlic like popcorn while we sipped a few beers," he said. "We must have eaten a pound apiece. When Mel, whose breath could have curled the wallpaper off a wall, walked up the steps to the plane, the stewardess nearly fainted. He took one look at her, laughed, and said, 'If you think this is bad, wait until you see my partner.'"

BELLI'S SUCCESSES IN the legal arena helped him accumulate a wardrobe second to none. "I had tailors doing variations on the standard lawyer's charcoal gray," he recalled. "They made me suits with a slightly rakish Western cut, all the jackets lined in red silk, high slash pockets on the trousers, no pleats and spare all the way down to my boots, which were not Texas cowboy boots, but Congress gaiters, calf-high black boots molded from a plaster cast of my foot by Peal's of London. Sometimes I wore a black homburg."

He wore spats and favored a pair of gold cuff links with "Robin Hood" embossed on them. *Life* magazine reporter Robert Wallace wrote, "The suits are mostly of blue and look as if they have been bought by mail order from an uninhibited tailor." He added, "His accessories, from the vermilion vest to doorknob-like gold cuff links, are in harmony with his suits."

Longtime secretary Joyce Revilla admired her boss' choice of clothes, though she felt that "sometimes they didn't exactly match." "The silk shirts, of every color," she recalled, "were custom made in Hong Kong, as were the matching ties. His suits, the Savilles, were imported from England. And his boots—there was a favorite bootmaker in Beverly Hills who made some of them. Of course, his secretary at the time also wore boots; that was a given." Belli owned hundreds of pairs of shoes, some made of exotic materials. One favorite pair was made of kangaroo leather.

Belli fell in love with a gold sport coat adorned with small concentric circles encased in squares. No one else thought much of the garment, but he wore it for weeks. A photograph shows Belli wearing it while carving a Thanksgiving turkey. When spraying juices soiled the coat, he was livid.

Belli's wardrobe inspired several fashion clones. Partner Bill Choulos's suits were red lined as well. At one point Choulos ordered suit coats that contained a red silk folding under the lapel. One secretary noted, "It was just big enough to hold three dubies and a gram of coke."

One Christmas season receptionist Maggie Quinn presented Belli with a *Book of the Himalayas*. He was furious when her gift to Choulos was a black club tie that, if inspected closely, read "Fuck You." Choulos loved the tie and wore it to Federal Court on a regular basis. Belli demanded a red one and Quinn marched off to the Embarcadero to order it.

Besides sharing a passion for clothing, both Belli and Choulos drove Rolls-Royces. The expensive automobiles indicated a man at the top of his profession. Belli's first Rolls convertible was maroon and black, the second a buttercup yellow, the third a white Cornische with a red top. Belli bought the second off the showroom floor, but ordered it be repainted eggshell at a cost of $5,000. Asked why he enjoyed different colored cars, he quipped, "The Rolls is the best car, but, after all, even a Rolls shouldn't be boring."

Maggie Quinn said being seen near her apartment in one of Belli's classy cars had its risks. "The owner of a corner grocery asked me what I did," she recalled. "I told him I worked for Belli. He said, 'Whew, that's good to hear. I thought you were a hooker.'"

While *The Adequate Award* was docked in nearby Sausalito, Belli's private investigator Jasper Watts said, "A local parking lot was called 'Mel's Place' after he dodged an imaginary dog on Bridgeway near Napa Street and crashed his Corniche."

A brand-new Rolls nearly cost Belli his life. On a trip to Los Angeles, the automobile, which he had owned for three months, began to smoke. He pulled to the side of the road, leaped out, and watched as the car caught on fire. He retrieved files inside then stood and watched in disgust as his prized Rolls went up in flames.

Belli drove his cars like he lived: fast. One colleague said, "Mel scared me to death with his driving." Police agreed, ticketing him on numerous occasions. Belli largely ignored the citations. To those who questioned his motives, he said, "I'm Melvin Belli."

13

THE RICH, THE POOR,
THE FAMOUS, THE INFAMOUS

VICTORY IN COURT meant a lavish celebration at Belli's San Francisco offices. First the Jolly Roger flag was hoisted up a mast on the roof of the building. Then two booming blasts were emitted from an antique ship's cannon out of one of the second-floor windows. "The boom scared the tenants and the neighbors," Joyce Revilla recalled. "If you weren't prepared, they jolted you right out of your seat."

These victories produced revenue, but the funds disappeared as quickly as they arrived. Belli never trusted bookkeepers, believing they all cheated him. One who actually had cheated him was a rather dim-witted fellow named Joe. Belli thought he was paying ghost employees and pocketing the extra money. Suspicions grew after Joe hosted a party featuring various exotic liquors. Other employees who attended the party couldn't believe Joe was dumb enough to display the beverages, since the liquors had been purchased or stolen by *Belli* on trips afar. Joe's display meant he had stolen them from the offices. He was fired shortly after the party.

Verdict funds helped purchased Maggie Quinn's "greeting desk"—an eighteenth-century mahogany bar that had been brought around the horn of Africa. Since she was only 5' 3" inches, Maggie had to grab the back of the bar and hoist herself up onto her chair. From there, she greeted the multitude of people who wandered in, all while manning a twelve-line telephone system that seemed to blinking at all times, in an office where one hundred new cases might be considered in a single day.

Quinn never knew whose head might pop into view in the court-yard or how Belli might react. On one occasion, she heard the roar of motorcycles on Montgomery Street. Her eyes widened as two mem-bers of the Hell's Angels rode their Harleys right up to her desk. Their leader, Sonny Barger, was a client. After their conference with one of the lawyers, they said "You're a cute blond. . . . We'd like to make you our mama for a weekend."

Quinn's job at the office was exasperating. "I had to keep track of the clients wandering in and juggle the twelve phone lines," she said. "My directive was to filter out the nuts, idiots, and crackpots who called from the regular clients and the celebrities. Those included Marlene Dietrich, Johnny Carson, Mickey Rooney, and Dick Cavett, people like that."

One episode nearly caused Quinn to pack it in. "It was on a Saturday morning," she remembered. "And I hated working then. But this guy slumbered in, and I noticed he had blood all over him. He had been in the office a week before and I recalled having to tell him to snuff out a joint he lit up. Two little ladies from Topeka on a bus tour were walking around and I thought they might be offended."

When the man approached Maggie, she noticed he had something in his hand. "I jumped a foot and muttered 'Oh, shit' as this bloodied man dropped a bloody knife on the desk," she said. "He said 'I just killed my girlfriend. She cheated on me. The other guy has a bigger dick than I do.'"

Startled by the knife, the blood, and the revelation that the man standing in front of her was apparently a murderer, Maggie eased her hand below the desk and tapped the buzzer that had been installed to signal trouble. It buzzed in a basement office where Gene Marshall and Craig Zerke, two "investigators" employed by Belli, were stationed. "Craig was on duty, and he came to the rescue," Maggie said. "The cops showed up, arrested the guy, and led him away."

On one occasion, a UPS man showed up holding his nose. Quinn knew something was amiss. "He was holding a small package with the tip of his fingers away from his body," she said. "He laid it in the courtyard, yelled 'This is for you,' and scampered off. I could smell something foul from my desk but I walked out to the package which had a Guam postmark."

The package was transported to the middle of Montgomery Street before it was opened. Inside was a dead fish. It turned out the present was for associate Jim Garlock who had flown to Guam in anticipation of filing a lawsuit for a man who had written the office seeking representation. Garlock dropped the case when he discovered the man was a Nazi. The greeting from the disgruntled client, alongside the rotting fish, was succinct. It read, "I will kill you when I get to the United States."

Many times complete strangers, including an Indian chief, roamed the office. They wandered in off the streets and were welcomed. "Streetpeople used to stop in for a sandwich," Carol Anna Lind recalled. "It was no big deal." One day the secretaries noticed a woman no one knew eating Chinese food out of the box at Belli's bar in his office. Associate Paul Monzione recalled working on a Sunday when two or three people waltzed in. "One of them picked up an object and said, 'How much is this?'" Monzione recalled. "And I said, 'Lady, we are trying to work here.'"

The presence of illicit drug users was not unusual. Dealers visited the office frequently. "One was called Morris," Maggie Quinn recalled. "He was a little peanut of a guy. He simply dropped by to take orders and there were plenty of those."

The Belli office prided itself on having the best "grass" in the city. One partner was credited with providing the best of the best. Employees loved to see Belli get stoned on Alice B. Toklas brownies. "They mellowed him out a bit," a secretary said.

Since the cast of characters-in-residence at the Montgomery Street office was an unusual mix, the night watchman, Tomas Minneweather, fit right in. "He was a 6'1" black man," Maggie Quinn recalled, "built like a brick shithouse." Belli first learned of Tomas through his letters to associate John Hill, sent from Soledad Prison where he was serving a lengthy sentence for double murder. Belli was impressed by the letters, and aided Tomas's efforts at parole. "He was intimidating as hell," Quinn remembered. "Reminded me of Michael Clarke Duncan in the film *The Green Mile*. Everybody knew Tomas was an ex-con. Nobody messed with him."

Quinn recalled that Tomas learned the whereabouts of the Symbionese Liberation Army (SLA), the group that had kidnapped Patty Hearst. "He knew they were in LA on their way to San Francisco," she said. "And one of our associates was John O'Connor, who was working on the case for the government. So I was listening to Tomas, and fielding calls from John. And an associate from F. Lee Bailey's office was around too. It was a mixed-up mess."

To be certain, Belli rubbed elbows with the rich and famous. During his heyday, not a day went by without the newspapers pairing the outlandish lawyer with a celebrity. If a famous person was in trouble or aggrieved, they telephoned Melvin Belli.

A fascinating case came Belli's way when he represented controversial comedian Lenny Bruce. Bruce first gained fame on the Arthur Godfrey television show. Some members of his audiences delighted in his performances while he offended others with his off-color material.

Belli hooked up with Bruce, whose real name was Leonard Alfred Schneider, after the controversial performer was arrested on drug charges. This appeared to be backlash for what the establishment believed was his filthy stage act.

To push the envelope, Bruce, a handsome man with silky skin, a hooked nose, spindly fingers, and long coifed eyebrows, became even more vulgar as critics lambasted his act.

In addition to Belli, San Francisco Chronicle columnist Herb Caen defended Bruce's off-color antics. He wrote, "They call Lenny a sick comic—and sick he is. Sick of the pretentious phoniness of a generation that makes his vicious humor meaningful. He is a rebel, but not without a cause, for there are shirts that need unstuffing, egos that need deflating, and precious few people to do the sticky job with talent and style."

When Lenny Bruce arrived in San Francisco to appear at the Jazz Workshop, he intended to present an unforgettable performance. Before a packed house, he began his performance by simply saying "Motherfucker." While the audience attempted to sort out their feelings, he said the word again, and then a third time. Then he added, "Now ladies and gentleman, to show you how silly this all is, the U.S. Supreme Court has just decided, so my lawyer, Mel Belli, tells me, that my act's obscene if it creates prurient desire in you. So I'm going to say motherfucker and you're going to see two of San Francisco's finest starred and blue-coated policemen come down and arrest me."

Bruce's prediction shortly came true. Two cops suddenly appeared, arrested him, and hauled him off in handcuffs. The next night, after the club owner had bailed him out, Bruce was back again. And he was arrested again.

Bruce's subsequent trial proved to be a landmark regarding First Amendment freedom of speech issues. He was acquitted, but the costs of that litigation and others in the future bankrupted him. He died in 1966 from a morphine overdose.

Belli considered Lenny Bruce a brilliant man. While they were working on his case, the entertainer frequented Belli's offices. "He came down to the basements, surrounded by all the law books," Belli recalled, "and read Supreme Court decisions. He didn't make a pest of himself . . . he had this ingratiating, almost little-boy quality. He'd get into the working girls [secretaries] working hours as well as their pants. Regularly. He had a fine mind and a marvelous glibness."

Bruce's choice of reading material stunned Belli. "He'd read dictionaries as I read novels," he recalled. "Once I went backstage at the Jazz Workshop and found him all excited over a big thesaurus, a whole new world of words."

If Lenny Bruce was considered controversial, then Belli wondered, what could be said about one of his former clients, the irrepressible Mae West? She had hired him when a San Francisco Broadway street "performer" advertised herself as "Diamond Lil." This was the name of West's Broadway play. Belli quickly put a stop to the use of "Diamond Lil."

Joyce Revilla said, "She was exactly what you expected from her films. She was a tough lady, no warmth there." Later, Belli exhibited a bit of senility while glancing over the invitation list for his annual Christmas party. To Joyce Revilla, he said, "Boy, I haven't heard from Mae in a while." Revilla replied, "Ah, Boss, she's dead."

Two other lovelies that Belli represented were Marie McDonald, the singer/actress known as "The Body," and blond screen siren Lana Turner. Joyce Revilla recalled talking with her after Belli had invited the sexy star to a Hollywood event. "She had throat cancer then," Rivella said. "And so she said, 'Joyce, I don't look very good, so make some excuse for me. But don't tell him its because of how I look.' I did that and Mr. Belli never knew." Turner told her one of the reasons she became hooked on cigarettes was that every month a tobacco company delivered four cartons to her mail station. "I really felt sorry for her," Joyce said. "She was so sad."

Belli had the chance to represent Timothy Leary, the self-styled drug guru famous for his LSD experimentations. Leary was sentenced to thirty years in prison for smuggling two marijuana cigarettes into the

United States from Mexico. He escaped incarceration and fled the country, but federal agents arrested him in Afghanistan for return to the United States.

Belli believed that Leary was a political prisoner and permitted a new associate named Kent Russell to oversee the case. Russell, working after-hours and on weekends, produced a first-class legal brief that was instrumental in reducing Leary's sentence. Belli commended his protégé's performance and Russell said he celebrated by "smoking a joint with Leary as they rode across the Golden Gate Bridge listening to Phoebe Snow."

Russell always remembered Belli's faith in him. "I doubt that any other lawyer would have allowed me to work on that case," he explained. "Mel was a great teacher if you allowed him to teach."

Cassius Clay, aka Muhammed Ali, was another client. Belli represented him when his conviction for refusing to be inducted into the military was under consideration by the United States Supreme Court.

According to Belli, Ali visited him at the Hilton Hotel in New York. When the boxer asked what he should do, Belli told Ali to offer his services as a spokesman for the Army and agree to several public relations appearances where he would enunciate his patriotism. Belli recalled that Ali loved the idea.

To aid his efforts, Belli contacted a Nixon administration higher-up. When he told the man of Ali's desire to speak out for America, he was ecstatic. All seemed to be on track until Attorney General John Mitchell rejected the idea. Belli thought that President Nixon had missed a great opportunity to show the world that he was a compassionate man.

Belli swore Attorney General Mitchell's wife, Martha, was as outlandish a female as ever walked the streets of Washington. Her outbursts had been an embarrassment to her husband and the Nixon administration, but Belli liked her from the first time they met.

"Martha was a tough lady," Belli said, "a sweet Southern girl in crinoline one moment and Gold-Tooth Gertie of the Klondike the next. She said she wanted me because she wanted a lawyer who wasn't afraid of Nixon and couldn't be bought off."

Martha and Belli met in Phoenix where she retained him as her divorce lawyer. "Then she showed up one night with my investigator," Belli said, "at the Plaza Hotel in New York. She was loaded. We were afraid to put her in her own room, so we got a large suite and put her in the corner parlor."

The next day, Martha talked about the Nixon administration. "She told me that the White House was in chaos; everybody was drinking, and when her husband, John, the attorney general, came home, he was so disturbed—she was the only level head in the inner coterie. After a few drinks, she elaborated—'Whom do you think was running the United States in those months? Me, Martha.'"

Belli thought he had the case settled, but against his wishes, Martha would not return, of all things, John's collection of black alpaca suits: "shiny, baggy at the knees, black, conservative, confidence—installing East Coast 'establishment' salesman suits. Hanging in the closet, they looked just like John Mitchell, without John Mitchell inside."

Nothing Belli could do convinced Martha to return the suits, so she dumped him for attorney Henry Rothblatt. Belli never did learn whether the suits had been returned.

"She died shortly thereafter," Belli said. "I missed her a helluva lot more than the fee that I didn't get because she died. . . . I hope most lawyers are like me—we continue to practice this wonderful profession even if we don't get a dime for doing so."

Belli later told colleagues he had a theory about Martha Mitchell's death. "I think she was offed," he said.

CAROL DODA HIT the big time by becoming the first stripper to wear a topless bathing suit. On July 19, 1964, Carol strode the stage at The Condor, a strip club in the North Beach section of San Francisco, with her chest bared for all to see. Described by *North Beach Magazine* as a "former prune picker, file clerk, and cocktail waitress," Doda fell afoul of the law. Believing that enough was enough, San Francisco mayor John Shelley ordered raids on fourteen clubs, including Chi Chi's, The Condor, and Big Al's. More than thirty strippers were arrested, including Doda, advertised as "The Girl on the Piano."

Belli and cocounsel Patrick Hallinan came to the rescue. Patrick's father was Vincent Hallinan, a revered San Francisco attorney. He had once called Belli, "Mr. Belly," during a trial. When the judge ordered him to use the proper pronunciation, Hallinan triggered laughter when he said, "Your honor, when I get into my favorite Italian restaurant must I now ask for a plate of 'spaghett-eye' with some 'raviol-eye' on the side?"

After a lengthy trial, Belli and Patrick Hallinan persuaded a jury that Doda was not guilty. Belli said she was "very appreciative" of the verdict.

By December she had taken her act to Las Vegas's Silver Slipper Club and visited London where she had her breasts insured for $1.5 million.

Later Belli returned to the strip clubs' defense. Doda was under fire for having performed in *The Rise and Fall of the World, as Seen from a Sexual Position*. It was a political satire at the Presidio Theatre that featured, among other things, Doda and the Bolshoi Ballet singing "Aida" while romancing King Kong atop the Empire State Building. Infuriated, the police cracked down, outlawing signs with the words, "nude," "stark naked," and "bottomless." Once again Belli's influence prevailed, and the clubs were permitted to present their topless acts. Carol Doda continued to perform, and became such a successful businesswoman that Harvard University astounded the world by announcing that she was their "Business Person of the Year."

Belli's prurient interests rose again when he defended the Kearney Street proprietor of Off Broadway, where waitresses bared their chests. In an effort to close the sultry hot spot, city officials had used the novel argument that "bare breasts are the kind of advertisement that leads to intemperate use of alcohol." To counter this argument, Belli, waving a copy of the playmate centerfold from *Playboy* magazine, extolled the virtues of what he called "an art form." "Looking at this," he shouted, "[will not] make me order a bottle of beer, a snifter of Jim Beam, let alone a double shot." In closing, he added, "As long as I can help it, the sun will never set on an exposed bosom."

ONE OF MELVIN Belli's great disappointments was film director Francis Ford Coppola's decision not to cast him as Don Corleone in *The Godfather*. Despite a screen test, he was passed over for Marlon Brando.

To be certain, Belli was proud of his relationships with mob-related figures. He was also a great admirer of their rigid code of conduct, based on loyalty, a quality Belli regarded highly.

To ingratiate himself with the mob, Belli rubbed elbows with Mafia characters from coast to coast. Belli represented, and became friends with, dangerous men who committed violent acts.

Among his friends and associates were thugs, scam artists, blackmailers, arsonists, strong-arm bullies, thieves, extortionists, and murderers. Milton Hunt said his boss was "enamored" of the mob and other corrupt individuals. "He loved for people to assume he was connected to the underworld," Hunt added. "And he was. For some time, Mel was what I would call an unofficial member of the San Mateo [city south of San Francisco] mob. He never went to court for them, but he was certainly an adviser."

Jeanne Belli said the attraction to mobsters was easy to understand. "He loved the fact that they got away with things," she said. Private investigator Jim Licavoli, who knew that his boss' bookkeeper had ties to the Bananno crime family, stated, "Mel loved the mob and they loved him." An associate who requested anonymity stated, "Mel was intoxicated with the Mafia. He loved the power, the money, the irreverence they had for authority just like he did."

Former associate John O'Connor witnessed Belli's representation of San Mateo beer distributor Andy Gatuso. Mimicking the deep voice and eastern accent of the stereotypical mobster, O'Connor said the client told Belli, "'Hey, I just want to make a living. Tell them I just want to make a living.' Next thing I knew, Mel made the problem go away."

To Belli, Las Vegas was a Mafia playground, one he visited whenever possible. Bob Lieff recalled that his famous colleague received first-class treatment no matter where he traveled in Vegas. "His connections were very extensive," Lieff said.

Former partner Seymour Ellis said, "Mel dealt with a great many lawyers there whom we knew were connected to the mob."

In 1972, Bob Lieff had witnessed firsthand what happened to people who crossed the mob. Operating out of Belli's San Francisco office, he and Las Vegas attorney William Coulthard were handling a divorce case. Opposing counsel, representing the owner of the famous Dunes hotel, was Lou Weiner, whom Lieff knew had affiliations with mobsters, including the notorious Bugsy Seigel.

Coulthard himself had interesting connections. He was a crony of Lester "Benny" Binion, owner of the Horseshoe casino, and his wife was the daughter of casino owner Pietro "P. O." Salvaging.

When Salvaging died, his son-in-law Coulthard inherited his real estate. That meant the lawyer was Binion's landlord. In early 1972, Binion had become aware that Coulthard intended to sell the land to his rivals, and a feud began.

To accelerate the divorce, Lieff planned a trip to Las Vegas to see Weiner. Coulthard agreed to pick him up in his new Cadillac. The two would then visit Weiner's office.

At the last minute, Lieff received a call from Weiner. "Don't come to Vegas," Weiner said. "I said, hey, we need to meet," Lieff recalled, "but Lou was insistent. 'DON'T COME,' he said again, this time in a stronger tone."

Heeding the instructions, Lieff canceled his flight. The next day he heard that Coulthard had walked to his Cadillac parked on the third floor of a parking garage near Glitter Gulch. He sat behind the wheel and turned on the ignition key. The car exploded. The lawyer was killed.

The bomb, "a trimble trigger with a guitar pick," was so violent, according to police records, that Coulthard was decapitated. He had to be identified by dental records. Gas tanks in five adjacent cars burst. The FBI blamed Binion for the car bombing, but he was never arrested. The murder remains unsolved.

After hearing the news, Bob Lieff gasped, then telephoned Weiner. "I simply said, 'Thank you, Godfather!'" he recalled.

When Lieff forwarded a memo to Belli, who was traveling in Europe, his partner took the incident lightly. Belli's return communiqué read, "Next time you are in Vegas, rent a motorcycle."

BELLI ENJOYED A friendship with Frank Ragano, the Tampa, Florida, attorney who represented Teamster boss Jimmy Hoffa and mobsters Santo Trafficante and Carlos Marcello. Ragano hired Belli in 1966 to represent him in a damage suit against *Time* magazine. It had failed to distinguish Ragano as an attorney and not a member of the underworld in a caption below a photograph of himself and several mobsters. Court delays continued the case for several years until the trial was set for May 1971.

In the meantime, Belli's relationship with Ragano flourished. In 1969, their friendship was so solid that Ragano played host to Belli on a deep-sea fishing trip aboard a forty-foot schooner. It slept six and was owned by Jimmy Hoffa's Teamsters' union. Hoffa was in prison at the time, but Ragano said, "The vessel was at my disposal; all I had to provide for a day's outing was food and drinks."

Ragano recalled the fishing trip less for the fish caught than Belli's escapades with a *Playboy* bunny from San Francisco. "[Belli] proudly introduced her as having posed nude in a recent *Playboy* centerfold," Ragano recalled in his best-selling book, *Mob Lawyer.*

During the voyage, Ragano's wife Nancy became annoyed with Belli's "friend." When she returned from below deck wearing only the bottom of a string bikini, Ragano complained, telling Belli, "Please tell her to put on her top." Belli grinned, but heeded his friend's request. The bunny was instructed to wear Band-aids across her nipples to satisfy the dress code.

MELVIN BELLI, DUBBED a "modern day Robin Hood" by the *Saturday Evening Post*, appeared most content when he represented clients he felt were being persecuted by the establishment. He was an attorney who simply could not tolerate people being taken advantage of, whether it was by the government, manufacturers, or their fellow man. To Belli, each case was unique, a new challenge, a chance to make new law.

In 1941, an ulcer had allowed Belli to avoid military service, giving him the opportunity to defend Horace Fong, a resident of nearby Oak Knoll, California.

Other residents of the town had attempted to evict Fong and his wife, citing Oak Knoll's restriction of people of Chinese descent. Belli stormed the courthouse with a lawsuit stating that Fong wasn't actually Chinese. Based on a precedent-setting case that ruled all residents of lands bordering the China Sea "Indians," Fong was an American Indian.

In an 1854 case, *People v. Hall*, a Californian was accused of murder. The only witness against him was Chinese. The defendant's lawyer had a unique theory: he asked the court to declare that the witness wasn't Chinese but Indian, since when Columbus had discovered America, he thought he had landed on one of the islands in the China Sea.

The judge bought the logic and ruled that the Chinese man was an Indian. In the 1850s, Indians couldn't be witnesses because they were believed to be "notorious liars, full of malice, and unsanitary." The Californian won his case and celebrated by blasting his revolvers into the air. Under the precedent, Belli claimed that Mr. Fong, though he looked and spoke Chinese, was indeed an Indian.

Before the Superior Court in San Francisco decided the case, Fong's wife left him. The distressed man moved into Belli's home. Soon after, the "Indian" and Belli opened a restaurant in Redwood City called Fong's Iroquois Village. Belli, who invested $50,000 in the venture, explained that "on the cover of the menus, a totem pole rose above a book labeled Law, 4 Cal. 399 [the citation for the pivotal case]. Centered around the book was a chicken, an ear of corn, a pumpkin, a fish, a big steed and bottle of booze. The inscription on the totem said, 'Ugh, me Fong.'"

The restaurant's dishes were as colorful as its owners. Belli created the menus, which included various flaming dishes, strawberry omelets, and expensive champagne. There was also boiled cabbage O'Fong, MacFong d'oeuvres, shirred eggs à la Fongstein, barbecued pork Fongstein, French prawns à la Fong, and abalone in oyster sauce Fongby. The restaurant closed its doors within six months.

The fault was not in the food, Belli said, but in the kitchens. "After dinner, which I always ate on the cuff, I would go out in the kitchen to see how the boys were getting along. They were all Chinese, and they would be running back and forth with frying pans full of money. I asked what they were doing and they said they were gambling. This struck me as a good wholesome thing for them, so I never objected. The only trouble was that whenever one of them ran out of money he would go and fill his pan from the cash register."

Belli's representation of "Father" William E. Riker again demonstrated his dedication to the persecuted. Riker believed he was God. During World War II, the self-proclaimed priest proclaimed his admiration for Adolf Hitler's racial policies. This led to an investigation into his leadership of a religious group south of San Francisco in the Santa Cruz Mountains city of Los Gatos. When sixty-eight-year-old Riker told a group of sailors visiting his commune to disarm and quit fighting, the government had stepped in. He was charged with sedition.

After his arrest Riker secured Belli's services. Belli, who privately called his client "the screwiest of the screwballs," said he took the case for one reason: "To allow any man to preach any crackpot ideas he wanted—to anyone." He let the prosecution present its case without objecting once. Then he went to work, comparing Riker with "all the other crackpots of American history from Ben Franklin to Woodrow Wilson" and asking why the government permitted Riker to continue speaking a year after the investigation began. He then challenged anyone to even understand what the "old kook" was saying and promised to pay $50,000 to anyone who could.

San Francisco Chronicle reporter Carolyn Anspacher described Belli's speech in glowing terms, adding that his client was moved to tears. Riker was acquitted, anointed Belli his "Second Typical God," refused to pay the lawyer's fee in lieu of saving him "a place in heaven," and then subsequently sued the attorney for labeling him an "old kook" during final argument.

Belli represented a merchant marine captain who he said "was not merely an occasional tippler, but a dipsomaniac." One afternoon, the inebriated seaman fell three stories through an open elevator shaft and landed on a cement floor. He broke both ankles, his knees, and his hip. Reports indicated a whiskey bottle in his pocket survived the fall intact. The captain said of the fall, "It was the last step I ever took on this earth with my own two feet."

The captain only survived after yelling "Man overboard!" for at least an hour. When Belli had him on the witness stand, he asked, "When you regained consciousness in the bottom of the elevator shaft, what did you think had happened?" The man replied, "Jesus Christ, torpedoed again." His honesty, in the eyes of the jury, must have been charming. They awarded him damages despite his drunken state.

When a client named Frank Sullivan sued for damages from a street-car accident, liability was uncontested. The jury was left to determine what the injury was worth. Sullivan, a red-haired war veteran with a wife and child, had suffered a crushed pelvis, fractured vertebrae, and a ruptured urethra. The latter caused young Sullivan to become impotent.

Debating the compensation issue caused Belli to ask, "What if while I am arguing the numbers, I deliberately make a miscalculation?" He decided to take the gamble. "I was hoping that some numbers freak on the jury would catch my deliberate mistake," he said, "and feel so proud of his discovery that he might become an advocate for this number inside the jury room."

The calculation involved multiplying Sullivan's life expectancy of forty-four years by his projected income, one hundred and fifty dollars a month. The total, Belli told the jury, was "sixty-six thousand dollars in lost income."

While watching the jurors carefully consider the figure, Belli was shocked to hear the voice of Judge George Schonfeld. "Wait a minute, Mr. Belli," he said, "you've made a mistake in your mathematics."

Without hesitation, the judge informed Belli that the proper calculation was seventy-nine thousand two hundred dollars. Better yet, he repeated the figure: "The young man should get seventy-nine thousand, two hundred dollars."

At once, defense counsel leapt to his feet and shouted, "Objection!" "You have just told the jury what they ought to allow," he argued. The judge, obviously pleased with his disclosure, overruled the objection. The jury agreed. When they totaled up the lost compensation and the pain and suffering, they returned a verdict of $125,000. An appellate justice later characterized the award as "the largest verdict that has heretofore come before an appellate court in this state."

The case became one of Belli's favorite examples when discussing insurance company's claims that verdicts were too high. "Would you swap places with [Sullivan] for the $125,000 he was awarded?" Belli said. "Or for a million dollars? Or two million? Ten million? I think not. Yet [the insurance companies], the noble, stalwart, simon-pure insurance companies, they say, are being victimized by fakers—just for losing a lousy arm or leg." He added, "When I started winning [big] awards, they began sending out letters and buying expensive ads aimed at potential jurors in personal-injury cases. 'Keep those awards low, or you'll force your automobile insurance to go up.' Bushwa! I say."

NEVER ONE TO consider advancing age as a deterrent, Belli was ready to take on all comers. He successfully defended members of the Free Speech Movement in Berkeley, including the legendary Mario Savio, the wiry, twenty-two-year-old student leader who organized "sit-ins" protesting restriction of civil rights on the University of California campus. The effort was a forerunner of the Vietnam War protests.

Having preserved Savio's rights, Belli then won a $550,000 verdict in the Virgin Islands for Harvey "Rip" Collins, a U.S. Navy frogman and former star athlete who suffered a brain injury when his motorcycle collided with a government automobile left unattended in the middle of a dark road.

Remarkably, Judge Walter Gordon said to Belli, after he had given his final argument, "Sir, would you repeat that, my wife just walked in and she missed it." Despite outrage by the defendant's counsel, Belli did just that.

Belli's appearance in the Virgin Islands was an event to remember. The headline, "BELLI DRAWS FULL HOUSE," appeared in the local *V.I. Times.* The first sentence of the articles read, "His fame had preceded him and when Melvin M. Belli, one of the world's most colorful and successful lawyers, appeared in District Court, the courtroom was packed by the curious."

BELLI'S TRANSITION FROM actor in the courtroom to actor in Hollywood seemed natural. He had already tested the waters with television appearances. The Los Angeles Metromedia station syndicated his interview program around the country. Regarding his guests, Belli said, "Name the people who were making the news in 1964 and 1965. I interviewed them." Among them was Papa Doc Duvalier, the controversial ruler of Haiti.

Belli enlisted nine-year-old son Caesar to star with him in the October 11, 1968, episode of *Star Trek*. It was Episode Sixty, "And the Children Shall Lead." The publicity release read, "An evil superbeing disguised as an Angel has taken over Triacus and persuaded the children to kill adults. Only the crew of the Enterprise can stop him from invading the galaxy. 'Friendly Angel' is played by the high-profile lawyer Melvin Belli whose son Caesar plays carrot-topped kid Steve O'Connell."

Belli also hit the game show circuit. In 1971, he and Caesar appeared on an episode of *All About Faces*, a program hosted by Richard Hayes. Comedian Rich Little and his partner squared off against the Belli boys.

He was also on a program called *Guilty or Innocent*. It aired on a Channel 44, a local San Francisco television station. Belli enjoyed bit movie roles in such films as *Wild in the Streets, Devil's Dolls* with Susan Hayward, and, most important, *Gimme Shelter*, starring the Rolling Stones.

He relished his celebrity status in the Hollywood community, one that led to an invitation to the Academy Awards. Jeanne Belli recalled how pleased he was, stating, "He loved to watch all of those pretty girls in the fabulous dresses."

Though he claimed to have mixed emotions about his celebrity, no one believed him. "I had become a celebrity," he wrote, "which was fun about one percent of the time and a bore the rest. Being a celebrity . . . meant sending a pair of my horned-rimmed glasses to the . . . Famous People's Eyeglasses Museum in Henderson, Nevada. It meant seeing myself caricatured in a 'Little Annie Fanny' cartoon in *Playboy*."

Secretary Joyce Revilla had a theory. "He loved the attention," she said. "Because of how he started out. He became so famous so quickly, internationally famous. And then as the years passed, he needed the acclaim and the attention. He loved to see his name and photo in newspapers, and he would do just about anything to get that."

Revilla also recalled that Belli didn't seem to mind bad publicity. "He didn't care what they said about him," she explained, "just so long as they mentioned his name." Others disagreed, recalling Belli's anger at stories that criticized him.

In 1971, Belli displayed his resolve to never shy away from controversy. When the book, *Angela, a Revealing Close-up of the Woman and the Trial*, was published, the cover, which featured a close-up of revolutionary black activist Angela Davis, was imprinted with, "Foreword by Melvin M. Belli." It read in part, "The life of Angela and her trial is a story of challenge and conflict. Whether or not she is found to be guilty, a substantial portion of our system of justice stands on trial with her."

MELVIN BELLI WAS quite the showman, whether it was emceeing a victory celebration for topless dancers or judging the Miss California Pageant.

A photograph shows the handsome lawyer outfitted in a black tux with matching bow tie standing between two blondes and two brunettes. To his right stands the winner, a statuesque brunette with bouffant hair and a wide smile. Belli is grinning and squeezing the bathing suit–clad Miss California close to him. No caption is visible, but someone might have written, "Belli in Heaven."

An encounter with Mick Jagger and the Rolling Stones nearly cost Belli his legal license. The group's manager telephoned him in December 1969 when plans for a free concert featuring the Stones, Santana, The Grateful Dead, and Jefferson Airplane went awry.

At first Belli wasn't certain exactly who the band was. "Who's this Mick Jagger?" he asked, before being told that his potential client was a pop star of international renown. Realizing there was publicity to be had, Belli hugged Mick and the boys when they walked into his office.

A motion picture crew shooting a documentary captured images of the sixty-two-year-old Belli standing behind his desk barking into a speaker while attempting to locate another concert venue. One minute he was talking to the sheriff in a nearby county, the next he was conversing with the promoter.

Belli's efforts paid off when Dick Carter, owner of Altamont Speedway, agreed to host what the media dubbed "Woodstock West." After the deal was struck, Belli spoke with Jagger. The rock star praised his work and invited him to attend the concert as a special guest.

When the night of the concert dawned, there was a thirty-five-mile traffic jam along the route. More than three-hundred-thousand people flocked to the woods. Jagger cranked up his guitar and strutted across the stage. The crowd went wild—too wild.

The event's "security" force was partly made up of Hell's Angels. The Stones had used them as security in London, though European Hell's Angels were said to look more like Jagger than their ex-con American counterparts. They began to scuffle with rowdy kids intent on storming the makeshift stage.

The result was a riot of huge proportions. The rowdiness began during Santana's first set, when an angry Angel began hitting a long-haired kid with a pool cue in front of the stage. A hippie named Meridith Hunter brandished a gun and actually fired a shot in Jagger's direction. He was surrounded by security and stabbed by an Angel. Taken to an ambulance, he later died.

Dick Carter found the gun, contacted Hell's Angels leader Sonny Barger, and then delivered the weapon to Belli's office in a shoebox. Belli turned it over to the district attorney investigating the event.

The Stones's set was interrupted several times by incidences of violence, but, to his credit, Mick Jagger kept rocking and rolling. Even a steady stream of Stones hits such as *I Can't Get No Satisfaction, Under My Thumb*, and *Angie* did little to quell the unrest.

Belli had been on stage during the melee, his ears ringing as hard rock blasted out of the huge speakers. According to Belli, he experienced his own encounter with the security force when one of them yelled, "Okay, Grandpa, get off the stage." Belli said, "I got mad and started after him, but he raised his pool cue."

By the time the madness ended, several spectators had been killed. It was a black mark on rock concerts that would never be forgotten. Whenever disturbances occurred in the future, Altamont was the standard of comparison.

After the smoke had cleared, the State Bar decided Belli should be held accountable. Word had spread that he behaved unprofessionally even to the point of having hot-wired a car in order to speed off to the concert. Belli had to appear at a hearing and call witnesses in his defense. The charges of impropriety were eventually dropped.

When *Gimme Shelter*, filmed by the Maysles Brothers and dubbed "a time capsule of the violent climate in 1969," was released in 1970, Belli was prominently featured. The "old man's" part in the tragedy was documented for posterity.

ONE OF BELLI'S most memorable cases involved the defense of Winnie Ruth Judd, aka "The Trunk Murderess."

Judd was the twenty-six-year-old wife of a physician thirty years her senior. When he left Phoenix for Los Angeles, Winnie Ruth befriended two young women living nearby. She also began dating a wealthy lumber owner named Halloran.

Sparks flew when disagreement arose over who was sleeping with whom. During an argument between the three women, Judd, in a fit of rage, shot and killed them. Halloran found her in despair and offered his assistance.

Together they devised the scheme to hide the bodies. One fit nicely in a trunk, but the other was too large for a second one. Cleverly, they dismembered the second body and rearranged the parts. The bodies fit perfectly.

Judd, after withdrawing a few body parts and placing them in a valise to lessen the weight of the trunks, then calmly told her landlord to transport the trunks to the train station. She said they contained "books that her husband needed."

With the valise at her side, Judd accompanied the trunks on the four-hundred-plus mile trip. The scheme might have worked, but a baggage handler, who nearly fainted from the foul odor, noticed a thick, red liquid oozing from one trunk. He notified his superiors. They looked for Winnie Ruth Judd, but she had vanished.

She was captured and returned to Phoenix. A jury decided she was guilty of murdering the woman who had not been dismembered. She was sentenced to death by hanging, but the double murderer was pronounced insane three days before her execution.

Judd then became an escape artist. Belli first heard from her after her last and most successful escape from Arizona State Hospital in 1969. She ended up in San Francisco where police arrested her.

When she telephoned Belli collect from her jail cell, Belli accepted the charges. "Through law school," he recalled, "W. J. R. had been a standing joke. She had been over the wall more than Babe Ruth."

After Judd begged Belli to represent her, he sent an associate to the jail in Contra Costa County. When he returned, the description of Winnie caused Belli to double over with laughter.

"Mel, it's here and she looks like . . . everybody's grandmother, Barbara Fritchie, and Florence Nighingale." Anne Horii, a dental hygienist who cleaned Judd's teeth, was not repulsed by her reputation. "She was just a nice, old lady," Horii said.

Based on the description, Belli accepted Winnie's call for help. He accompanied her back to Arizona and after several attempts, finally secured her release for time served. Appreciative, she left Arizona and moved to within a few miles of Belli. She eventually returned to Phoenix, where she died in 1998, at age ninety-three.

Following his representation of Winnie, Belli spent time in Rome. Then it was off to Kenya for a safari. His companion was a tall blonde, the Countess Nieti Von Der of Munich. When Belli didn't pay enough attention to her, she burned all his credit cards and cash and left for Germany.

Nevertheless, a photograph snapped during a big game hunt on Mount Kilimanjaro depicted "The Great White Hunter" having a hell of a good time. Wearing a dark cloth fedora, and smoking a thin cigar, he was captured sitting in a wooden washtub in the buff with his upper torso lathered in suds, his ornery grin on display.

While his romance was a total disaster and the hunt only partly successful, a side trip to South Africa gave Belli a great thrill. There, he watched Dr. Christian Barnard perform open-heart surgery, a revolutionary procedure at the time. "When he removed the ligatures to see if the bypass had worked," Belli recalled, "everyone in the operating room yelled, 'Hurrah!'"

While in Vietnam, Belli was honored when the Green Berets presented him with an AK rifle that he hung in his San Francisco law office. The inscription read, "Presented to Melvin M. Belli, by the officers and men of Co A, 5th SFT (ADN), RVN, captured by 3rd Mobile Strike Force Command, Rang Rang, 28 January 1970."

NO MILITARY WAS involved, but in 1976, Belli traveled to Saudi Arabia for a civil case involving a member of the royal family. In a *San Francisco Chronicle* article titled, "Notes from a Saudi Journal," Belli wrote, "The cruelest fate of all is to be born a woman in Saudi Arabia." He noted the absence of civil rights, and discussed his view that severing one's hand for stealing in accordance with the principles of the Koran was excessive punishment. Belli was even more emphatic when he described the obstacles presented in transporting his legal target, a wealthy emir, to the United States for a deposition. To do so, he wrote, involved "my leasing a 747 or at least a 707 for him, his six body guards, his ten ministers, his wives and friends, two of his cooks and at least a dozen sheep which would be slaughtered, probably in the bathroom at the Mark Hopkins and cooked, barbecue style, in the drawing room."

14

TROUBLE WITH J. EDGAR HOOVER

NO MATTER WHERE Melvin Belli plied his trade, professional legal authorities, especially the American Bar Association, monitored his activities. His successes spoke for themselves, but his flamboyant style and media attention offended many within the legal establishment. Jealous of his success, and determined to make him behave according to their standards, they were intent on reining him in.

Belli's appearance in ads for a new Scotch called Glenfiddich gave the California Bar a chance to punish the lawyer. The ad's headline read, "Melvin Belli is onto unabridged Scotch." Underneath in small print were the words, "This isn't the first time he knew something others didn't know."

When the ad appeared in the *New York Times*, the copy read:

Melvin Belli is the famous trial lawyer who first employed "demonstrative evidence" in the courtroom. Rather than simply stating his case, he demonstrates it so conclusively that the case is almost won at once. To give you an example, we asked him to interrogate a conventional Scotch drinker. Six lengthy Q and As followed, with Belli slowly but surely pressing his case that Glenfiddich was a remarkable new Scotch.

In summation, the ad quoted Belli as saying,

> Then perhaps you can understand why I am an advocate of Glenfiddich. It had been distilled from 100% malt barley in handmade copper stills since 1887. And I will abide no abridgment. The converted Scotch drinker replies, May Glenfiddich remain forever unabridged.

The ad concluded with the words, "Wild applause in the courtroom." Belli's photograph appeared in the upper left-hand corner of the ad. When the California Bar Association saw it, they threatened to suspend Belli from practicing law for a year if he did not submit future commercial opportunities in advance for approval. When he refused, they ordered the suspension.

Promising to strike back at what he believed was denial of free speech, Belli turned to associate Kent Russell to represent his interests. The California Supreme Court ruled in his favor in 1974. Russell believed the case was of historical significance. "It showed that lawyers were protected by free speech, First Amendment Rights," he said.

To placate the establishment, Belli believed, the court suspended him from the practice of law for one month. Receptionist Maggie Smith said Belli was a nervous wreck during that time. "I told Bill Choulos, Belli's partner," she recalled, "that Mr. Belli was standing by me monitoring all of the calls. He was driving me nuts."

BELLI'S BOXING MATCH with the American Bar Association or other legal organizations did not go unnoticed by one of the barrister's leading adversaries—FBI Director J. Edgar Hoover. In Belli's six-hundred-page FBI dossier, secured under the auspices of The Freedom of Information Act, Hoover was constantly informed about Belli's activities both domestically and abroad.

THE ACCOMPANYING LETTER to the file from John M. Kelso Jr. stated, "The enclosed documents were reviewed under the Freedom of Information/Privacy Acts (FOIPA). . . . Deletions have been made to protect information which is exempt from disclosure." The dossier was riddled with cross-outs. On occasion, entire paragraphs were excluded. One page was missing. Another was completely marked out. Several times, mark-outs were adjoined by the words "Consulting with CIA." It was unclear whether the notation meant that Belli was working with the CIA or that the CIA had been consulted regarding the text. According to notations on the pages, the material had been declassified in 1980.

Belli's file portrayed a troublemaker whose behavior was closely monitored by the Bureau. In 1956, he came under suspicion of the FBI regarding potential communist sympathies. Belli was opposed to a California Senate Bill that would have required members of the bar to swear to a test or loyalty oath as a condition to practicing law. An attached *Daily People's World* (*DWP*) newspaper article read, "A group of prominent Bay Area residents, headed by Attorney Vincent Hallinan, protested the prosecution of twelve Communist leaders to Alben Barkley during the vice president's visit here."

In a December 14, 1956, FBI memo, the California State Bar alleged that "Belli was unethical in soliciting his clients." He was also accused of representing the children of an individual who made a "hidden donation to the Communist party." A memo dated three days later from L. B. Nichols to Clyde Tolson, Hoover's personal assistant, notes that Belli was representing State Director of Education Pearl Wanamaker, falsely accused of being a communist. The accuser, Fulton Lewis Jr., had asked the FBI for assistance in "learning about the attorney." Nichols promised his cooperation.

By September 1959, the FBI was closely monitoring Belli. A memo from around that time read, "The director has instructed that our San Francisco office keep alert for any violation of law by Belli in view of his questionable record. Attached is a brief letter to San Francisco with appropriate instructions." Unfortunately the entire text of the instructions is marked out.

Belli's hoax at the ABA convention in Miami precipitated the memo. Under "BACKGROUND," it read, "The attached clipping from the *New York Times* reflects that Attorney Melvin M. Belli . . . introduced West Coast Mobster Mickey Cohen at a seminar on legal tactics during the current American Bar Association Convention. Cohen was introduced as 'Professor O'Brien,' expert on tax evasion and other criminal cases." The latter reference was exaggerated: Belli merely introduced the professor as an expert on taxes.

On March 18, 1960, an eight-page report was issued on Belli's personal life. Chronicled were his marriages to date, his most famous cases, a recap of the Cohen incident in Miami, Belli's defense of Cohen's girlfriend Candy Barr, Belli's crowning as "King of Torts" by *Life* magazine, and the material regarding his communist activities.

On August 9, 1960, Belli was the subject of an FBI memo that linked the FBI to the ABA effort to disbar the attorney. Agent H. L. Edwards, who called Belli "a notorious publicity seeker," quoted an ABA source as saying, "He has been trying in every possible to 'make a case' which would justify ousting Belli from the ABA for unethical practices although Belli is apparently smart enough to stay within the ethical rules." Attached to the memo was a May 15, 1960, letter on Belli's law office stationary informing them about the "Tenth Annual Belli Seminar" scheduled in Washington, DC. A bizarre section of Belli's file dealt with a 1961 case involving a Downey, California, judge's "leniency for love" escapades. Judge Lynn Johnston was charged with bribery, since prosecutors said he granted probation if female defendants "paid him little visits." Belli's defense featured allegations that Police Chief Ivan Robinson framed the judge.

The name of the individual who contacted the FBI about the case was marked out, as was a huge block of text. The references to Belli were derogatory. According to the report, the "source" stated, "Belli was one of most vicious and unscrupulous individuals that he had ever encountered." The report advised that, "Every care will be taken to avoid our being interjected into this matter."

Belli must have shocked the FBI in March 1963, when he penned a letter of inquiry to Dr. Fred Miller, a noted Bureau forensic scientist. Belli requested a reading and review of *Modern Trials*. Miller sent Belli a polite letter declining. In a later memo, Special Agent M. A. Jones quotes J. Edgar Hoover as saying that Belli was a "shyster." Added under the banner OBSERVATIONS was, "In view of Belli's unsavory reputation, we certainly do not want to offer him any kind of cooperation nor do any thing to encourage further contact of Bureau personnel by him."

The first indication of the FBI's interest in Belli and the Jack Ruby case was a copy of a newspaper clipping dated December 10, 1963, seventeen days after Ruby shot Lee Harvey Oswald. The headline read, "Ruby's Plea to Be Based on Insanity." Belli was labeled a "spectacularly successful San Francisco attorney."

The next day, an interoffice memo from Special Agent S. Rusen bore the designation, "For The Director's Information." It announced Belli's representation of Ruby. The memo also mentioned his representation of

Jean Kidwell Pestana, "a Los Angeles attorney who is active in the Communist Party."

In February 1964, an FBI memorandum titled "ASSASSINATION OF THE PRESIDENT" reported that "alleged sources" were indicating that both Lee Harvey Oswald and Jack Ruby were informants for the FBI prior to the assassination of President Kennedy. The memo added, "Belli additionally told the reporter that Ruby informed on gamblers and people of low character, and that Oswald was a security-type informant."

Special Agent C. D. DeLoach denied the allegations in the memo. He said he told the inquirer, "this was an old, old story without a scintilla of truth to it." Among the sources he cited for the misinformation was an employee of Senator Strom Thurmond.

After chastising Belli for being a lawyer who wanted to "get publicity for himself," DeLoach, under the ACTION paragraph of the memo, stated, "consideration should be given to immediately interviewing Belli concerning [his] allegations." True to that suggestion, FBI files indicate that Belli was interviewed on February 28, 1964, in his hotel room. The memo chronicling the meeting said that agents informed Belli that there was "absolutely no truth" to the rumors about Oswald or Ruby.

According to the memo, Belli then informed the agents where he had heard the rumors. He cited various reporters and "people around the courthouse." In the RECOMMENDATION paragraph of the memo, Special Agent Branigan stated that he believed the source of the rumors was, in fact, Belli himself. A note also indicated that a transcript of the interview and the rumors would be passed along to the Presidential Commission, i.e., the Warren Commission.

Fifty-two pages of Belli's FBI file dealt with a threat he received shortly after the Jack Ruby trial. A letter postmarked Starkville, Mississippi, was sent to Belli on March 24, 1964—ten days after Ruby's conviction. It read, in part, "Old Dago Belli says of Dallas, 'This city stinks!' We have news for you, jelly belli—that's your upper lip you smell. Furthermore, if you're not careful, somebody's going to put a slug of hot lead between those beady eyes of yours." Below the message was the typed signature, "The Committee." Below it were the words, "Remember, San Francisco is no sanctuary."

Investigation by the Bureau, including fingerprint analysis, uncovered a suspect named R. A. Wagner of Jackson, Mississippi. On September 7, 1964, the suspect forwarded a typewritten letter to the Bureau. In a rambling text, Wagner stated, "My 'crime' is not extortion but—to a very small degree—pointing an accusing finger at those who would [and may] bring social disaster to this nation—out of hypocritical financial and political opportunities as well as out of a warped equalitarian philosophy which has *no* basis in fact to the philosophical foundations of the country." No mention is made as to whether or not Wagner was arrested.

THREE MONTHS LATER an FBI memo detailed the account of Shields Mitchell, "a freelance cameraman and producer of motion pictures in Dallas." Belli had employed him during pretrial interviews with Jack Ruby.

Mitchell told a colleague that Belli claimed he wanted to record Ruby on tape so as to "ascertain the personality and character of [his client] for his assistance in preparing Ruby's defense." Mitchell went on to say that Belli was more interested in "compiling an immense film library for future exploitation," and "hoped that Ruby would 'crack up' during one of the interviews so it could be recorded. Belli's belief was that such film would become priceless as a historic document in the future and that he would personally reap rich rewards."

The cameraman swore that "Belli frequently referred to the unethical approach he was taking, stating that if it became known he would 'go to jail.'" Mitchell said he resigned because of the job's unethical climate. The author suggested that the information be forwarded to the Warren Commission. No record of it exists in their final report.

IN OCTOBER 1964, the FBI monitored a San Francisco debate between Belli and controversial author Mark Lane. A four-page report was issued on their subject, "IS OSWALD THE LONE ASSASSIN OF THE PRESIDENT?" The moderator was San Francisco attorney Jake Ehrlich, passed over as Ruby's attorney because of his Jewish heritage.

In attendance, the report said, was "a Special Agent of the FBI" He detailed Belli's praise for the Warren Commission, his belief that Oswald acted alone, and his belief that Oswald was a "psychotic person."

Belli's personal battle with J. Edgar Hoover intensified in December 1964. During a speech at Rice University, he said, "Hoover has long since outlived his usefulness."

Whether he knew the FBI had compiled a dossier on him is unknown, but Belli lambasted the Bureau on that subject. "The portfolio and dossier Hoover has on so many Americans is frightening," he said. "And one sees with dread the building up of a federal police force. It is a dangerous trend."

In May 1965, he ridiculed the FBI director in *Playboy* magazine. He charged that the director's "ideology is fascism," and "The FBI director is a 'dangerous, dangerous man whom we should have gotten rid of a long time ago." This triggered a May 11 memo from Special Agent M. A. Jones, which said, "It [the interview] was another typical example of the thirst for headlines so often evidenced by this egomaniac."

A week later Special Agent Jones followed up his memo. Attached to it was the entire Belli *Playboy* interview. The first sentence read, "Melvin Belli, the San Francisco attorney and the most notorious charlatan in the legal profession, has blasted, in the current issue of *Playboy*, the Director, Bobby Kennedy, the American Bar Association, and the American Medical Association, with the Director receiving top billing."

Jones's disapproval of Belli increased with each sentence. Under OBSERVATIONS he wrote, "This 'two-bit' Barnum and Bailey barrister grossly distorts the role of the FBI in law enforcement. . . . His reasoning on every count is typical of his nature of an egomaniac. . . . This is another case of where the Director and the FBI can well be proud of their enemies."

After Belli had once again called Hoover a fascist during a speech that was chronicled by the *Miami Herald*, Special Agent C. D. DeLoach wrote, "Belli is obviously a mentally disturbed and intemperate attorney." In a July 28 memorandum, DeLoach boasted that a movement was in progress to oust Belli from the American Trial Lawyers Association. Quoting Florida Judge Jim Floyd, DeLoach wrote, "Former Agents desire to take Belli apart because of his stupid allegations."

When *Playboy* presented a PANEL DISCUSSION: CRISIS IN LAW ENFORCEMENT in February 1966, Special Agent M. A. Jones was not pleased. He wrote, "Captioned magazine [attached] includes a panel discussion on alleged infringement of constitutional rights of individuals. Taking part are shyster lawyer Melvin Belli, subversive pervert Bavard Rustin, disgraced ex-Agent William Turner, American Civil Liberties Union Executive Director John Pemberton Jr., Judge George Leighton of Chicago, the notorious [marked out] Fred Cook." Regarding Belli's participation, Jones said, "[He] alleges the Director and others are greedy for power and want a police state." In the OBSERVATIONS section of the memo, Jones wrote, "The best interests of the Bureau would appear to be served by officially ignoring this cheap attempt to enmesh the Bureau with their petty grievances."

If J. Edgar Hoover believed that Belli would halt his scathing comments, he was wrong. In February 1967, Belli told the *Cincinnati Enquirer* that "he was amazed that the American public hasn't sent this American Franco packing years ago." A month later, he told the *Albuquerque Tribune*, Hoover was "a fraud" and "that there were links between the FBI director, chief racketeers, and politicians."

Belli would have been proud to know that his latest barrage triggered action from the FBI director himself. On March 27, 1967, over the signature stamp of J. Edgar Hoover, he wrote to an unidentified inquirer, "I would not consider making any public answer to the statements attributed to Melvin Belli . . . and regard them as being too ridiculous to warrant further comment."

BELLI'S FBI FILE contained a copy of a forty-two-page article that he wrote titled, "Are Our Courts Coddling Criminals." The subtitle read, "(No, They're Protecting the Accused)."

The first paragraphs must have intensified Hoover's hatred of the attorney. Belli replied, "I don't like Edgar Hoover. One of the reasons I don't like him is that he has designedly through his high-powered public relations organization created such an image of himself that even honest American politicians are un-American in their fear of him and afraid to criticize him even though they know he is an ideological fascist." Later in the text, he added, "Bobby Kennedy and Mr. Hoover and their strange bedfellows in this instance, the Far Right, want to tap my telephone. They want to know what I'm saying, what I am thinking."

In February 1968, Belli dubbed Hoover a "fatuous old dictator," and alleged that he "has set up a little storm troop empire." The lawyer then acknowledged his belief that he was being monitored, writing, "I am one of a number of attorneys who have had FBI agents checking into their past." Special Agent M. A. Jones followed up the tirade with another memo, writing that the criticisms were "nothing but cheap, undocumented, slander against Mr. Hoover and the bureau."

Belli's discontent with Hoover extended across the Atlantic Ocean. According to FBI memorandums, the lawyer made various complaints about the director to the *London Daily Mirror* and in South Africa. Then he returned to the United States. Addressing a college crowd in Mobile, Alabama, he criticized not only Hoover, but also Richard Nixon. "There is no such thing as the new Nixon," Belli said as the 1968 Presidential campaign neared. "It is just a case of a trickier Dick." He then added, "To know Dick Nixon is to distrust him. . . . I'd rather have George Wallace than Nixon. At least we know where he stands. We know he is no good and we know how to handle him." Of Hoover, he said, "The director is a hypocrite."

In August 1970, Belli attacked Hoover on radio station WKAT, Miami. Offered a chance to rebut the remarks, the director wrote back saying, "I feel these scurrilous charges should not be dignified with a reply."

While FBI records indicated that the Bureau monitored Belli's appearance on the *David Frost Show* in October 1970, an interview in the *Omaha World-Herald* drew the ire of an unidentified special agent. The article, titled "Belli on Hoover," began with the words, "Melvin Belli came to town the other day and casually slandered three American presidents. The lawyer's thesis: that J. Edgar Hoover keeps his job because he knows dark secrets about his superiors."

Embellishing, the reporter quoted Belli, who had called Hoover "as dishonest as Dick Tracy" during a Honolulu interview, as saying, "How much he has got on the present guy [Nixon] I don't know. The reason the Kennedys didn't get him out of there and Johnson didn't get him out of there is that he had too much on both of them." Apparently those words riled the preparer of the memo, causing them to write in longhand "Belli is a well-known ass!" at the top of the copy of the article. What was written on the second page of the memorandum was not evident, since the entire text was crossed out with the explanation, "B1."

Belli's obsession with J. Edgar Hoover ended when the seventy-six-year-old director died in May 1972. He had been head of the FBI for forty-eight years. Upon his death, the FBI apparently lost interest in Belli; the file reflects no further monitoring of his activities. Maybe they were bored, or maybe Belli simply wore them out.

15

FAME, FRIENDS, PARTIES, AND PRANKS

FORMER LAW PARTNER John Hill noted, "In our dot.com society, fame lasts a few years at most. Mel was a genuine celebrity for more than sixty years." Melvin Belli was so famous he even had a song written about him. Titled, "Lone Ranger in a Three Piece Suit," it was penned by Belli associate Kent Russell. The first stanza read,

> Back in '55 the magazine of *Life* crowned him the King
> Juries were his subjects—and verdicts they did bring.
> He was help for the helpless—as he traveled far and wide.
> Claims agents and adjusters—saw Robin Hood alive.
> Takin' from the powerful the reckless and the cruel
> Awarding to the injured, the beggar and the fool.

A chorus followed:

LONE RANGER IN A THREE-PIECE SUIT AND TRIAL WAS HIS GAME
HIS CALLING CARD READ LAWYER AND BELLI WAS HIS NAME.

Belli was notoriously irreverent. While in Jordan, he insulted King Hussein and was asked to leave the country. Asked on England's most popular interview program what he thought of wigged lawyers and judges, he answered, "They're all full of bullshit." Telephoned by a deputy prosecutor in San Francisco and asked about the plethora of parking tickets left on his Rolls-Royce, he said, "I didn't think that law applied to me."

"He didn't respect any institutions," Bob Lieff said, "whether it was the ABA, the government, the church or J. Edgar Hoover. He attacked them all. I recall him saying on occasion, as if Hoover were listening, 'You hear that, J. Edgar?'"

Belli loved being recognized and attended to as a celebrity. Saturday lunches were a ritual, as Belli worked nearly every weekend. Most times they were held at Jack's, a famed San Francisco eatery. Time was never a concern, especially since, as Maggie Quinn put it, "Belli ate a full dinner at lunch."

At the lunches, Belli enjoyed ordering for everyone. A sign that an associate attorney had gained stature was that they were allowed to order their own meal, instead of having Belli do it for them. "Belli would choose the Sorrell Soup," Ellison recalled, "which was bitter, perhaps the Lamb Riblets, and normally a Pumard, a French Burgundy. Mel wasn't a big drinker, and he never got more than a few hours of sleep.

"Mel had a round table in the center or sometimes we'd sit at a large table in the rear," Seymour Ellison recalled. "Lou Lurie, one of the wealthiest men around, had his table, too. The waiters always seemed to be the same, Dominique waited on Lurie, and John, father of the later owner of John's Grill, waited on us."

Belli enjoyed the spotlight at restaurants and normally demanded a table in front where everyone could see him. There, as at Jack's, he would hold court, talking about the law while sipping liquor as admirers wandered over to pay their respects. "Belli chose the same places a lot," Ellison said. "So it became known that if you wanted to see him, then you went to Jack's at a particular time."

Belli loved to have as many people around him as possible. "Mel couldn't stand to be alone," said Seymour Ellison. "He loved people and he wanted company." John Hill said, "Mel never had real close friends, so he made up for it by having hundreds of not-so-close friends."

On one occasion Belli barged into a packed Doro's, the hangout next door to his offices, and co-owner Don Dianda refused to give him a table.

Since Belli's crew often ran up tabs of more than $10,000 during an evening of food and drink, he was understandably upset.

The result of Dianda's snub was an infamous Belli memo sent to all employees. It read: "TO ALL HANDS: NO ONE IS TO GO TO DORO'S UNTIL FURTHER NOTICE." On another occasion, when Belli was trying to save money, he issued another memo, instructing employees to "UNSCREW LIGHTBULBS WHEN DONE WORKING" to cut down on electricity costs.

With fame came arrogance and distasteful behavior. When Belli had a spat with famous San Francisco private investigator Harold Lipsett, he marched downstairs and announced, "I want to know if that man is in the building because if he is, I will leave because I don't want to be in the same building with him." This statement became a memo as well.

Milton Hunt said there were two occasions when it was "smart to hide from Belli . . . One was when he sent out one of those damn memos," Hunt said. "And the other was when he lost a case. In either situation, we all knew he would be on the rampage."

Seymour Ellison said Belli paid his respect to a person by calling him "Dr. so and so." "When people addressed him as Dr. Belli, he liked that," Ellison said. "And when he called me Dr. Ellison, I knew he was sincere."

People attempting to pattern their lives after Belli's were abundant, but Seymour Ellison said the most ardent was a Boston attorney named Irving "Chickie" Sheff. "He emulated Belli his hero like you wouldn't believe," Ellsion said. "Right down to the pinstriped suits, the custom shirts and ties, the red lining, everything. At one point, Mel asked me, 'Is he better looking than I am. Is he still dressing like me?'

"I told Mel that Sheff said, 'When you're a lawyer with a briefcase, you can go anywhere and to any whorehouse in the world.' Belli said, 'I knew I liked that guy.'"

Belli's colleagues were amazed by his stamina. Paul Monzione recalled that he and the attorney had flown to Hawaii for a trial. "We landed after the long flight, talked to our clients, had dinner, and drinks," he said. "Afterwards, I was exhausted, but Mel looked out the window and said, 'Boy, that ocean looks great. Let's get up early and take a swim.' At 5:30 the next morning, I was fast asleep when I heard someone pounding on the door. When I opened it, there he was in swimming trunks, ready for the swim."

"Mel's energy was boundless," Seymour Ellison said. "We had a case in Chicago and Mel couldn't be there. I had to explain his absence to a very angry judge who became more angry when he saw Mel on the *Johnny Carson Show* live in New York City. The next day the judge's quip was, 'Well, if he [Belli] thinks that Johnny Carson is more important than me, then tell him to try the case in front of Carson.'"

After selection of the jury, Ellison said Belli finally arrived in Chicago, despite his hectic schedule. Accommodations were at the fancy Palmer House. "That evening we went to dinner and who's performing, but Jack Benny," Ellison said. "After the show, he came to our table. I was just in awe. He and Mel talked about Errol Flynn and we had our picture taken. The following morning the judge castigated Mel for not showing up the first day of trial. He said, 'Damn it, Mel, if you're not going to show don't go on national television.'"

Belli's opening statement impressed Ellison and shocked the judge. "Mel didn't know a thing about the case," Ellison recalled, "And so he said to the jury, 'We're going to get educated together.' The judge didn't like that at all."

The case was finally settled in the midst of a Chicago snowstorm that prevented the weary travelers from escaping the windy city by air. "Mel said, 'Hey, one of the state senators said if I was ever in the neighborhood to come down to Springfield,'" Ellison recalled. "I was exhausted, but he wanted to drive four hours down there and so we did. When he walked into the chambers, the whole place came to a screeching halt. Everyone, both in the Senate and the House, came up and shook his hand and had their pictures taken. The Lieutenant Governor heard Mel was around and he came down, too. Then we drove to St. Louis and flew out of there. I could barely keep up with him. What energy he had! It was nonstop."

"His ego was insurmountable," John O'Connor said. "At one point, F. Lee Bailey, a Belli rival, became involved as an investor and publisher with *Gallery* magazine," O'Connor said. "That upset Mel, and so he had me work out a deal with a magazine in Chicago called *CoQ*."

For legal reasons, O'Connor persuaded Belli not to become publisher, but he was an investor and named general counsel. "Mel agreed to that," O'Connor said, "but I was surprised when I learned that the name of the magazine, published by George Santo Pietro, was not a play on 'cock,' which I figured, but a play on 'cocaine.' It only lasted a few issues, but Mel was proud of his name being on the masthead."

Jeanne Belli recalled her father's passion for being important. "We'd walk into a restaurant and he'd say, 'Let's see how many people know who we are,' but I knew he didn't mean me. One time he called a number demanding something from some office and when the woman wouldn't acknowledge him, he screamed, 'Don't you know who I am? I'm Melvin Belli, the most famous lawyer in the world!' When he figured out he was only talking to some poor telephone operator, and not some secretary, he was embarrassed."

John Hill recalled a lawsuit and Belli's obsession with *San Francisco Chronicle* columnist Herb Caen. "It was a perfect Mel case," Hill said. "A gigolo in his thirties married to a rich woman in her seventies in Vegas. The guy, who had broken his foot by falling off a bar stool, got drunk and high on pills, sent his fourteen-year-old son out to retrieve lighter fluid, and then torched his wife while she was in bed. He also had beaten her with the crutch."

On behalf of the dead woman's brother and sister, Belli filed suit against the killer. Under Nevada law, he could not inherit her fortune if he was the murderer. Tissue samples taken from the crutch showed that the woman had been alive before she was burned.

When the gigolo appeared in court, Hill said that Belli's first suggestion was to buy the guy a suit so he wouldn't warrant sympathy from a jury due to his jail clothes. Hill and Belli bought a Zoot suit at a nearby Goodwill store. This done, Belli confronted the killer on the witness stand. "It was hilarious," Hill said. "The guy and Mel sparred about whether Mel had selected the right cause of action, collateral estoppel. The gigolo actually quoted from one of Mel's books seeking to prove his theories wrong, that it was not the proper remedy."

Once the evidence was in, the gigolo argued, "I may have killed my wife, but I gave her more in her lifetime than her brother and sister ever did." "That was unbelievable," Hill said laughing. "The jury came back with a verdict of $1,452,000, the exact amount of the inheritance."

The coup de grace, Hill recalled, was the telephone call Belli placed to Caen after the verdict. "He told Herb it was his fourth million dollar award," Hill said, "but it was actually his first."

Bob Buich, co-owner of Tadich's, the legendary downtown San Francisco grill and self-proclaimed "Original Cold Day Restaurant," fondly recalled Belli as a humble patron despite his inflated ego. "Even though he was famous," Buich said, "he never asked for a preference. Most times he was with a group of people, but sometimes he'd just sit at the bar alone and write on a notepad. He wasn't intimidating to talk to, but I could tell he was very bright."

When a court victory merited celebration, Belli's crew retired to one of the booths to the side of Tadich's. "They partied long and hard," Buich said. "But they never caused any trouble."

"People would look at him and I'd hear them whisper, 'That's Melvin Belli.' They'd point and ask for autographs. He liked that," Buich remembered. "He didn't like it much," Bob Lieff said, "when some yokel would walk up to the table and say, 'Aren't you F. Lee Bailey?'"

Lieff recalled that whenever Belli was asked, "Who is the greatest lawyer who ever lived?" he would mention some obscure attorney in Chicago that no one ever heard of. "By doing that," Lieff speculated, "he obviously intended the listener to realize that he thought the greatest lawyer was none other than Melvin Belli."

Buich said Belli's fame meant that his Christmas parties were the talk of San Francisco. "Being on that list was special," he said. "There were always so many good-looking women there. And the building, it looked like it was something out of New Orleans." Asked about the Christmas parties, attorney Seymour Ellison said, "They were attended by seven to eight hundred of Mel's closest friends. The world would be there."

Sharron Long, who, along with several other Belli employees, called the days at the offices "magical," recalled the Christmas party number being more like "three thousand of Belli's intimate friends." Carol Anna Lind said the Christmas card list included more than *ninety-thousand* names. Belli later said it reached 110,000. Each card had to be hand-addressed.

The highlight of any party hosted by the famous barrister was the renowned "Pisco Punch," a deadly brew made from a carefully guarded secret recipe. Belli described it on invitations as "A famed San Francisco concoction from the original Peruvian recipe by way of Rome, improved by Anna Mouron, California's first woman druggist, and further later improvements by Caesar M. Belli and Dr. M. M. Belli after secret expeditions to the headwaters of the Amazon."

Belli once traveled to the Bolivar Hotel in Lima, Peru, with partner Bill Choulos. They reported the original recipe for "Pisco Sour Cocktail" called for "3 laces Pisco [Prune Brandy], 2 huitte eggs, 3 lemon juss, 1 asspun Sugar, 1 Rags Price, Very Shaquel For Cervis drop cingculu." Those who drank the brew said that translated to 100 proof rum, fruit juices, and grenadine with most anything else thrown in for good measure.

Simplified, the recipe was, "Put some pineapple in the bottom of a crock and let ferment for two or three days. Then pour straight pisco Peruvian prune brandy over it and let ferment for a couple more days. Crush the pineapple and add fresh orange, pineapple and lemon juice, some angostura and lots of ice, and if necessary, sugar. Stir with an ossick [a petrified pizzle of a walrus Belli found on in Alaska]."

Those in charge of preparing the concoction, including Sharron Long and "maintenance engineer" Art Jackson, stayed up nights watching the deadly brew marinate. Party guests found the "Pisco" positioned in strategic spots around the office in huge crocks. Those who weren't aware of its potency soon discovered they were significantly drunk. Even consumer crusader Ralph Nader, a longtime friend of Belli, wasn't immune. At Belli's seventy-fifth birthday bash, he bartended and, according to guests, became woozy after a few nips of Pisco.

Jeanne Belli said there was danger in her father's "testing" of the brew. "By the time the testing was over," she recalled, "he was three sheets to the wind and the party hadn't even started."

AT THE HEIGHT of his fame in 1969, Belli and fellow attorney Nathan Cohn embarked on a trip around the world. Cohn, founder of the American Board of Criminal Lawyers, handled many controversial cases.

Cohn and Belli belonged to a handful of San Francisco lawyers of great notoriety. Others included Jake Erlich, Leo Friedman, Vincent Hallinan, Charles Garry, and James Martin MacInnis. Cohn wrote about the select group, stating, "They created law in an open, unsettled tradition. They tested the limits of the courtroom itself. They sometimes took to their fists to make a point. They recited verse. They turned the courtroom into a theater and they had fun. Sometimes even the judge and jury had fun, too."

The adventure took the two lawyers from San Francisco to London, Paris, Amsterdam, Stockholm, Leningrad, Moscow, and then, on the Siberian Transcontinental Railroad, to Yokohoma and Tokyo.

Cohn was impressed with Belli's capacity to travel. "He was an absolute delight," Cohen said, "despite being on crutches during the early part of the trip. He had stepped on a nail in his apartment, and was suffering, but that didn't stop him from gallivanting around Europe and Asia."

Highlights of the four-week excursion included Belli's affair with a beautiful Danish woman in her twenties and an interview during which he informed reporters that Richard Nixon was "no fucking good."

They traveled on the Siberian Railroad. Cohen said it had "bad food, bad accommodations, and stunk to the high heavens." He purchased a Russian newspaper he couldn't read just to cut it up and use it as toilet seat covers.

During the final days of the cross-country trek, a gang of "huge lumberjack-types" boarded the train, drunk on vodka. They argued with Cohn over the size of his salad, and forced him to drink vodka before finally releasing the two to their bunks. "All the while," Cohn recalled, "Mel was as cool as could be."

Belli's saving grace on the trip was his resisting temptation of one of his favorite things: stealing. At every stop, per his usual routine, he had stolen hotel keys, but Cohn warned him that if he did so in Russia, they both would be arrested, incarcerated at some Stalag prison, and never heard from again. When soldiers searched the two, Cohn froze in fear, but they found no stolen hotel keys.

BELLI WAS THE ultimate prankster. On one occasion he brought coconspirator Art Jackson, a black janitor who worked in his office, to the opening of the San Francisco Opera. On the evening of the big event, Belli dressed Jackson in a tuxedo with a red sash stretching across his chest. He affixed a gold medal near the breast pocket of the tuxedo.

Belli introduced Jackson as an African ambassador, a diplomat from "the emerging country of Rutabaga." He told anyone who wished to speak to Jackson that his dear friend didn't speak English. This worked until Art spied a television set, saw the Giants playing, and blurted out something in English.

Regardless, one of Belli's favorite photographs portrayed him standing with "the diplomat" and a San Francisco member of high society. "If those big shots," Milton Hunt said, "could have only seen Art mopping the offices four hours later, they would have died of embarrassment."

Seymour Ellison experienced Belli's pranks firsthand. "I was staying at the Princess Hotel in Vancouver on a reconciliation trip with my wife," Ellison recalled, "and there was a knock on the door. I opened it to discover the Manager and the Chief of Security, among others. 'Excuse me,' the manager said, 'can we search your room?' I asked what that was all about and he replied that he'd received a telegram that informed them that I was an Indian tribal chief in cognito. It also stated that I would be involved in a tribal ceremony that involved a campfire. The final words were, 'Don't let him burn the hotel down.' When I asked Mel about it, he said, 'Telegram, what telegram?'"

Business manager Harry Cobden was a prime target of Belli's. After he stayed at a hotel during a trip to Los Angeles he made without his wife, Belli telephoned a friend in LA. The friend stole some hotel stationary and Belli wrote a note stating, "Mr. Cobden, we certainly enjoyed having you. The lipstick and underwear Mrs. Cobden left is being sent to you." When Mrs. Cobden received the note, Harry had some explaining to do.

Cobden returned the favor while Belli was on a hunting trip high in the Sierra Mountains. He arranged for a forest ranger to deliver a telegram to Belli, who had chastised Cobden for begging out of the trip due to sickness. It read, "Cobden is dead. He wanted you to be a pallbearer. Please return immediately." Belli rushed down the mountain, drove back to San Francisco, and showed up at the address Cobden's "widow" had provided. It was a African American funeral parlor.

Paul Monzione recalled the attorney's fun-loving ways. "On the yacht trip to Santa Barbara for the cigarette trial," he said, "we saved a small vessel that had called 'Mayday.' The captain gave Mel two big five-gallon pails of live sea urchins. I was sick as a dog from the tossing and turning in the waves, but Mel took a cleaver, chopped one in half, and began eating it. 'Want one of these?' he asked laughing as I tried not to throw up."

Belli was impressed by the gift. Believing it was an "adequate award," for his kindness, the idea suddenly struck Belli to change the name of his yacht. From that day forward, the S.S. *Fifer* became the *Adequate Award*.

Attorney Bob Lieff noticed Belli's sense of humor his first day at the firm. On a wall, Belli taped a worn cardboard sign that read in Belli's handwriting, "Rob't Lieff, Lawyer!!!, Trials, Briefs, Tax, PI, Domestic, etc. etc. (Money)."

Attorney Safford also recalled fondly pranks played at the office to keep things light. "When Mel was deeply into the tobacco cases, someone planted a cigarette in Elmer's mouth," he said. "On another occasion, an investigator was playing around with an unloaded ten-gauge during an office meeting. Someone had loaded it and it went off. Knocked a picture off the wall."

* * *

GIVEN BELLI'S REPUTATION as lady's man and hard partier, it was only natural that he be interviewed for *Playboy* magazine; the issue became a best-seller. More important to Belli was the fact that respected journalist Alex Haley, later of *Roots* fame, was the interviewer.

Alex Haley's eleven-page interview, titled "MELVIN BELLI, a candid conversation with the embattled, outspoken attorney who defended Jack Ruby," began on page 77. The introductory paragraph read, "The mad genius of the San Francisco bar . . . a court jester . . . a publicity-mad pettifogger . . . the S. Hurok of the legal profession—these are the kinder things said about San Francisco attorney Melvin Mouron Belli." Haley then wrote, "That he is unquestionably among the greatest living trial lawyers however, is conceded even by Belli's legion of enemies." The author then lists the ABA, AMA, most insurance firms, J. Edgar Hoover, Robert Kennedy, Richard Nixon, and the city of Dallas as members of that legion.

To Belli's delight, he and Alex Haley became great friends. The writer had retired from the Coast Guard after twenty years of service. He said he learned to write by penning "Dear John" letters for fellow seaman to hometown "honies." Haley also swore he had worked seven days a week for more than seven years before *Playboy* gave him his first big break.

Regarding "Alec," Belli said, "[Haley] became a constant companion and lived there on Telegraph Hill, with me and my pet rooster and occasional visitors like The Great Impostor, Ferdinand Demara."

"He was as black as my mahogany bar," Belli wrote. "He was an editor for *The Reader's Digest* and a contributor to *Playboy* and an author of the mighty best-seller *The Autobiography of Malcolm X*. What impressed me most about Alex was his unfailing good sense and his sensitivity."

So close were they that Haley persuaded Belli to collaborate on a book. Attorney John Hill said the whole episode was a nightmare for the noted journalist. "Alex would write and write and then give the manuscript to Mel," Hill recalled. "But Mel would scribble in the margins and mark it all out, Alex told me, discarding any mention of sensitivity or redeeming qualities. Finally, Alex said the project was hopeless and gave up. He told me he was going to finish his life's work. That turned out to be the tracing of his family history. That turned out to be *Roots*."

Bob Lieff kept a letter from Haley discussing the book collaboration dated September 30, 1970. Haley expressed his sorrow that he and Belli coud not go forward, stating, "I am so close to Mel, so emotionally warm toward him that indeed I cannot really deal with him as a subject in the detached, abstract way one should be able to deal with subjects." Haley inserted an asterisk after the word "him." At the bottom he noted, "Though at certain times he makes me so mad I want to kick his ass."

Joyce Revilla said Haley traveled extensively with Belli. "Belli used to introduce him as 'my butler,'" she recalled. "They got quite a kick out of that. And this was after Mr. Haley was famous for *Roots*. For a time, wherever Mr. Belli went, Mr. Haley went. They were very close."

Revilla recalled Haley's visit to the offices after his return from a trip to Europe and Africa to discover his ancestry. "He laid out all of these photos and such," Revilla said. "It was quite impressive, and he was so excited. 'This is my family, my ancestors,' he said." Haley ironically told Belli associate John Hill, "It's my life's work. I have been working on this book for twelve years and I will never make a dime off of it."

She believed that Haley was indebted to Belli. "He told me at one point that 'if not for Belli, I couldn't have finished *Roots*.'" Revilla believed he was referring to money that Belli had lent him for his research trips.

Haley acknowledged Belli's assistance in a March 1986 letter. He wrote, "Each time I'm in Paris—probably a score of times since you sponsored my first visit. . . . You were/are, I believe, the most giving, selfless, truly cosmopolitan, truly a–ethnic person I've ever met."

16

LADY'S MAN

THOSE WHO KNEW Melvin Belli best knew that he was better at choosing jurors, playing practical jokes, and performing in the courtroom than he was at choosing women. A lady's man extraordinaire, Belli was nonetheless clueless about love.

Regarding the split with his third wife, Joy Turney, Belli said, "That marriage ended after nine years on the grounds that I seemed to be married more to my law practice than to my wife."

The friction with Joy bothered Belli later on. When *San Francisco Chronicle* columnist Albert Morch asked for marital advice, he said, "No matter how angry you are at your wife at the time of the divorce, restrain yourself. If not, every verbal blow will be reflected in your children. I see it in Caesar's traumas."

Belli issued a list of particulars as a part of the filing of the divorce. Among other things, he charged his wife with adultery. He added that she was "keeping company with a rather unusual interior decorator," throwing "worldwide temper tantrums," and "making indecent suggestions to comedian Jerry Lewis."

Belli charged that Joy became intoxicated at parties and embarrassed him in New Orleans, Houston, New York, Vienna, and Hollywood. In Vienna, Belli alleged, "she deliberately extinguished a cigarette on the hand of their cute guide, who was the granddaughter of one of Vienna's great surgeons." Summing up, he alleged that Joy "never performed wifely duties, never sewed a button on his clothes, never cooked or shopped." He quoted her as saying that she stayed married to him "'because you are older and will die first.'"

Joy denied her husband's allegations and retaliated with charges of extreme cruelty. A year later, the divorce was acknowledged by the *San Francisco Chronicle* headline, "The Belli's Quick, Unusual Divorce." On the day the decree was entered, Belli was in Los Angeles presenting a speech. Joy, wearing "a two-piece gray woolen dress lined with chinchilla," testified that her spouse had "rarely had dinner at home, refused to admit her to his social life, kept a bachelor apartment away from their Twin Peaks home, called her filthy names in front of their children and others, threatened to blow her head off, and boasted of other women with whom he was keeping company." She added, "He kept me in a continually upset state."

Belli's lawyer Nathan Cohn recalled that his client told him, "'I'm in love with another woman so you've got to get me a divorce.'" This woman was stately brunette Pat Montandon, a San Francisco socialite, television personality, model, and writer with heavy lips and a stately manner. One magazine characterized her as "the queen of the jet set." On October 12, 1966, the two had exchanged vows in a Shinto ceremony in Japan. Belli's best man for the wedding was Japanese Supreme Court Justice Toshio Irie.

Belli told reporters the location, the Jozankel Inn on Hokkaido, the northernmost island of Japan, was chosen since "it reminds me of my native Montana," which made no sense at all. Performing the services was a Shinto priest, who officiated "in a singsong cadence of formal, archaic Japan." Belli and his fourth wife then offered a twig of the sacred sakaki tree to the altar. They also drank "san-san'kudo," described as "three times three cups of rice wine."

The photograph of the marriage ceremony was humorous. It depicted Belli in a ritualistic black silk kimono and hakama shirt standing beside a Japanese compatriot dressed in authentic garb. Belli, in true tradition, had left his Texas boots outside the Shinto shrine. When no white socks could be located big enough to fit his feet, Belli donned black hose.

Pat Montandon, described by onlookers as "as lovely as a Christmas decoration cake," wore a colorful kimono; a high, lacquered headdress that appeared to be off center; and a dagger, signaling she would defend her honor at all costs. Both she and Belli had rather confused looks on their faces.

Montandon was a strong woman, determined to control Belli's amorous intentions. Receptionist Maggie Quinn recalled her as "top drawer" and remembered what she had said before the wedding. "'He [Belli] is a mother-fucking son of a bitch,'" Quinn quoted Montandon, "'and if he wants to get in my knickers, he's going to marry me first.'"

And so he did. When the lucky couple returned to San Francisco, the *Chronicle* printed a photograph of a beaming Pat, fashionably dressed, with Belli beside her snuggling his nose close to her ear. "They touched down," the reporter wrote, "holding hands, and bussing cheeks." Belli's client Yvonne D'Angers threw rice at the couple. "I'm glad it isn't cooked," Belli quipped.

Despite the apparent bliss, the marriage failed miserably. Pat discovered that Belli had, she believed, never properly recorded their union in Japan and therefore they weren't really man and wife. Belli swore his action wasn't deliberate, but agreed to an annulment. Attorney Bob Lieff remarked, "Hell, he should have known what the law was. He wrote *Life and Law in Japan*!"

Seymour Ellison said he had warned his colleague that he had to register the marriage with the proper authorities in Japan. "I sent him a telegram," Ellison said, "reminding him that otherwise all the little Bellis would be bastards. He kept that telegram up on his wall after he returned."

Days later, they decided the whole affair was a big mistake and an annulment was granted. Belli called the marriage "little more than a footnote" to his marital exploits. Columnist Herb Caen, noting that the marriage lasted all of thirty-six days, dubbed Montandon "wife number 3 1/2." He called the mess, "Thirty seconds over Tokyo."

Belli's battle with Montandon's attorney, George T. Davis, turned personal. Belli had mocked him for losing a high-society murder case that Belli believed should have been his. After the verdict the two crossed paths, and Belli said to the highly respected Davis, "You did good George, but I could have lost the case for a lot less money." Belli liked the quote so much he telephoned Herb Caen's assistant Jerry Brunson. It was included in Caen's column the next day.

When Montandon hired Davis, whom she knew hated Belli, she apparently had no money to pay him. Davis asked if she had other assets. She told him she had a pair of gold cuff links that belonged to Belli.

When the case arrived in court, Davis stood next to Belli, flashing the cuff links proudly for all to see. Finally, Belli noticed them and said, "Hey, you're wearing my cuff links," to which Davis replied sprightly, "They are not yours anymore."

Feelings between Montandon and Belli darkened after the annulment. Lawyer Hunt said Belli ran into her at KGO-TV when both he and his client were going to be interviewed. "She said, upon passing us, 'Well, they don't care who they let in here, do they?'" and Mel retorted, 'After you were in there, they'll have to fumigate the place.'"

Asked why women adored Belli, Bob Lieff said, "That's easy. He was good looking, had high energy, was flamboyant, famous, fun, and smart. And, of course, he appeared to have money which was a great attraction in itself." Attorney Nathan Cohn disagreed, saying that Belli's chief asset was "confidence." "Woman loved that about him," he said. "He was just so confident that they wanted to be with him."

Author Robert Wallace agreed with that observation, but said Belli's lure was the look in his eye. He wrote, "Belli's effect upon women has always been approximately that of a cocktail made of gin and catnip."

Following his fourth divorce, Belli exposed personal feelings about his dismal marital record. In *Divorcing*, written in 1988 with psychological counselor Mel Krantzler, Belli wrote, "I was born in 1907 and grew up in a time when divorce was an unmentionable subject. . . . 'Fallen woman' was the term used to label any divorced woman, a diseased person to be feared, scorned and avoided." He added, "On the very rare occasions when a divorced person's name would come up (I remember listening to the comments as I hid under the table after a big family dinner), one of my parents or relatives would inevitably label the divorced man a 'villain.'"

REGARDING HIS RELATIONSHIPS with the fairer sex, Belli remarked, "I love women and I do not like being alone, but after a while with one woman, things begin to dull for me (and maybe for her, too). Then I make a vow of perpetual bachelorhood. Soon, though, I find adventure with someone new—and wind up married again, full of optimism that this time my own neuroses will mesh with hers."

Wife number five was a brunette named Lia Triff. Born in Detroit, Michigan, Lia was a cheerleader and president of her high school class. Her father was a Teamster, and her mother hosted a radio talk show.

Belli said she "charmed him" when they met at the Washington, DC,

Kennedy Center for Performing Arts in 1971. He swore he had spoken to Lia earlier, but to no avail.

Later, according to his story, she approached him and, with tongue in cheek, asked if he was "the famous lawyer." When the sixty-four-year-old Belli grinned and told the twenty-three-year-old lady "I guess I am," she asked, "Does your name start with B?" Belli played along and provided another "yes" answer. Then Lia, a bright woman who said she had been awarded a Fulbright Scholarship, teased him by saying, "F. Lee Bailey." This exchange sparked a mutual interest leading to a romantic relationship.

Seymour Ellison told another story. He said Lia was simply a "janitor" at the Smithsonion and that after an office investigator named Gene Marshall "was done banging her," he turned her over to Belli who stayed with her at the Mayflower Hotel. Lia became pregnant and a wedding followed shortly after.

Lia's boasting of her academic credentials became an issue. When it was discovered that she was not a Fulbright Scholarship recipient, associate John Hill, among others, was upset. "I was offended," he said, "since I was one." He added, "She was a pathological liar."

Milton Hunt, who alleged that Lia's mother talked her into the marriage, said Belli was smitten with his new bride. "He said to me," Hunt recalled, "'Look at that beautiful ass on her.' He compared it to an Italian rump. Later, he pulled up her skirt and said, 'Look at the meat on there.'"

When Belli arrived in San Francisco with Lia by his side, he told pal Herb Caen, "I don't know whether to keep her for myself or turn her over to Caesar." He decided on the former.

After months of wooing, Lia became Mrs. Lia Belli on a lovely June day in 1972. The ceremony was conducted at the Tuolumne County Courthouse in Sonora, California, Belli's hometown. Judge Adelle Mueli presided. Belli, whose face appeared a bit bewildered in a *Union Democrate* photograph, wore a three-piece suit while Lia, her hair pinned back under a scarf as she held a lovely bouquet of flowers, had a pensive look.

The nuptials were celebrated at Pastorini's Restaurant. Belli hired musicians to play Italian folk songs. When the party grew dull, Nathan Cohn decided to liven up the place. "I told the band to strike up the Jewish song, *Hava Nagila*," he said. "That woke everyone up and got them dancing."

With Caesar in tow, they traveled the globe on an extended honeymoon, visiting Switzerland, Italy, New Zealand, Madagascar, and Brazil. Soon Belli's sixth child, Melia, was born.

Later, Lia became obsessed with politics, campaigning against liberal Republican Milton Marks for the California State Senate. During her campaign she became embroiled in controversy over misstatements concerning her academic credentials when Marks charged that she had not been awarded the Fulbright scholarship, or graduated with a master's degree as claimed. Lia finally admitted this was true, but said it was due to "sloppiness" by campaign workers.

Marks further challenged Lia's creditability by questioning claims that she had been President Jimmy Carter's "director of protocol." Lia produced a telegram to back up her claim.

When the election occurred, Lia was soundly defeated. The State Election Board later fined her $75,000 for the misrepresentations. They charged her with hiding more than $300,000 in donations. Some was simply left off required election reports; others, the Fair Political Practices Commission alleged, were laundered through friends and acquaintances. These people were given money by Belli family members and then asked to donate the money to Lia's campaign. It would thus appear that her family was not financing the entire campaign.

Concerning love, romance, and law, Belli said, "Am I a romantic? Of course, I am. Show me a good trial lawyer who isn't. Good trial lawyers have a quest for life, a penchant for all good things bright and beautiful, kinky and flawed, for good wines, great tables, wide travels, and beautiful women." He added, "There's a great lust for life in many of us, we are always learning, storing ideas and images in our imaginations—from whatever source. When I stand up to argue a case, heaven knows what knowledge and what experience I will call upon to make a point. It may have been something that happened at sea years ago while I was standing watch on the foc'sle head. It may have been something I learned while riding the rails during the depression."

A TRUE MAN'S man in the ilk of Ernest Hemingway, Belli had an insatiable appetite for the ladies, though some alleged Belli was bisexual. One lawyer said he had seen a register at a gay club with Belli's name on it. "I wouldn't be surprised if Mel experimented with all that," Bob Lieff said.

Even though he was in his sixties, Belli visited the infamous Mustang Ranch in Nevada. When he returned to the office, John O'Connor recalled him boasting of his sexual exploits while relaxing in his office chair. Ten minutes later the worn-out Casanova was fast asleep and stayed asleep for the rest of the day.

Attorney John Hill said Belli loved to boast of his conquests. "'I've fucked a hundred women a day,'" Hill quoted Belli as saying. "And I don't know how many at night." According to Hill, it was important to Belli "that people saw him that way, realized he was in control and got what he wanted." Seymour Ellison recalled one of Belli's favorite expressions, "If you want to get fucked, you ought to pay for it."

Milton Hunt was a "lookout" for many of Belli's amorous escapades. "I sat in the living room to make certain there was a witness around," he said. "Mr. Belli wanted to make sure none of the women decided to charge him with some foul deed, rape or something. He didn't want any lawsuits."

Belli was also a member of a group of successful men who passed women around. It was called either the Plato Club or the Zero Club, depending on who was telling the story. At one meeting a nude lady with long flowing hair played the harp as the men looked on.

"Those guys were a bunch of big shots," Milton Hunt said. "They had a black book and a red book filled with women's names. Many of them were what were called 'arm dressing,' chicks that looked good on your arm. They went to the Poodle Dog, Zach's, Tadich's, all over. They were all VIPs."

MELVIN BELLI'S ROVING eye intensified as the years progressed. He would do almost anything to meet women.

Former partner Bob Lieff recalled a "recruiting trip" to Europe he and Belli took. "Mel decided he wanted to hire European secretaries to spice up the place so he had ads placed in the *International Herald Tribune*. Several woman responded so Mel and I set up appointments in Frankfurt, Munich, Zurich, Geneva, Paris, and London."

The schedule called for the attorneys to stay two nights in each city. Belli, who always stayed in the finest hotels, reserved a suite in each city, complete with two bedrooms and a sitting room. The women were to be interviewed beginning at nine in the morning at half-hour intervals. "I took one girl into my room, while Mel interviewed another," Lieff recalled. "The trick was to pick one or two and tell them that the interviews would continue on the train the next day. That worked as we made our way from city to city. It was quite a time, I must say."

The ruse to meet women actually did result, Lieff reported, in the employment of two captivating young ladies. They traveled to San Francisco and worked for a short time in the offices. "One day Mel came in and said, 'You've got to get rid of them.' I don't remember the reason, but I guess he had tired of them. He wasn't good at confrontation or firing someone so I had to handle it. I told bookkeeping to buy them nonstop tickets home, but somehow they swapped them, got off on the east coast, and then showed back up in San Francisco. I never did know what happened to the poor girls."

Perhaps it is private investigator Jim Lacovoli who best summed up Belli's incredible magnetism with women. "[Even in the late stages of his life] he always had an eye for a young broad. Hell, I saw twenty-, thirty-year-old women who just loved him. He was the ultimate charmer."

17

TAKING ON TOBACCO

"NINETY-NINE PERCENT OF the doctors I've met," Melvin Belli wrote in 1976, "are great guys, doing their best and working hard. Young doctors I've met recently seem particularly dedicated. But the individual doctor has a far higher code of ethics than the physician acting in convention, through his association. With lawyers *and* doctors, it seem there's some sort of collective amorality, a callous mob psychology, that takes over the individual practitioner's ethics and honesty."

Among Belli's first malpractice cases was one that left a bitter taste in his mouth. It involved a young man whose physician prescribed enemas and cathartics as treatments for appendicitis. When the condition worsened, the doctor ordered him transferred to a hospital, but then abandoned his patient. The boy's appendix burst, and he died.

Belli alleged negligence occurred not only at the hospital, but also during the doctor's initial house call. He believed the doctor had been heavily intoxicated at the time. But despite his efforts, Belli could not find a single physician who would testify regarding the doctor's competence or physical condition. His face flushed in anger, he later said, "Five doctors testified in his behalf including the head of one of our largest university hospitals."

The verdict was a predictable not guilty. Belli later learned that the physician in question became a habitual drunkard and dope addict, and eventually committed suicide.

This "mob-psychology" occurred yet again, Belli believed, in the "case of the lost penis." A man named Edward Spraker discovered a small lesion on his penis, which his doctor diagnosed as a wart. Treating it gave no relief, and several months later, another physician informed Spraker that he had cancer. A subsequent operation was needed to remove the penis. Spraker sued his first physician for malpractice.

When it came time for final arguments, Belli, with a straight face, told the jury: "King Farouk recently bought a racehorse for seven hundred thousand dollars. Had the racehorse lost his male organ, King Farouk would have no hesitancy going to court and suing for seven hundred thousand dollars. Now I am *not* going to tell you that this boy would have sired a racehorse or even an Abraham Lincoln or an Einstein, but he could have sired a human being." The statement would be quoted for years to come.

The jury returned a verdict of $100,000, but the judge in the case set it aside. A second trial proved disastrous: When multiple doctors testified that the physician acted properly, the jury returned a verdict for the defense. Belli was furious.

During his early years of practice, Belli had been outspoken on the reluctance of doctors to testify *against* other doctors. In *Playboy* magazine, he said, "Good old Doc Frebush may have staggered into the operating room dead drunk, carrying a rusty knife and wearing a pair of overalls, but as long as he's a member in good standing of the AMA, not one doctor in 10,000 will testify against him." The lawyer's strong words made a difference: In the future, doctors would indeed have the courage to stand up against their brethren.

While making it clear that he felt most doctors were competent, Belli chastised those who weren't. In the *Playboy* interview, he was asked whether he exaggerated his condemnation of the medical profession. He answered, "Listen, an entire book has been written about things left in patients—not just sponges and forceps, but rings, wristwatches, even eyeglasses, for God's sake. 'What time is it, nurse? I've lost my watch? Just, a minute, I'll put on my glasses. Where *are* my glasses?'"

He continued his tirade against corrupt physicians. "There's a leading specialist." he said, "No matter what's the matter with the plaintiff, murmurs, arrhythmic beatings, leaky valves, he can't hear them. You can fire a cannon under his stethoscope and he won't even blink."

As more medical malpractice cases appeared, Belli decided he wasn't educated enough in medicine. To rectify this, he "began to haunt the University of California Medical School, charmed my way into autopsies and the operating rooms and donned green surgical pajamas. I tried to learn as much as I could about the human body and the kinds of things that doctors can do to foul up its normal functioning."

Belli shadowed an impressive list of noted international doctors: Bellevue hospital pathologist Dr. Milton Helpern, Italian physician Dr. Cesare Gerin, Viennese physician Emil Brietenecker, Dr. Keleman Endre of Budapest. In a photograph displayed in the second edition of *Modern Trials*, the barrister is shown with Endre in a morgue. The caption reads in part, "The author, Melvin Belli, (holding leg), gowned and gloved with the world famous Dr. Keleman Endre (left) at the Budapest Morgue."

As his knowledge of medical procedures grew, Belli began to understand the challenges physicians faced. After he sued one physician for negligence regarding a blood transfusion, the doctor asked to show him how the procedure was performed and why the potential existed, through no fault of his own, for error. Shortly after the doctor completed his explanation, Belli decided he was *not* responsible and withdrew the suit against him.

During one case Belli outwitted a doctor bent on confusing jurors with medical lingo. Throughout the trial the physician kept sloughing off blame because he said his male patient suffered from "amenorrhea." The jury accepted his explanation because no one had any idea what the word meant.

Just before final argument, Belli did a bit of homework. When he addressed the jury, Belli lugged a huge blue Webster's dictionary to the lectern. Midway through his argument, he read the definition of amenorrhea: "abnormal absence of menses." Needless to say, the doctor lost his case.

A noted San Francisco physician was once asked, "What man has done the most for medicine in the past century?" The interviewer suggested Louis Pasteur and Joseph Lister, among others. But according to Belli, the doctor answered, "No, Melvin Belli, because the son of a bitch has made medical men conscientious about their courtroom testimony, and has made lawyers learn medicine."

Physicians everywhere were certainly aware of Belli. No one wanted to incur the famed lawyer's wrath, and this was possible in nearly every small town and large city around the world. At one point he was associated with law firms in Forest Hills, New York; Sacramento and Los

Angeles, California; Chicago, Illinois; Dallas; Washington, DC; New York City; Munich, Germany; Rome, Italy; Paris, France; and Tokyo. Belli's satellite offices acted as watchdogs, ready to pounce on those who wronged others.

Regarding Belli's popularity, and his formidable presence in a case, author Robert Wallace wrote, "Well, whom would you rather have in your corner, Mel Belli or Benjamin Bunny?" Belli learned, to his amusement, that some lawyers informed their adversaries, "We are bringing Mel Belli into the case." They didn't actually know the famed lawyer, but were attempting to scare opposing counsel into settling a case. Most times that ploy proved successful; simply the mention of Belli connoted an expensive battle with the legal street fighter.

BELLI DERIVED SATISFACTION from helping others, and loved taking pro bono cases. This led Maggie Quinn to say, "He loved the law more than the money." Joyce Revilla added, "He had no hobbies, the law was his life. The 'other woman' in his life was his law office."

Long before it became fashionable to do so, Belli turned his attention toward America's tobacco companies, natural targets for the modern-day Robin Hood.

Belli strongly believed that if other manufacturers were held liable for unsafe products, then tobacco companies should be no exception. He set out to prove that they should be held accountable for causing cancer, emphysema, and other respiratory diseases. This quest would continue for more than four decades.

Belli's files indicate that he was researching cases to pursue in 1959, years ahead of anyone else. In May of that year, correspondence with attorney Alva Brumfied of Baton Rouge was accompanied by an article titled, "Man Charges Smoking Cause of Cancer; Seeks $1 Million."

The man's name was Joel H. Yowell, a former seaman who claimed that smoking two packs of Camels and Salems a day for nearly twenty-four years gave him larynx cancer. He was suing the R. J. Reynolds Tobacco Company.

Belli charged that R. J. Reynolds was "willfully, wantonly, and grossly negligent and reckless, careless and with total disregard to the health of the public and particularly this complainant, in selling, advertising, and distributing their cigarettes without warning." He stated that Reynolds "warranted that the products were wholesome when in truth, they were not."

Belli next filed a suit on behalf of a man named Jerzy M. Szyfer. This time, his target was Phillip Morris. The allegations were similar to those in the first suit, but Szyfer had smoked English Ovals for ten years, not Camels or Salems.

Winston-Salem Journal reporters Frank Tursi, Susan E. White, and Steve McQuilkin wrote, "To Melvin Belli, a personal-injury attorney from California, suing the tobacco industry was the most rational idea in the world. More important, it was a crusade. And unlike other plaintiff's attorneys, Belli truly frightened the cigarette companies."

Each of the early cases Belli filed fell by the wayside. "If we don't get them soon, we'll never get them," he exclaimed. In late 1960, Belli succeeded in forwarding what in all likelihood was the first cigarette case ever to go to trial: A claim filed by a New Orleans widow named Victoria St. Pierre.

St. Pierre's husband, Frank Lartigue, had chain-smoked Camels, King Bees, and Picayunes for fifty-five years. At age sixty-five, Lartigue succumbed to cancer of the larynx. On his behalf Belli sued R. J. Reynolds and Liggett and Myers based on his belief that the companies failed to properly warn Lartigue that cigarettes could cause cancer. The judge permitted contributory negligence as a defense, but the jury disagreed with Belli's arguments that the tobacco companies had a duty to manufacture a safe product.

Associate Paul Monzione was quoted in the *Winston-Salem Journal* story as having said, "He [Belli] used to say that the jury told him that 'If we let you have this, the next thing you'll be doing is suing Elsie, the Borden cow, for too-rich cream and Jack Daniels for cirrhosis of the liver.' And Mel would say, 'Elsie, the Borden cow maybe, but never Doctor Jack.'"

Disappointed, but undeterred, Belli pressed on. In the 1960s and 1970s, Belli wrote letters to physicians and clinics requesting that they look for "the perfect case" where he could test his theories in court again.

Since Belli was taking the tobacco cases pro bono, he could solicit clients. In one advertisement, a gruff photograph of him appeared above a caption that read: "Wanted: squamous-cell lung cancer victim. Object: to take on the tobacco industry in a multi-million dollar damage suit."

Pressing ahead, Belli became involved with an organization called "Citizens Against Cigarettes." Based in Las Vegas, it sported an impressive array of talent on its Board of Directors, including Barron Hilton; chief justice of the Nevada Supreme Court John Mowbray; Belli; and Harry Wald, executive vice president of Caesar's Palace. The celebrity Board of Directors featured such famous names as Mohammed Ali, Joe Namath, Ed Asner, Barbra Streisand, Donna Summer, Kenny Rogers, Robert Wagner, and Natalie Wood. The group's motto was "Cancer Hurts Before It Kills."

Citizens Against Cigarettes proved to be a worthy organization, but Belli was itching to match up once again with a tobacco giant in the courtroom. He finally decided to try a case against R. J. Reynolds in Santa Barbara, California, despite having sued Reynolds unsuccessfully twenty-five years earlier. Their good fortune in the courtroom had continued. They boasted an undefeated record in 145 similar cases.

The case would be tried before Superior Court Judge Bruce William Dodds. He and Belli had tangled over two chief issues: Belli's determination to present evidence regarding tobacco industry advertising and use of the surgeon general's report on smoking. Belli was livid when the judge slammed the door on his efforts. His relationship with the strong-willed, no-nonsense Dodds worsened when he publicly criticized the judge, telling reporters, "He keeps threatening to hold me in contempt. Maybe he thinks that if he puts me in the can it will make him famous."

Several times Belli and Dodds engaged in shouting matches in court. He was upset when the judge scolded him for a perceived violation of questioning procedure *before* the attorneys for Reynolds opened their mouths. Belli stated, "This is the worst judge I've had in fifty years."

At stake, as it had been with previous Belli cases, was the attorney's attempt to open the door to a flood of lawsuits against the tobacco companies. If he could win just once, then the corporate giant's immunity from damages would be wiped out.

To a *Santa Barbara News and Reviews* reporter, Belli spelled out his hopes: "I don't care whether cigarettes are taken off the American market or not. All I want is for an American jury to say that they are carcinogenic, and you should be damn well advised before you smoke them, then if you want to kill yourself, you can jump off the bridge."

Concerning his quest to hold tobacco companies liable for their actions, Belli said, "I think nothing does more to make a safer life than whacking a corporation and having its president explain to his stockholders how much money it cost them. You get some guy than finds a rock in a can of beans up in Maine, he sues and wins, and that'll make that can of beans safer down in San Diego."

The judge restricted Belli's attempts to prove that cigarettes caused cancer, that the tobacco industry did nothing to warn people, and that smoking was addictive. In the end, the jury, which included two smokers and five ex-smokers, agreed with defense lawyer Thomas Workman, who argued that plaintiff John Galbraith should be responsible for decisions he made that affected his health. The final vote was nine to three in favor of R. J. Reynolds. Monzione, who tried the case with Belli, believed the source of the loss was that their client was sick with so many illnesses it was difficult to prove that he died from cancer caused by the cigarettes.

Reynolds used twenty-two lawyers and more than twenty paralegals during the case. Belli's firm had spent nearly $200,000 on the case. Frustrated, he told *Law Journal* reporter Deutsch, "I can't compete with the millions and billions of Reynolds' dollars. I don't think you'd ever get the number of lawyers to match what they're willing to put into a case like this." To his surprise, and delight, his prediction was wrong.

Nearly ten years later, Belli became part of the most monumental effort ever mounted against a single industry. No one was ever clear on whose idea the campaign was, but Belli was a leader from the outset. Triggering the effort was an announcement from the surgeon general of the United States: Cigarettes were indeed addictive.

The moment the nation's highest medical officer declared that cigarettes were "habit-forming," Belli telephoned Bob Lieff. Together with several other high-profile lawyers, they began to assemble a select group of law firms dedicated to tobacco litigation. Sixty-four law firms banded together to take on the tobacco kings.

The *Associated Press* article accompanying the announcement included Belli's statement, "We will prove that the tobacco industry has conspired to catch you, hold you, and kill you . . . all without a moment of remorse or self-examination."

Law firms were asked to contribute $100,000 to build a "superfund." As a first payment, Belli invested $25,000. This money was critical, for a tobacco memo released during congressional investigations disclosed an R. J. Reynolds's attorney's boasting, "To paraphrase General Patton, the way we won these cases was not by spending all of [R.J.R.'s] money, but by making the other son of a bitch spend theirs."

While the army of lawyers pursued the groundbreaking "class action" test case, Belli was determined to involve the whole world in the lawsuit.

In a June 1994 letter to an attorney in Australia, he wrote, "We would like to join some Australians in the class so that we can show that the Australians feel as we do about these bastardly cigarette companies and the people they've killed."

Belli's participation in the lawsuit was critical to its potential success. Elizabeth Cabraser, a San Francisco lawyer, said Belli believed "it was the duty of tort lawyers to use the court system to make tobacco companies accountable. And to do so, he believed strength was in numbers. That included his participation since just the name Belli was inspirational and made people sit up and take notice."

Cabraser marveled at Belli's skill even at his advanced age. "When Mel talked to people about products liability, people listened," she said. "He was fiery, dedicated, and without his cheerleading, the effort would never have been possible."

Belli's stature, Cabraser insisted, was confirmed when the tobacco industries hired Griffin Bell, a former U.S. attorney general and legal giant in his own right. "They brought him in to offset Belli and his magic name as a crusader," she said. "We were heading toward a clash of the legal titans."

To educate the formidable group of attorneys, Belli was asked to speak when they met in New Orleans. Cabraser said Belli's words mesmerized the audience. "He talked about history, and the importance of the litigation," she said. "He was brilliant."

Though the case itself was dismissed, the effort on the part of the legal firms persuaded the tobacco industry to settle with attorney generals across the country. The result was a multibillion–dollar award to be disbursed to those involved in the litigation.

When a final award was made in the case, Lieff's firm, representing Belli's interests, argued that a share of the damages were rightfully his. "Mel was the true pioneer who led the charge toward liability on the part of the tobacco companies," Lieff said. Cabraser added, "Mel was the catalyst, the headwater of the cascade. When it is decided who gets what, the unsung heroes will be singing and in those voices one should be heard for Mel Belli."

18

RECOLLECTIONS

THOSE ATTORNEYS WHO were mentored by, or worked with, Melvin Belli, never forgot his graciousness.

"I limped into San Francisco in a dying Fiat with a quarter in my pocket," attorney Tim Palm recalled. "When Mel heard my story about being a small town farm boy from Ohio who crossed the country, he said, 'Son, you got balls.' The next thing I knew I was trying a case where the mother of Bennett Alley fell out of a hospital bed. Everybody else thought that case was a loser, but I won the damn thing and became his fair-haired boy thereafter."

San Francisco attorney Patrick Hallinan recalled his father Vincent's "high respect" for Belli, and that he considered him "a great lawyer." This was a special accolade since Vincent Hallinan, one of the finest attorneys ever to practice law, was a true legal pioneer like Belli.

"I recall on that one occasion," Patrick Hallinan said, "my father and Mel had been invited to speak by the students at Gonzaga University. Just prior to the engagement, the school canceled my dad, since he was considered a renegade and not Catholic. Mel heard about it and refused to appear."

Patrick Hallinan also recalled that Belli was quick to share credit. "We were involved in the high-profile topless cases," he said. "And together we managed to ruin the North Beach section of San Francisco. But what I recall is that when we took the cases, it was Mel Belli assisted by Pat

Hallinan. Then he let me take over, and the newspapers all said it was me assisted by Mel Belli. He let that happen and I appreciated it."

John O'Connor, who worked for the U.S. Attorney's Office in San Francisco after leaving Belli's office, recalled a man not afraid to let new associates sink or swim. "The ABA was coming to town," O'Connor said, "and Belli wanted to make a big splash. He told me he wanted to sue Martindale-Hubbell, the company that published a directory of attorneys. They, in his opinion, were very silk-stockingish, very clubbish, and he had instinct that they were doing something wrong."

O'Connor said Belli ordered him to create a complaint without a cause of action or a client in place. "It was my first case, and so I researched antitrust laws and found that they didn't sell ads to anyone that wasn't 'rated.' So I conjured up a client named Israel Steingold in Virginia, who had been wronged, and prepared the complaint."

When it was finished, O'Connor showed it to Belli. "He basically said it was boring," O'Connor recalled. "Then he proceeded to redo it with all sorts of hilarious, insulting comments such as calling Martindale/Hubbell a 'Knickerbocker, silk-stocking, split-fee club.' It went on like that for paragraph after paragraph. He called it a 'speaking complaint.' I filed it, and he held a news conference, and after all the hoopla, I think the case got settled."

Such showmanship with the law, O'Connor believed, tainted Belli's true professionalism. "The outrageous publicity stunts, performing for the cameras," he said, "obscured that he was one of the most spectacular lawyers ever. There was nobody like him."

O'Connor said, "He operated at a level where he tried a case like he was stoned. He connected with everyone at a deep level. And that voice, modulated, what a beautiful voice. It projected across the room almost like he was singing." Attorney John Hill added, "It was foghorn-like voice. You could hear it three tables away and know it was him."

Maggie Quinn said Belli's voice depended on what mood he was in. "When he was mad, the intonation brought fear to anyone's heart," she recalled. "It was booming, from his soul, way down deep. But when he was kind, he had the smoothest, most melodious, calming, smooth 'nothing can hurt you' tone I ever heard."

Author Robert Wallace wrote, "The lawyer had a fine command of the English language and magnificent voice: his words fell upon the jury like particles of silver iodide on a fat cloud and often produced the same result." Las Vegas attorney Gary Logan said Belli's voice was "silky." "If I heard that voice in hell, I would recognize it," he said. Kent Russell recalled, "He never mumbled, or whispered. His voice had the cadence of an orator. It was easy to listen to, at times booming." Associate Bob Ingram called Belli's voice, "like a Wurlitzer, a huge organ."

During one case, two female jurors complained to the judge about Belli's mannerisms. They alleged that he had hypnotized them during his final argument, causing them to award his client an overabundance of money. The judge laughed and had his bailiff remove them from the courtroom.

BELLI WAS NEVER one to take failure lightly, and John O'Connor knew firsthand how courtroom losses affected him. "In 1972," he recalled, "we lost a case against a fish company. We should have settled it, but the client was greedy. After the loss, Belli was severely shook up. It shattered his confidence, he felt so bad."

O'Connor wondered whether Belli could recover, since he was sixty-five at the time. "He had great instincts, but I was worried," O'Connor remembered. "But he wanted to get right back up on the horse. We had a case coming up for trial, but I didn't know if he could handle it. Then we went to Doro's next door, drank wine, and got drunk." In the middle of our stupor, he pounded his fists on the table, and said, 'I've got it, I understand the story.'"

"The story" that unfolded at trial involved the wrongful amputation of a high school music teacher's leg. The teacher, who had left his false teeth at home, was mistaken for a wino and whisked off to the county hospital, where a series of mix-ups resulted in the removal of his leg.

O'Connor was impressed with Belli's ability to assess the case, to consider new approaches and strategies. "He decided to hone in on the bias shown to the teacher, that he was considered to be a common drunk due to his having no teeth and so forth. Then he pointed out that the music teacher aspired to be an opera star and that he couldn't very well be on stage hopping around singing with one leg."

To emphasize that point, Belli called to the witness stand baritone opera star Maestro Barati, who testified to the difficulty of performing. Belli then played for the jury *This Nearly Was Mine*, from South Pacific. "It was a tearjerker," O'Connor said, chuckling. "Then the jury awarded a big verdict and Mel was at the office gloating. He'd sing a verse, like

'One girl for my dreams,' then add 'ca-ching, ca-ching,' like a cash register as people howled."

O'Connor also remarked that Belli loved young lawyers, because they weren't "corrupted yet." This was fine with associate Bob Ingram, who started as a young lawyer and appreciated being given a chance. However, he wondered whether the client was being adequately served. "Here I was," he recalled, "two years out of law school and suing General Motors in North Dakota."

Attorney John Hill thought Belli's trial tactics and tips were invaluable. "He taught me to make certain that every day of trial, when we entered the courtroom, to look at the jury and say 'Good morning, ladies and gentleman of the jury.' I also noted that he never addressed opposing counsel in front of the jury by name. It was like they didn't exist."

Seymour Ellison echoed Hill's comments. "Mel believed he was the total presence in the courtroom, like there was nobody else there," he said. "And he liked lawyers to take him on personally. If they did, he was the master of the one-liner. He could cut someone to size without raising his voice, except for emphasis."

Kent Russelli said Belli's confidence in the courtroom was unmatched. "He had a purpose for everything," Russell recalled. "I was sitting second chair during one trial and I kept walking around the courtroom while questioning a witness. During a break he laughed and said, 'What the hell are you doing?' I answered, 'I'm walking around like you do.' He chuckled and said, 'Listen, you have to have' what he called 'purposeful movement. You can't just walk around with nowhere to go.'"

Russell was a good pupil. "I noticed he used his glasses a great deal," he said. "He'd put them down, pick them up, leave them, go get them, pick them up, put them down, all for emphasis. During a trial in Montana, I emulated him and a newspaper story about the case said that was the best thing about my performance!" He remarked that Belli was the "quickest study" he'd ever seen.

"He was fearless in the courtroom," Russell said. "By the third day of trial, he controlled everything, the jury, the judge, the witnesses, all of it. Most judges loved him because he overly deferred to them, made them feel important."

Attorney Alessandro Biccari had fond memories of Belli's legal prowess. "He was the last of a breed, one of a group I called the rebel lawyers," he said. "He and Jake Erlich, George Davis, Vincent Hallinan,

Joe Alioto, others, they left their initials on the legal profession. They were always stretching the law, not only the limitations but the potential."

"They were mischievous, theatrical performers, two-fisted warriors," Biccari continued. "All came within inches of being thrown in jail. And their dress, they wore cuffs so starched they could crack walnuts. And boots that gave them an extra two inches of height in the courtroom. When those lawyers got together for dinner Mel called it the Last Supper. They'd eat like animals and tell stories. It was a grand time."

Bicarri's recollection of Belli in the courtroom was vivid. "He used gestures to hold the attention, used his hands, his whole body, it was so theatrical. Mel's idol was actor John Barrymore, and he wore collars like the actor's even when they weren't in fashion. He'd prance around the courtroom like he *was* Barrymore, deliberately turning his head so that that curl of his would flop down on his forehead as he emphasized a point. Then he would whirl around so it flipped back up. All for emphasis. He even cut his hair or left it long depending on where he was trying the case."

Bicarri was always impressed with Belli's pretrial rehearsals. "He'd scout the courtroom," he said, "and then practice walking around from one area to another. It was like that was his stage, and he was preparing his performance. And when the trial came, nobody performed like Mel. He once told me the role of the lawyer was to convey a psychological message. And he did that, often quoting famous scholars or great legal minds like Oliver Wendell Holmes. He'd bellow, 'Holmes said in 1903 that' and then he'd quote him verbatim. What a memory that man had."

Belli's sixth wife, Nancy Ho Belli, witnessed her husband's courtroom prowess in his later days. She said he was "like magic." "He could put people at ease," she said. "And he was very quick in responding, a good listener who understood what people were saying. And he was charming. He was a natural actor who could charm the birds right off the trees."

Seymour Ellison recalled that Belli never took notes in the courtroom. "Mel always had his head up," the attorney noted. "He was always watching, never wanting to miss anything. He watched the jury, the witnesses, the judge, carefully recording their nuances. He thought that was very important."

Milton Hunt believed Belli's chief advantage in the courtroom was his ability to bluff. "It was amazing the number of things he got away with," Hunt said. "He was a true genius at his craft, but one time after he pulled something, I said, 'Hell, Ray Charles could have seen you were bluffing.' He laughed, but he knew I was right."

Hunt said Belli was a master at keeping the focus on himself during a trial. "When anyone began to nod off or not pay attention," Hunt said, "he'd drop a book or open his suit jacket and show off the red lining. And he always wanted me to tell him how he did. I'd say you really kicked their ass and he'd holler, 'You bet I did.'"

John Hill noted that Belli was an expert at finding the lowest common denominator to base his case on. "He would ask, 'How can we sell this case?'" Hill said. "Then he'd find a metaphor so that the jury could understand the tragedy that had been occurred and say, 'Yeah, Belli's right.' He was truly a nuts and bolts guy who focused in on the simple elements of a case."

Paul Monzione recalled Belli's ability to create in the courtroom. "The first case I tried where I assisted the master was first degree murder," Monzione said. "The accused was an heir to the Kimberly diamond fortune. During jury selection, the prosecution questioned an older woman. Her husband was a captain in homicide in San Jose, and so I wrote 'no' next to her name."

Monzione added, "When it came time for Mel to question her, I nudged him and showed him my notation. But he began talking to her and before I knew it he was discussing ballistics, trajectory of bullets, whether it took 4.3 or 5 pounds of pressure to squeeze the trigger on the gun, that sort of stuff. I was afraid he was going to keep her, but then he simply said to the judge, 'We thank the juror and excuse her.' What I had witnessed was his laying out his whole ballistics case to inform the jury. He never intended to keep the woman, but he used her to assist the other jurors in understanding the case."

John Hill believed Belli could be compared with a Hollywood director. "Mel truly choreographed his cases like he was directing a movie," he said. "He planned all the moves, all the strategies, like he had an outline in his head." Hill's associate Mike Guta said Belli escaped punishment because, "back then trial was the most important aspect of the case. Now it's the pretrial stuff, the motions, and discovery. That's why there's no room for any more Bellis. The law has changed too much."

Former associate Morris Beatus had the chance to work with Belli on a case involving a fourteen-year-old boy who had been injured on a Strategic Air Command base. "The issue was whether the boy who

broke his neck and became a quadriplegic was negligent for not heeding signs to stay off the trampoline when no one was around," Beatus said.
"I handled most of the trial, but when we got to final argument, the judge
told Belli he expected him to give it, since all the people in the town
including himself wanted to see the great orator in action."

The final argument was superb, Beatus said. "The night before Mel had
the idea to quote God's words. We hauled the Gideon Bible out of the
drawer in the hotel room and he looked up the verse in I Corinthians:
13. It read, 'When I was a child, I spoke like a child, I thought like a child,
and I reasoned like a child. When I became a man, I gave up my child-
ish ways.' The next day, he told the jury he was going to read from the
'oldest law book there is.' He then read the verses and the jury was mesmerized. We ended up getting the highest damage award in the history
of North Dakota at that time."

Beatus agreed that the law passed Belli by during his final years, but
that didn't taint his memories of the big man in the courtroom. "When
he was at his peak," Beatus said, "he was the best I ever saw. He was the
sharpest guy I ever met and possessed the quickest mind. Mel could grasp
the meaning of facts, and bore into the issue like you wouldn't believe.
When he didn't know the facts, and you schooled him, right away he
began to ask the right questions."

Nearly every attorney who worked with Belli agreed that his main
strength in the courtroom was cross-examination. "He wasn't great at
direct, or even at opening statements," Bob Lieff said. "Final arguments
were very competent, but it was cross where he shined. He was the master, always knowing where to probe for weaknesses and what questions
to ask that led the witness to reveal information most critical to his case."

Beatus said when Belli cross-examined, "He could get away with
things no other lawyers could because he *was* Belli, but he was very
imposing to a witness, very intimidating and he could devastate a witness." Belli had addressed this in a previous text, writing, "[As a cross-
examiner] you must watch for telltale signs, for the too-bold look, the
quick flush, the tilting of the chin, tapping of the foot. Never ask a question you don't know the answer to. Begin with a question that captures
the attention of the jury, and if possible, disconcerts the witness."

AT THE MONTGOMERY Street offices, Belli presided over weekly meetings to assess cases. Every member of the firm was required to attend and

outline their cases. "Many times the meetings were held at 4:00 pm," Seymour Ellison recalled. "Or right after Mel came back from a trip. He'd go around the room and each attorney would discuss what they were working on. He didn't remember all the names of the cases, but he knew the facts of let's say 'the tire case' and he'd expect a full report. I was amazed at his memory for both past and present cases."

Attorney Tim Palm witnessed the remarkable memory firsthand. "He asked me to look up a case in the library," Palm said. "I looked everywhere, but couldn't find it. I told him so, but he said, 'I know it's there.' Then he quoted an exact passage, a quotation from the case. When I found it, I was in awe."

Elizabeth Cabraser, who had witnessed the aging lawyer's magnificence during the Castano tobacco litigation, observed, "When I first met him [Belli], I thought he's past it, doesn't understand the simple nuances of the cases," she recalled. "But I didn't appreciate him, he was in the realm of big ideas and was no longer interested in the day to day stuff."

Cabraser said Belli "had a synthetic mind." "There are classical lawyers and jazz lawyers," she surmised, "and he was a jazz lawyer. There aren't any more around like him. He was a great figure from a bygone era, an actor without a stage since he watched the profession turn into a business and that didn't interest him. He simply ran out of time, and he couldn't get a continuance."

In an interview with author Norman Sheresky, Belli was asked about the important of having a killer instinct in the courtroom. He replied, "Your opponent may be your good friend, but never in the courtroom. Fuck 'em if you can. They expect you to do it." Addressing his reputation for staying focused and ignoring self-analysis during trial, Belli said, "You keep away from all that stuff when you're trying cases. You've got to be a mechanic. The niceties of why you do things, who you are, where you belong in life, interferes with your being a mechanic."

Belli told Sheresky the qualities he believed a great trial lawyer must possess: sense of legal history, skills of voice, jury presence, grace, and timing. Belli also emphasized the need for "a warm feeling for the client." He added, "We [lawyers] marry our clients." On another occasion, when asked to define the makings of a great trial lawyer, he replied, "First, you gotta be smart. Then you've got to have a lot of imagination. A little law knowledge will help, but then you've got to have the guts to stick with your client, whether you are winning or losing."

Those who practiced with Belli agreed with his assessment. Attorney George Safford, a former Navy pilot, said, "Belli was full of more bullshit than any man I ever met in my life. He could get away with things, but his main weapon was being able to pick out a cogent fact in a case, a small point, and weave the whole case around that. He had a great talent."

Asked why Belli had problems with his type of courtroom behavior during the later years of his life, Safford said, "He resisted the modern concepts of discovery and pretrial motions. He was used to matching wits with the other side when it was trial by ambush and neither side knew what to expect. As time passed, that changed and pretrial tactics became more important. Belli liked it better the other way."

Attorney Safford was right. In an interview with the *San Francisco Chronicle*, Belli said, "In the old days, lawyers used to carry their brains in their briefcases. It was trial by ambush." Asked about an attorney's demeanor in the courtroom, he replied, "Oratory is now extinct. For juries raised on *Kojak* and *M*A*S*H*, reference to the Bible and Shakespeare fall on deaf ears."

19

TOUGH TIMES AHEAD

ASKED ABOUT HIS former associate, attorney Frederica Sayre told the *Chicago Tribune*, "He [Melvin Belli] was like a big Howitzer. You had to get him pointed in the right direction."

During the 1990s, Belli appeared to have been misdirected. Many of his courtroom battles were with family, friends, and legal associates. Most were due to matters of pride, causing the *San Francisco Chronicle* to surmise, "[Belli] allows a burning ego to eclipse a first-class legal mind."

This ego and his love for the law caused Belli to practice the profession far too long. During the 1980s and the early 1990s, Belli's name continued to be linked with high-profile cases, but with spotty results.

The downturn didn't mean Belli had lost his touch for success. Belli and his firm represented victims of the Korean Airline Flight 007 crash, the Las Vegas MGM Grand Hotel fire, the Kansas City Hyatt Walkway disaster, and the Benedictine birth defect cases. In the Bhopal/Union Carbide isocyanate gas disaster in India, he and his colleagues represented more than twenty-four-thousand victims. He won a $200 million verdict in the Dow Corning silicon breast implant controversy.

Four California women hired his firm to file a $10 million claim against the Navy, alleging that they were sexually assaulted during the Tailhook conventions in 1990 and 1991. The case was also a success.

In 1992, Belli successfully represented Phillipinos tortured and killed under the regime of President Ferdinand Marcos. He based the case on a "piracy in high seas" allegation whereby the victims had been robbed and pillaged by Marcos. Joyce Revilla said the idea showed "what a genius Mr. Belli was." Sharron Long added, "He was incredibly brilliant. Other lawyers would have liked to know as much as he forgot."

Belli instituted the lawsuit in 1986 and formally served Marcos with a summons when he landed in Hawaii. Six years later, U.S. District Judge Manual Real awarded the staggering sum of $2 billion to those aggrieved. Marcos had died in 1989, but the judgment against his estate withstood legal challenge.

But any success he had at the time was marred by a nasty divorce from Lia. "He was angry when he heard about it," Joyce Revilla said. "And he was angry after it was over."

BELLI'S VIEWPOINT TOWARD his fifth marriage was mixed. In *My Life on Trial* he wrote, "Lia is a multi-faceted woman who can be the soul of horn-rimmed efficiency from nine to five and the warmest woman I have ever known when the sun goes down....I am proud of her and I love her."

Despite the kind remarks, Belli disliked Lia's spending habits. As John O'Connor discovered, so did his associates. O'Connor attended an office meeting where Lia was present. "Lia sat in the Louis IV chair, up high, behind Belli, like a fly on the wall," O'Connor recalled. "When we went around the room, I noticed that all the attorneys were playing down their cases, being pessimistic. It took me awhile to catch on, but later I understood when I found out that Lia was spending $8,000 a month just at Sak's Fifth Avenue and up to $30,000 a month on clothes alone."

Ironically the civil lawsuit was filed in 1988, the same year Belli coauthored *Divorcing*. In chapter one, he wrote about his four failed marriages and his new marriage to Lia. Belli was optimistic that this fifth marriage would last a lifetime. Certainly his fondness for Melia shone through. He wrote, "Having a thirteen-year-old daughter at age seventy-eight keeps me from feeling old; she's a delight."

REGARDING LIA, BELLI wrote, "That my marriage to Lia has lasted as long as it has, and continues to become better with each passing year, reinforces my conviction that divorce, painful as it can be, can be a stepping-stone to a better life."

Obviously, some time after Belli penned those words, the relationship between husband and wife soured. The "Lia War," as Belli called it, began. The split was fueled by high-octane arguments about nearly everything.

The crowning blow was struck when the aging lawyer felt he needed to protect himself from liability in pending malpractice suits. Anticipating a huge verdict against him in one such case, he deeded his $8 million Broadway Street mansion to Lia, and his office building to son Caesar and daughter Melia.

Las Vegas attorney Gary Logan said the mansion was amazing. "It had a view from the bedroom that was unbelievable," he recalled. "The Golden Gate bridge, everything. The picture windows must have been ten feet by twelve to fifteen feet." The spacious twenty-five room, seven bath, red brick English Tudor mansion at 2950 Broadway had a backyard swimming pool, built by Belli to keep Melia at home entertaining her friends. The house was decorated with Chinese wall scrolls, bronze dragons, African masks, Russian icons, and antique silver boxes.

The mansion was the setting for many lavish parties. At one Thanksgiving feast, friends and family enjoyed unusual hors d'oeuvres; someone had provided "pot" brownies. Lia sampled several, believing her guests were joking when they said marijuana was a key ingredient. When she stood to give a Thanksgiving greeting to the thirty-plus guests, she found she couldn't say a word. Belli, himself under the influence, stood shakily and told the crowd, "Lia, you're screwed up!"

These special times were quickly forgotten when the malpractice suit verdict was rendered in Belli's favor. Delirious with joy, Belli ask that his wife and children return the properties to him. They refused. Belli was enraged, the family structure forever fractured.

Belli was especially incensed after the 1989 San Francisco earthquake severely damaged the office building. He wanted to repair the dwelling so he could move back into his cherished office, but Caesar and Melia wouldn't cooperate. Belli would never return to practice law from the world famous office.

The divorce proceeding lasted for three years, producing ill feelings that bordered on hatred. At one point Belli accused Lia of having affairs with South African Bishop Desmond Tutu, Zsa Zsa Gabor, and a housekeeper (the latter responded, "I am proud to say I am gay and I've never had sex with Mrs. Belli."). Lia, resplendent in a white turban and huge straw hat, said to reporters, "Please kill the rumor that I am rushing off to have an affair with Mother Teresa."

As the public arguing continued, Belli charged that Lia had thrown Momba, one of his precious dogs, off the Golden Gate Bridge, and that while in Poland, she had "fucked Lech Welesa."

These allegations stemmed from Lia's bizarre relationship with a young Australian man named Lord Alexander Montagu. Montagu, who claimed to be a viscount, doubled as a limousine driver.

When Desmond Tutu visited the United States in the late 1980s, Lia organized a charity fund-raiser in Los Angeles during which a rare pearl was auctioned off. Whoopi Goldberg and other Hollywood celebrities were in attendance. Belli, ever aware of making a fashion statement, appeared in a dark suit, no socks, and Dockers.

Montagu was invited to the event. Smitten with Lia, and unable to get her to return his telephone calls, he appeared in the lobby of the Hilton brandishing a gun. The crazed "viscount" threatened to kill his true love, but unable to find her, ended up shooting himself. He survived a chest wound, but missed the charity event.

Later, when Montagu was arrested in Australia, he prevailed upon Belli to assist his efforts to be freed. If he did so, the viscount promised to testify that Lia had threatened to, or had actually thrown Momba off the Golden Gate Bridge. Belli passed this on to the media in an effort to show how evil Lia really was.

Lia, in turn, charged the octogenarian Belli with domestic violence. She accused him of "pushing her into a mirror, throwing a dish at her, hitting her in the eye with a newspaper, and with having affairs." He had admitted to one such affair, with Elena Yee, an heiress to the Lilly pharmaceutical company fortune.

Lia also indirectly accused Belli of having an intruder attempt to shoot her. Before the divorce was filed, Lia told police that a mysterious gunman had attacked her. A front-page story in the *Chronicle* on June 29, 1988, was headlined "Lia Belli Says Intruder 'Was Trying To Kill Me.'"

She said she was awakened at 5:15 PM by her husband's four barking dogs, secured in the basement for the evening. Waking, she heard a key being positioned in the door lock to her bedroom. Belli was in Russia at the time.

Lia yelled, "Mel, is that you?" Receiving no answer, she grabbed a heavy brass vase and fled from the room by jumping on the balcony, smashing the vase against the glass door of her husband's adjacent bathroom and slipping inside. Then she entered his bedroom and set off the burglar alarm.

Lia told police that when she opened the door, she saw "a young man wearing a black T-shirt and neon-red gloves standing by the stairway with a gun in his hand. He pointed the gun at me and fired." Investigators later recovered one bullet from the door and another in a pile of broken glass.

After the intruder, described as being "wiry, over six feet, built like an athlete with straight, dirty-blond hair and bushy eyebrows," fled on the fire escape, Lia said she ran screaming from the house in her nightgown. She attempted to secure help at the Gordon Getty museum down the block, but no one was there. Finally a police car, lights blazing, came to her rescue.

Asked for a possible motive for the break-in, Lia said, "My heart wants to believe this was a robbery, but the facts scream otherwise." When asked to elaborate, she said that while she had received no death threats, her husband received one three months earlier from a caller who said, "Are you prepared to die? I am going to put a bullet in your brain."

When Belli was contacted about the break-in, he said that threat came from "an Australian friend of his wife who is mentally disturbed and who describes himself as an English lord." This, obviously, was Lord Montagu. After accusing the viscount of "beating my wife, causing her black eyes," he said Montagu had "poured sand in my gas tank twice." Montagu countered with the accusation that "Belli smashed her head against the wall of the yacht. Blood was pouring out everywhere."

Belli said, out of fear of Montagu, "I now sleep with a shotgun beside my bed." Concerning the accusations that he was abusive, he proclaimed "I never laid a finger on Lia. I love her like my mother." This comment was perplexing to those who knew that Belli hated his mother.

Lia disputed Belli's claims, telling police, "I'm glad my survival instincts were intact," adding "I have hired a full-time bodyguard." Later, as the divorce proceedings grew more intense, she hinted that perhaps her husband or "a hit man" hired by an unidentified family member with designs on her share of the Belli fortune had ordered the intruder to kill her.

Regarding the incident, "a prominent San Francisco socialite, who asked not be quoted by name," told *Houston Post* journalist Mark Mac-Namara, "Mel Bellicose did the impossible four times—he married women noisier than himself. Lia—or 'Liarbell' as she is called—makes up so many stories she could qualify for a fiction award."

Even though Belli told police he was certain Montagu was the "mad shooter," no suspects were ever arrested in connection with the break-in. The viscount maintained that he was innocent and had spent the entire evening in question in Los Angeles with director James Cameron. He also stated that he was going to sue Belli for $10 million and "paint his offices bright pink and turn them into public toilets." Belli then issued a statement suggesting that Lia was pregnant with Montagu's child. Lia denied the allegation and showed reporters a six-inch scar on her arm, claiming it was proof of Belli's savagery.

Lia's petition for separation was filed three days after the incident. She said the final straw was Belli's lack of sympathy over the attempt on her life. "I have been heartbroken that throughout this entire issue my husband has not called home. He has called his office, but his only question was about the safety of the dogs, nothing about me."

Belli was in Russia when he learned that he was being sued for divorce. The proceedings were media fodder for months. On July 7, 1988, the *San Francisco Chronicle*'s front page featured the headline, "Lia's Being a Pussycat." Under a photograph of her bodyguard Michael Evans holding the dog Welldone Rumproast IV, the story continued under the banner, "But Mel Says She's Got His Dog." Accusations flew back and forth, with Lia saying she kept Rumpy for protection and Belli swearing that the poor animal had been dognapped and was forced to sleep on a "cold, stone floor."

"She does not like the dog and the dog does not like her," Belli, living on his yacht at the time, said. Belli said he was ashamed to have to go to court to ask for visitation rights to see a Dalmatian, but Lia finally agreed. Two days later Rumpy was delivered to the yacht, safe and sound. When the custody of the dogs was at stake, the *San Francisco Chronicle* ran a poll to see how readers felt. To his delight, Belli won.

Those who observed the roller-coaster marriage had differing ideas about whose conduct was worse. Joyce Revilla called Lia "conniving," but recalled Belli insulting his wife in front of employees and embarrassing her. "He treated Lia like he did some of the employees," Revilla recalled. "When the honeymoon was over, he would step on people. And if he found out he could do that, then he lost respect for that person."

Sharron Long said it was simple: "He loved her, and she didn't love him." Bob Lieff simply said Lia was "a gold digger who used Belli to further her own interests." Milton Hunt's explanation for the breakup, "She was in the newspaper more than him."

Long also believed that Belli married Lia, whom she described as "a bitch," because he wanted a child. "He asked me, and I'm sure he asked others to have a baby," she recalled. "But I just laughed and said, 'No, way.' When Lia became pregnant, he married her. That was a big mistake."

Belli wanted to fight the divorce settlement for the rest of his life, but it was finally settled in 1991. Reopening the divorce case with Lia cost him an estimated $500,000 in additional legal fees. He was ordered to pay her $20,000 per month in support. Concerning the agreement, Belli said, "She cost me fifteen million."

Two years later Lia informed the judge handling the case that Belli was more than a quarter of a million dollars in arrears in support payments. His attorneys responded that Uncle Sam was first in line: Belli owed the government more than $400,000.

Richard Brown, who briefly practiced with Belli, said, "Belli was his own worst enemy." The former associate pointed out that Belli had "to keep fighting, it kept him alive."

After the divorce Lia fled to London, where she studied business at Oxford University. In 1996, she married Prince Paul, said to be the heir to the throne of Romania. Her title, "Princess Paul," one pundit observed, was chosen since "Princess Lia" might evoke memories of the *Star Wars* character. Regardless of the moniker, the prince's father was dubious of the relationship. He dubbed Lia a "title digger."

In 1997, Lia was arrested in London. Three million dollars' worth of jewelry she had borrowed from her friend Countess Stephania von Kories was not returned. Instead, it ended up for sale in a jewelry store. They had been pawned for 280,000 pounds.

Lia professed innocence, but Scotland Yard detained her. Then von Kories called the entire matter "a misunderstanding," and Lia was released.

In 1998, daughter Melia sued her mother for unlawfully confiscating $90,000 in stock from her trust fund. Asked by journalist John Rhine about her relationship with her mother, Melia said, "We haven't spoken in five years. I think she's pathological."

20

FINANCIAL RUIN

ONE OF THE great disappointments in Melvin Belli's life was the adverse effect the divorce proceedings with Lia had on his daughter Melia.

Belli was sixty-six years old when she was born, but there was a special bond between them. The aging lawyer attempted to learn from his mistakes and include his children, Caesar and Melia, in his life. To that end, he wrote in *Divorcing*, "I made her [Melia] a part of the office. I gave her a mailbox, in which I put advertisements in her name, pieces of gum, candy, and toys. . . . She has had her own chair and desk and drawing pad in the Belli Building since she was five."

Belli explained that he included the kids in any discussions about future renovations to his building. He wrote, "Melia and Caesar are both very proud of that; they speak of the building as 'their' building, and their advice is asked about what flowers are to be planted, what painting is to be done, what furniture and computers and such are to be gotten." Melia, Belli mentioned, had now become part of his Saturday lunch with associates and friends.

Continuing his attempt to be a good, caring father, he ordered a sign for the front of the building that read, "Belli, Belli, and Belli," hoping Melia and Caesar might carry on in his tradition. It would never occur.

Belli was constantly worried about Caesar. Before partner Bob Lieff left the law firm in 1972, he said Belli became quite emotional. "He gave me a big Belli bear hug," Lieff recalled. "He made me promise not to leave, which I did, and to make sure that Caesar would have a place in the firm to practice law."

While working on the Exxon Valdez case in Seattle, Lieff was forced to be frank with his partner about son Caesar. "I told him Caesar was a bum," Lieff said. "Because of the way he was raised. He won't make it at all. Mel urged me to put Caesar on some committee that was important. I did so, but it didn't work because Caesar was lazy and so full of himself. He was a spoiled brat and that was Mel's fault for giving him everything and taking him everywhere when he was growing up."

Through the years Belli and daughter Melia were close. As time went by, however, she began to suspect that he was cheating her. She sued him for unlawfully cashing a $1 million bond belonging to her. Its present value was more than $300,000. He discounted her claim, alleging that the bond was only due if she met certain criteria, such as graduating from law school and becoming a lawyer. A settlement was finally reached, but the gap between father and daughter had widened.

WHEN CLIENTS, WIVES, or family members weren't suing Belli, his associates were. In 1984, several charged him with defamation, fraud, negligence, intentional infliction of emotional distress, and breach of contract. These lawsuits were the most recent outcome of the poor relationship Belli had with his colleagues.

In the 1950s, his first attempt at partnership, with attorneys Lou Ashe and Van Pinney, ended in turmoil. Regarding the split, author Robert Wallace wrote that the two left the firm after "deciding they would rather practice law in a closet full of exploding skyrockets than with Belli."

Associate David Rosenberg claimed Belli held meetings where "he would rage, bellow, excoriate, damnify, slander, humiliate, and oppress his own staff." Belli called the accusations, "scurrilous, false, defamatory, scandalous, and irrelevant."

Belli told the *San Francisco Chronicle* that his ill temper could be attributed to "episodic headaches that have plagued me for fifty years. They made me a miserable son of a bitch." But, since "brisk walks, twisting his neck, and deep breaths" had eased the pain, Belli said proudly, "I am no longer obstreperous and deliberately controversial."

In 1995, five lawyers in Belli's office filed suit against him and partner/son Caesar. The associates charged that they were doing all the work, while the Bellis took all the money. Belli was most irritated by their allegation that he was too senile to practice law. Regarding the suggestion that he retire, he quipped, "What, and let some bum lawyers step into my shoes and do a bad job for my clients. I love the law. No one in this office is allowed to say the word 'retirement.'"

Belli told *San Francisco Focus Magazine* in December 1984, "I admit I was wrong. I made a mistake. I should have called their mothers, taken down their pants, spanked them, and sent them home in a taxi with a guard. I shouldn't have yelled at the poor dears." He added, "See, I was coming into the office before they got there, going to court before they got there, and then I'd work at night and I had no idea how lazy they were. Finally, it dawned on me, and I got rid of them. . . . One of them I threw out of the office physically."

Milton Hunt believed the associates were simply using Belli as "a letterhead." "He'd tell me," Hunt recalled, "Those Goddamn vultures, they're sitting on the fence waiting for me to die. They wish I was in a rest home. I never get my due respect."

Daughter Jeanne Belli echoed those thoughts. "He hired people who weren't as good as him to make himself look good," she said. "And they weren't. The fights were about distrust, power, and money. He used to tell me, 'The money comes in the front door and all the vultures are there waiting. I get nothing.'"

After working beside her father as a paralegal, Jeanne finally left the law firm. "I couldn't take it," she said, "all the infighting. It was awful. Dad was furious when I left, but I had to do it for my own sanity."

Belli was melancholy and angry. "I built up this law practice," he lamented, "built up my estate, and now it's all gone." After abuse allegations on both sides, the suit between Belli and the associates was settled. As with all Belli disagreements, it became personal. "There were simply too many egos running around the office," one former associate said. "All of them greedy to the point where backstabbing was a common daily occurrence."

The settlement with the five associates didn't stop litigation by other former associates. Sacramento lawyer Glenn Spitzer, an employee in Belli's office for nearly three years, filed suit for back wages and won a $40,000 judgment. Frustrated in his attempts to collect, he finally convinced a judge to authorize him to confiscate Belli's prized Rolls-Royce. Spitzer discovered Belli was in Marysville trying a case, but arrived a split second too late to seize the automobile.

Bob Ingram witnessed Belli's erratic behavior. "I should have decked Mel fifteen or twenty times for what he said," he recalled. "One time he threw a wadded up piece of paper at me. I took a step toward him and he backed up. I took another step and he backed up again. I thought 'What a chicken shit son of a bitch,' but of course I was just a kid and he was in his early sixties."

Such incidents caused Ingram, a self-proclaimed "straight-guy" amongst what he called the "user-abusers" in the office, to sum up Belli in three words: "erratic, nuts, and unpredictable." He added, "But I loved the man."

At times, Belli simply did not want to confront attorneys he was going to fire. He once sent a memo to Bill Choulos that read, "FIRE EVERY-ONE AND THEN FIRE YOURSELF." On another occasion, an attorney named Charley was fired and demanded to see Belli. The boss locked himself in his office and refused to come out.

Belli's disputes weren't confined to associates. Nearly all his partners ended up becoming his enemies for protracted periods of time, if not forever. Leaving the office for any reason was deemed disloyal, and the offender was banished. After Seymour Ellison departed, Belli issued a scathing memo that read, "IF YOU HAVE ANYTHING TO DO WITH THIS MAN, THAT IS GROUNDS FOR IMMEDIATE DIS-MISSAL."

Lieff's separation from the firm was typical of disagreements that forbade Belli from enjoying any continuous partnership that wasn't filled with calamity. At the time, revenue was divided between the partners thusly: Belli, 40 percent; Ashe, 20 percent; Ellison, 15 percent; Choulos, 15 percent; Lieff, 10 percent. When Lieff, who felt he was earning a significant amount of revenue for the firm, asked that his share be raised, his request was ignored. He quit, taking several associates with him. His departure became front page news in the *Chronicle*.

Belli was livid. "I can remember Mel standing in front of the building on television blasting me as not even being a partner," Lieff recalled with a laugh. "And right behind him was the sign on the building that showed I *was* a partner."

Belli chastised Lieff in public, but in private he was even more vehement. "He told friends," Lieff said, "that I was gay and fucking the receptionist." After suing Belli for compensation, he was ostracized for more than fifteen years.

Finally, Belli and Lieff spoke, and to Lieff's delight, became good friends again. The turnaround was symbolic. Except for the continued disintegration of Belli's relationship with Bill Choulos, time healed wounds and former associates and partners once again became Belli's friends.

The same men who Belli relished as legal associates, he treated with utter disdain. Lou Ashe, a confidant of Belli's for years, was ridiculed on a regular basis. One attorney described him as "Belli's whipping boy."

"Lou Ashe was a Rabbi, a scholar," lawyer/economist J. Kelly Farris, whom Belli affectionately called, "The Prince of Torts," recalled. "He was highly regarded but Mel treated him like shit. He wouldn't have taken it if he hadn't loved Mel so much."

When Ashe quit out of disgust for Belli's actions, Belli had a change of heart. He and another attorney journeyed to Ashe's new San Francisco offices, removed the furniture, and took it to his old Belli Building office. Ashe returned as if nothing had occurred.

Farris knew a thing or two about the bad seed Belli. "One time he asked me how the receipts in the office were," Farris said. "And I jokedly told him they're up, but the black girl on the receptionist desk is pocketing them. He said, 'You racist son of a bitch.' That upset me since I was joking, and we yelled at one another. Finally, I said well, I don't give a diddly fuck about you or your office, and I walked out. We didn't speak for two years. Then I received a postcard from him in India and he wanted to make up. We settled our differences and we were friends again."

Bob Lieff said Belli looked for weaknesses in those who worked around him. "He was an expert and knew the potential for spotting masochists, people who he could pound on. And then he took advantage."

Lieff believed most Belli associates sucked up to him. "Even at lunch," Lieff said, "there would be five guys around the table, and they'd all say the steak looked good. Then Belli would decide to have a chicken dish and all at once everybody decided that the chicken looked pretty damn good and that was what they ordered."

John Hill, the attorney who had Belli's ear perhaps more than any other, believed that the famed lawyer relished calamity. "He continually surrounded himself with sycophants," Hill said. "People who were sleazy. He loved the raucous lifestyle, loved having those kind of corrupt people around. They were ones who were going to steal from him, or take advantage. They all wanted something from him, to share in the glory, and they caused him all kinds of problems."

Bob Lieff agreed. "Mel was a narcissistic to the extreme," he said. "He had this grandiose personality like Hitler, Mussolini, or General McArthur. And he was surrounded by sycophants, all of whom were scheming to get rich off of him."

Hill believed Belli enjoyed the psychology of it all, the psychodrama. "He was always playing psychological games," Hill explained. "Trying to figure people out. He'd say, 'Goddamn, it John, we've known each other for thirty years. Why don't you steal something from me so I can get angry at you?'"

"Mel loved to collect good people who had personality flaws," said Seymour Ellison. "He recognized talent, and he wanted those around him who cared about others. That was the most important trait he looked for."

Despite Belli's tirades and flair for agitating those around him, Hill saw more positives than negatives in the aging lawyer: "Belli was a creative genius in law, one of the great legal minds ever. He could take a fact situation and develop it and strategize it as well as anyone who ever practiced law."

If those were Belli's positives, Hill recognized the negatives as well: "Mel was creative and a genius, but he lacked discipline and organization, lacked judgment. That is what caused his downfall."

Hill also believed Belli should have retired years earlier. "During the last fifteen years or so," he said, "it was apparent that his time had passed. The legal system had changed and he couldn't change with it. He was out of touch with what juries wanted to hear from lawyers. It was important not to overplay things, but underplay them. And that wasn't Mel's way." Hill added, "In the final years, Mel didn't charm jurors and he antagonized judges. After one case we lost, I talked with the jurors. One said, 'Why did he keep yelling at us?' The acoustics were bad, but I knew it was because he was hard of hearing and so he talked louder than he had to."

When asked why Belli didn't quit, Hill responded, "Because he loved the law so much. I never saw anyone so passionate about the law, never knew anyone who loved the law the way he did. It was his life."

IN DECEMBER 1995, Belli stunned the legal world by announcing that his law firm was filing for bankruptcy protection under Chapter XI. This was the result of his messy divorce from Lia, the breakup of the firm and subsequent legal action by associates, and a decision by the Dow Corning

Corporation to file for bankruptcy, preventing the firm from receiving its settlement.

Belli's public relations spokesman Edward Lozzi read a statement. It said, "The Belli firm was to receive over $200 million prior to Dow filing bankruptcy." He added, "That's the case that got us in trouble."

Lozzi said Belli insisted on not filing for Chapter XI until the last possible moment. He finally filed after being contacted by several creditors, including the doctors and hospitals owed money from the Dow Corning case.

"He didn't want to do this," Lozzi said of his boss. "He's from the old school where they think this is disgraceful. It's not." Nancy Ho Belli, Belli's sixth wife, confirmed that he hated the thought of bankruptcy. "I'd rather die before I file," he told her. She said, "Mel, they're coming to lock the doors." He relented and filed the action, saying, "If Dow can do it, and Donald Trump can do it, then Belli can do it."

That bankruptcy wasn't filed until well into the 1990s was a tribute to Belli's efforts to keep the firm solvent. It was always on the brink of financial disaster. "We were forever in debt," attorney Seymour Ellison said. "Many times payroll was pending and Mel would say to me or Bill Choulos, 'Go see Al at Lou Lurie's back and get a loan.' Mel gave new meaning to the words, 'deficit spending.'"

Belli was certainly no stranger to bad investments. Never one to turn down a get-rich-quick scheme, he was easy prey for screwball ideas. At one point, his office safe was packed with Twisto Toothbrushes. They featured cylindrical handles full of toothpaste. With a flick of the finger, a gob released from the cylinder landed on the brush like, as an ad stated, "a frog on a lily pad." Belli invested several thousand dollars in the venture, but soon discovered that the inventor couldn't keep the trigger mechanism from malfunctioning. Every so often, toothpaste would shoot out with machine gun rapidity, covering the user in toothpaste. For a time Belli carried a miracle toothbrush in his pocket and provided demonstrations whenever possible. His expensive clothes often had white toothpaste stains. "Once when I was summing up in a jury trial," Belli said, "I lifted my hand to gesture and got an armpit full of Pepsodent."

Belli once considered an investment in Alaska. According to lawyer/economist J. Kelly Farris, "Belli and I and a lawyer named Alva Brumfield flew to Juneau to investigate a whorehouse that had been turned into a church. We traipsed through the mud to find it and Mel was intrigued with the history and so forth. Fortunately, he never bought the damn thing, but we did get drunk as all get out. On the plane back, Mel sliced open a pillow in the cabin and released the feathers into an overhead fan. They were flying everywhere, but luckily the stewardess couldn't identify the culprit and we were saved."

When Belli discovered the ghost town of Garlock, California, was for sale, he immediately bought it. His rationale was simple: One of the lawyers in the office was named Jim Garlock.

In 1965, Belli had purchased the *Delta King*, the paddle wheel sister to the Mighty Mississippi's *Delta Queen*. Belli intended the *King* to operate as a floating restaurant/hotel running between Sacramento and San Francisco. He spent five years in litigation when the investment didn't pay off.

Continuing litigation by Belli was a means of avoiding paying his bills. Bob Lieff, a partner during the *Delta King* days, defended him in numerous lawsuits. "If vendors filed suit in state court," he recalled, "we stalled by removing the case to federal court on the basis that the *Delta King* had an engine that was operable and thus the boat fell under federal admiralty laws. If the case was filed in federal court, we chose to remove the case to state court stating that the boat had no operating engine and thus was not susceptible to federal admiralty laws."

Fellow attorney John Hill scolded him for his poor choice of investments, saying, "Mel, you can't keep throwing millions of dollars away." Belli replied that when you stoop over to pick up an object, "You never know whether it will be a brick or gold."

"Belli's financial decisions were made strictly on emotion," Hill said. "He was impetuous, and he wouldn't listen to anyone. That character flaw had serious consequences."

Former associate Bob Ingram reacted to the bankruptcy with sadness, but admitted he wasn't surprised. "Mel had an enormous self-destructive streak," he said. "One time he accepted defense of a case where the client was charged with passing bad checks. When the partners asked him the state of the retainer, his face broke into a smile and he said, 'I took a check. Of course, the check bounced.'"

The firm only made money when judgments or settlements were made in their favor and they received payment. Meanwhile, money poured out, spent on investigating cases, hiring legal experts, and other costs. It was feast or famine for the law firm, and famine finally prevailed.

Among the 127 creditors listed on the bankruptcy form were accountants, printing companies, personnel agencies, insurance companies, deposition services, telephone providers, automobile dealers, Federal Express, and the Beverly Hilton Hotel. Even Lozzi was listed: The firm owed him $19,000.

Pending litigation claims were also reflected on the petition. In all, thirty-one lawsuits against Belli were noted.

Undaunted and unapologetic, the eighty-eight-year-old Belli said in a statement that he was forced to file "to protect the valued interests of my clients as we continue the legal crusade against corporate interests who include gross negligence as an acceptable way of conducting their business. We shall prevail against them as we always have." Lozzi added, "Dow eventually will come through with something. In the meantime, this will keep the jaws from snapping."

Belli's inability to deal with financial matters was legendary. When the cash box was full, Belli was given ten brand-new ten dollar bills by his secretary in the morning. He kept the roll of bills in a solid gold money clip. By the end of the day, the money was gone. Belli never kept track of where it went.

In response to a question as to whether he had won over $600 million in jury verdicts and settlements as of the early 1980s, Belli said, "Well, we've tried cases for over fifty years. . . . I do drive a Rolls-Royce. I'm a millionaire many times over—but I've made a lot of people millionaires many times over, and I've given away a lot of money."

Privy to the inside workings of the firm, Maggie Quinn knew that money was always an issue. She said, "Some months there was no money to make the payroll, others there was something like $4 million sitting in the bank. It was flood, famine, feast."

Belli's bankruptcy drew emotional reactions. Attorney Richard Brown, who had tangled with Belli, told William Carlsen of the *San Francisco Chronicle*, "It's tragic. He's given so much to the law. I fear he's going to end up like that famous San Francisco character, the Emperor Norton, wandering the streets penniless before long."

San Francisco Chronicle columnist Herb Caen learned firsthand of Belli's plight. On December 8, 1995, he wrote, "Atty. Melvin Belli on the horn yesterday sounding mournful. 'I'll take you to lunch if you'll pick up the check.' [he said] His way of confirming that he has put himself and his firm into Chapter XI, and whew, it's a long story." Caen then

recounted Dow Corning's decision to file bankruptcy as the main reason for Belli's downfall before writing, "but that's not the only problem,
laments the lachrymose lawyer. 'La Trampa'—his loving nickname for his
ex-wife—'cost me fifteen million,' one of the largest divorce settlements in history. Sounding more morose than bellicose, Mr. Belli signed
off with 'No Christmas cards this season. Scrooged again.'"

Kent Russell, who continued a friendship with Belli long after he left
the firm, wasn't surprised by Belli's downfall. "He had the worst judgment with wives and partners. Wives screwed him one after the other.
Partners screwed him one after the other. Instead of a legacy as a legal
scholar, which he truly was, there was a haze of ineptitude all around him
during his final years."

Attorney John Hill saw the situation firsthand. "He wandered in my office
one evening at five o'clock," Hill recalled with sadness. "He didn't have any
money for dinner. I didn't want to have him feel embarrassed to ask for
it, so I quickly suggested I loan him two, three hundred dollars that he
could pay me back. This was around the time his house had been foreclosed on two or three times. It was a tough time for him."

Despite his woes, John Hill witnessed the old fashioned ethics that
were ingrained in Belli. After a successful malpractice case in Atlanta, Belli
was due $3 million.

Hill knew that Belli owed creditors much more than that, and if the
money was sent to San Francisco, it would be confiscated and Belli would
get nothing. He thus urged Belli to deposit the money in an offshore
account and hire an attorney to negotiate settlement of debts so that Belli
would have sufficient funds to take care of himself. "The answer was an
absolute no," Hill recalled. "Mel really got angry with me. 'You must be
crazy,' he bellowed, 'You want me slinking around back alleys like a criminal trying to keep from paying people I owe?'"

During the bankruptcy proceedings, Belli suffered a stroke. His personal physician told the court that he "was not competent to read and
comprehend complex documents." John Hill defended Belli, saying,
"I've been seeing him on a daily basis, and he is gradually improving."
Asked whether there was still a spot for Belli at the office, Hill said, "We
want him in here, dispensing sage advice to the lawyers and talking to
clients. . . . He was still working seven days a week up until his stroke."

In early July 1996, U.S. Bankruptcy Judge Thomas Carlson declared
that the barrister was no longer fit to handle his legal practice. He
ordered an independent examiner to take control. San Francisco busi-

nessman David Bradlow was appointed with the power to "sell Belli's assets, terminate Belli's employees, and lease his offices."

More information was forthcoming on Belli's financial status. According to Patrick Murphy, who represented him, his assets were listed at $2.6 million; his liabilities totaled $3.2 million. Richard Adler, the lawyer for the bankruptcy, said he knew why. "He was great at creating liability," Adler suggested, "and at diminishing assets."

Later many of Belli's prized possessions were sold at a bankruptcy auction. Joyce Revilla called it "a sad day." The auction program read, "Over two hundred items of memorabilia will be offered, including framed photographs, both signed and unsigned of Melvin Belli with a selection of famous people [one pictures Belli and Jack Ruby], many framed certificates honoring Belli, a selection of books he wrote, an archive of articles about Belli, a wooden gavel, his personal office desk and executive chair, and faux human skeleton that was in his office the day he died and that was of the type he used in court as demonstrative evidence." Beside the ad for the sale, there was a photograph of "Elmer."

Bob Lieff purchased Elmer, along with several volumes containing text from the famed Belli Seminars, an Indian headdress, two deer heads, a water buffalo head, and an antelope head. They were displayed alongside Elmer on the main floor of Lieff's law firm at their corporate offices in San Francisco. Asked why he bought the items, Lieff simply smiled and said, "Sentimental reasons. I don't want people to forget one of the greatest lawyers who ever lived."

NANCY HO WITNESSED Belli's financial woes firsthand. She met Belli when he was seventy-three years old. "I was a law student at the University of Florida in Gainesville in 1979," she recalled. "I read that Mr. Belli was appearing in court in Orlando. I decided to drive there, watch, and learn something."

To Ho's distress, she learned from Belli that the case had been continued. They chatted, and Belli, on the prowl even at age seventy-three, asked for her telephone number. Nancy did not give it to him, but that didn't stop Belli from contacting her. "The next day," she said, "a secretary at the law school came running into a classroom and said, 'Melvin Belli's on the phone for you.' I was shocked."

Belli used a familiar phrase to attempt to seduce the law student, nearly four decades younger than him. "He said, 'Oh, honey, I'm going to New York, do you want to go?'" Ho said. "I didn't want to be a groupie, so I said no, I had to study for graduation, but I did give him my phone number."

Four years later, after some persuading by Belli, Ho joined the law firm in San Francisco as an intake attorney. She witnessed the good and bad of him. "There was a lot of backstabbing in the office," she recalled. "And Mel liked to blow off steam. Shouting was like breathing to him."

Nancy Ho noticed other characteristics about Belli. "He was easy to take advantage of, masochistic," she said. "When people took advantage of him, he found that *interesting*."

By 1992, Nancy left the offices and ventured into real estate development. According to her, Belli kept pursuing the romance. "We became soul mates," she said. "I was very independent, a strong person and he liked that. He got involved with all those dumb-blond types who looked good to him in the beginning but then he tired of. They were all dependent and I wasn't."

The relationship grew, Ho swore, out of a caring for each other's minds. "I think I intrigued him," she said, "and I know he intrigued me. We saw each other a lot and I fell deeply in love with him. He loved me, too."

Gradually, Ho became aware of Belli's poor financial status. "I learned that he was basically broke," she said. "After the divorce from Lia, he had no place to live. I bought a house on Union Street for him and constantly helped to pay his bills. I simply couldn't see him penniless and no one else seemed willing to help him."

At one point, Belli was so financially strapped that he and friend/chauffeur Milton Hunt shared a jar of peanut butter when neither had enough money for lunch. "Some days I was the one," Hunt said, "who bought the lunch. He'd say, 'Milt, how much money you got?' and I'd say twenty bucks. We'd go out and have lunch. Sometimes I had to stop him from spending it on the dogs. He'd buy some veggy dish with chicken, and I'd eat the chicken before he gave it to the dogs."

Regarding those times, Joyce Revilla said, "People fed off of him his whole life, and then there was no one there to help him when he was in need."

By all accounts, Nancy Ho finally stepped in and took charge of Belli emotionally and financially. Milton Hunt paid her the ultimate compliment when he said, "I wish Mel would have been with her years before."

When Ho began dating Belli, she was a wealthy woman in her own right, but also courtesy of family wealth in Singapore. Her career in real estate had been extremely successful through operation of a company called Pacific Bay Holding. Attorney John Hill confirmed that Ho had loaned Belli considerable amounts of money during the last years of his life.

Belli proposed in 1995. "I traveled to Hong Kong on business twice a month then," Ho said. "One time Mel went with me, he loved Hong Kong, but we got stranded at the airport when the plane had to turn around after two hours in the air. While we were waiting, Mel beat around the bush but the essence of it was that we ought to get married."

Nancy Ho decided she did not want the publicity that surrounded Belli's previous marriages and insisted the wedding be private. The two were married in a small church in the town of Auburn, California. The mayor of Auburn assisted Nancy with her privacy wish: When Belli had to sign the marriage license at the courthouse, a clerk walked to a van where Belli was hidden so he could sign without fanfare.

The ring Nancy wore was a family heirloom, and since the two were married on short notice, a ring for Mel was secured at a pawnshop. Later, she took him to a San Francisco jewelry store and bought him a new ring. To commemorate the purchase, Belli's cousin Linda Mouron, a CNN reporter, filmed the event.

The two kept their marriage a secret. But one day, when Nancy was attending an office meeting, the doctor called with the results of Belli's medical tests. All those in the meeting heard him say, "How long do I have?" and "Is there anything I can do?" When he hung up, Nancy hugged him and said, "Honey, I think we should tell them about us."

Belli then said, "I have good news and bad news. The bad news is I have cancer, and the good news is Nancy and I are married."

21

BELLI'S FINAL DAYS

MELVIN BELLI, FALLEN legal giant, died on July 9, 1996, twenty days short of his eighty-ninth birthday.

On the final day of his life, Belli's family surrounded him. Ex-wife Betty Ballantine and sons Rick and Johnny were present. Jeanne Belli was by her father's side as well, despite the hurt she endured when her dad refused to attend her wedding in Tiburon. They had all patched things up. Belli was survived by his wife Nancy, three sons, three daughters, two stepchildren, ten grandchildren, and two great-grandchildren.

Most everyone who knew Belli believed he had, for the most part, been a failure to his kids. Many chose to blame it on his upbringing as an only child who wasn't close to his mother. Others said it was because he was simply too selfish, too self-centered, to care about and provide time for his children.

More likely was the fact that the man married to the law simply didn't know how to be a good dad, to love and cherish, to be compassionate where it counted. Time and time again, he found ways to keep from spending time with his kids. To Belli, it was the law first, the dogs second, adventures third, and family fourth. "It's no wonder that most of the kids turned out to be dysfunctional," one former legal associate said. "When their mother wasn't around, they were left to fend for themselves in the company of strangers, or office employees, never their dad. He wasn't there for them and it showed. It was his greatest disgrace."

The Internet headline for the *San Francisco Chronicle* tried to pay proper homage to the legal icon. It read, "Melvin Belli, King of Torts, Dead at 88, S.F. Lawer Known for His Flamboyance, Celebrity Cases." If he had been alive, Belli would have probably sued the newspaper for leaving a year off his age and the "y" out of "lawyer."

In the second paragraph, reporter William Carlsen wrote, "The world-renowned attorney had pancreatic cancer and suffered from a stroke and pneumonia in the last few weeks. The exact cause of death is not known."

Carlsen quoted Belli as saying, "I can love a big rich man as much as a poor little man, but there are just a lot more of the poor little men." On another occasion he had called himself, "the poor man's ticket to the courtroom."

He wrote that Belli "practiced law with an enormous gusto that made him the best-known attorney in the country." "There may be better lawyers than me," he quoted Belli as saying, "but so far I haven't come across any of them in court."

One quote that appeared in several news accounts of Belli's death across the country was apropos. "The greats of the past needed words, needed biblical stories and poetry to hold the jurors," Belli had said. "I started the shift from the literary forays to the thing itself. Now we inform juries with models, skeletons, and films."

Chronicle columnist Herb Caen said Belli liked "women, big cases, big cars and big houses." Caen also recalled memories with Belli in the 1940s at El Prado, the barrister's favorite hangout. "He was already wearing custom-made Italian suits," Caen recalled. "He loved it when I called him Mellifluous Belli, a tribute to his melodious voice that snake-charmed so many juries. He was not so fond of Bellicose, which I coined after experiencing his awesome temper."

Carlsen wrote that "former associates [unnamed] said Belli should have retired years earlier. . . . They described him during his last years as paranoid and lonely, isolated by his ego and in his ability to let anyone get close to him. They said his memory was slipping and that he had succumbed to periods of rage when he lashed out arbitrarily at those around him." He added, "His defenders, however, said that even toward the end, Belli showed flashes of the genius that had made him such a powerhouse in the courtroom."

A *Chronicle* editorial read, "Let's put aside for now the snarling quarrels and growling delusions that overwhelmed Melvin Belli in the final years of his eventful life.... [His] was an astounding legal career that mixed brilliance with bombast and memorable shrewdness with world-class self-esteem." The final sentence read, "We shall not see the likes of him again."

Attorney John Hill, who served as a pallbearer at Belli's funeral, recalled the good times. He said, "Mel had a great sense of humor. He caused me to laugh more than anyone. And he was the best storyteller I ever heard. He truly lived life to its fullest."

After recalling Belli as a "city icon [who] had a shock of white hair and thick, black-rimmed glasses," *San Francisco Weekly* journalist Lisa Davis wrote, "[He] was a bonafide wisecracking, stunt-pulling, headline-generating, one-of-a-kind character, wrapped inside a lawyer."

Revilla recalled that before Belli's death, he had turned into a hypochondriac. "We were checking out everything," she said, "eye clinics, hearing clinics, sleep clinics. He also went to the Mayo Clinic. All to fight off the inevitable." Jeanne Belli echoed Joyce's comments, saying, "Dad was pulling pills out of his pockets. Pop. Pop. Pop. It was very distressing."

John Hill believed two stories about the fabled man summed up Belli's zest for life and love for the law. "A year before his death," Hill recalled, "he hired a woman in her early fifties to help him out. He was eighty-eight at the time, but it didn't make any difference since the woman told me that while she loved the job, Mel was chasing her around the office trying to have sex with her. She told me she just didn't know what to do. Knowing Mel was always respectful of religious beliefs, I told her to say that she had been a nun and that while she wasn't one any more she couldn't have amorous relations. She did, and later Mel came to me and said, 'I like that woman but she used to be a nun.' I had trouble keeping a straight face."

John Hill's second recollection concerned a telephone call he received from Belli ten days before he died. "He knew he didn't have much time to live," Hill said. "The cancer had gotten him. Nevertheless, he wanted to discuss a medical malpractice case that we had considered the week before. He thought it had merit and I did not, so we had passed.

"He asked me if I would come over and talk to him at his home in North Point, and so I did," Hill said. "We sat there with the dogs and talked the case through. He suggested legal theories and so forth, but we reached the same conclusion as before. Regardless, I saw once again what love he had for the law and how deeply he cared about people. He was a marvel."

ELMER THE PLASTIC skeleton had popped into the news almost immediately after Belli's death. He became a symbol of the tug of war between Nancy Ho Belli and Melvin's son Caesar. Trading hurtful accusations about nearly everything, the two managed to soil a time when all of the good things about the courtroom innovator should have been foremost in everyone's minds.

As plans were being formed to hold a wake at the Grace Cathedral in San Francisco, Caesar questioned whether his father had died of natural causes. Of specific interest he said, was Belli's trip to Mexico for a "laetrile treatment" forty-five days before his death. Caesar demanded a coroner's investigation.

Inflamed, Nancy Ho, who had married Belli eleven months before his passing, retorted that Caesar and wife Gretchen, a former Belli office secretary, "had hastened the death by pressure to obtain assets and maintain the family law practice." She charged, "They killed Mel."

Based on her beliefs that her husband's relatives were "up to no good," Nancy Ho Belli said she would forbid Caesar and Gretchen to sit with the family at the funeral. "He is not part of the family," Nancy said. "Mel does not want him."

Caesar and his father had parted company over many factors, but in recent months, the son had surprised even those who knew him best by accusing his dad of being incompetent. He and Kevin McClean, an associate, had attempted to wrestle control of the law firm from his father. Father and son became bitter enemies.

Ho said the deterioration of the relationship helped worsen Belli's condition. "They got me, I'm finished," she quoted him as saying in reference to Caesar and Gretchen. She also said Belli told her of Caesar, "He's evil." Another time, she quoted Belli as saying, "I have cancer and it's my son."

Nancy Ho was disturbed to hear that Caesar and Gretchen had entered Belli's office several hours after his death despite a court order not to do so. According to the police report, Elmer and several photographs were stolen. When Caesar was notified that the items had been removed, he relented and returned them. Elmer was apparently back where he belonged, though he did make an appearance as a special guest, appropriately enough, at Gretchen's gala Halloween party.

When the flamboyant barrister was honored with a memorial service at Grace Cathedral, "The place was packed," John Hill said.

Belli was eulogized as a true San Francisco treasure at the memorial service. More than five hundred people attended to catch a final glimpse of the legendary figure. The Right Reverend William Swing, Episcopal Bishop of California, presided over a televised service.

Former Mayor Joseph Alioto's tribute from the pulpit was stirring. He compared Belli to Harry Truman and Earl Warren, saying, like them, "he was a fighter for social justice." He commented on the accusation that his friend only defended the rich and famous. "Sure he had celebrity clients," Alioto said. "Celebrities naturally flocked to him. But as a practicing attorney, he fought for the common man and the common woman."

San Francisco Mayor Willie Brown's comments were poignant. "San Francisco is more like a museum and in that museum are some very choice pieces that have been framed and sculpted by God. Mel is one of those pieces."

In a tribute to their leader, several family members wore red handkerchiefs or red scarves. Nancy Ho and Caesar and Gretchen Belli sat far apart, never acknowledging one another's appearance.

Belli would have been proud of the Right Reverend Swing's final comments. Before "Amazing Grace" was played, Swing said, "Melvin Belli, a man of law against the chaos of life, a man of chaos against the laws of life, may you, by the mercy of God, see the sunrise."

Caesar informed the press that as his own special tribute to his father he would fire a shot from the cannon atop the Belli building. A huge photograph of Belli was nearby when the firing took place. Musicians playing violins added to the celebration.

Journalist Bobbe Vargas provided an apt description of Belli's funeral. In the *Coastal Post*, she wrote, "Belli's funeral drew, as it should have, a mob! The Bishop in full mitered cap and gown presided. As we sat in that beautiful cathedral, we hoped all the concrete was well enforced in case a shaker came along. . . . A reception held at the Mark [Hopkins Hotel] was mobbed with all sorts of folk, even a monk in hassock and sandals. Farewell, Mel!"

22

WAR AT HOME

CAESAR BELLI DID not attend his father's burial in Sonora. "Sure I wanted to be there," he said. "But I wasn't invited. They didn't bother to tell me when it was." Family spokesman Michael Woodson disagreed, saying, "Caesar chose not to come. He was more than invited. The idea that he didn't know when it was is ridiculous. Everyone in Sonora knew when it was." He had hosted his own reception at the Huntington Hotel in San Francisco after the service at Grace Cathedral.

Those who did attend the twenty-minute service at Sonora's Odd Fellows Cemetery shed tears as the casket was slowly lowered into the ground. Momba and Sky, Belli's dogs, were close by, sniffing and wagging in honor of their master. The images of the Italian Greyhounds were imprinted on the black marble headstone below and on either side of a black-and-white photograph of Belli. He stood stately in a three-piece suit in front of the bookshelves in his office, his left foot arched on a stool so that a high pantleg exposed a black leather boot. His left arm was extended across his body, and his hand held the trademark black horn-rimmed glasses.

Nancy spoke fondly of her husband and his undying spirit and love. She told the *Union Democrat* Belli was "a romantic to the end. Even at eighty-eight, he talked of having 'some little ones.'" Jeanne Belli said of her dad, "He was a loving, devoted father and a mentor."

Before the service, Sonora Police Sergeant Glenn Roberts was prepared for a media onslaught. "If there are a bunch of satellite trucks and a big crowd, we'll be able to handle it," he said. Sonora police were on alert for any disruptions, including Caesar and his clan, and the area was swept of any "outsiders and crackpots." Sergeant Roberts was intent on a "civil" ceremony. He told the Sonora *Union Democrat*, "We don't want one of these guys [the dead] waking up and rising from behind a neighboring grave in the middle of the ceremony."

Sergeant Roberts shouldn't have worried. The crowd was sparse and satellite trucks were nonexistent. The man who made headlines around the world during his prime was buried with little fanfare.

Belli's expensive inlaid maple wood casket arrived by hearse. His would be the final casket in the six-grave plot, surrounded by those of his mother's family.

Momba and Sky were permitted one final sniff as Belli's chauffeur Milton Hunt accompanied them to the coffin. Family members then placed red roses on the casket before it was lowered. By 10:00 am on July 15, six days after his death, Melvin Belli was left alone.

IF OBSERVERS OF the Belli family feud believed the participants would put aside their differences after the funeral, they were wrong. Immediately there was conflict over who would get what remained of his estate. A line by Julian Guthrie of the *San Francisco Examiner* summed up the war between Nancy Ho Belli and Caesar Belli: "First, there were angry words. Now come the dueling wills."

Caesar based his claim on a handwritten will, dated January 24, 1993. It was barely legible, but Caesar swore it was his father's last will and testament.

In the handwritten will, Caesar was named executor of Belli's estate. It provided a fair split of Belli's estate. Ten thousand dollars was given to each of Belli's four dogs, with the remainder of his estate to be divided equally between his children and charity.

Also included was a clause that read, "I charge my executors to see that nothing, but absolutely nothing, goes to Lia Triff, and I charge them to contest ultimately any claim by this miserable, deceitful person."

"All Caesar is doing is trashing me," Nancy told the *Examiner*. "For him to come up with a will dating back to 1993 is ridiculous. They're trying to destroy me. But they're going to fail."

Nancy countered Caesar's claims by revealing not one, but two more wills. One, she said, had been prepared shortly after their marriage in late March 1996; a second was dated April 24, 1996. This will indicated that she was to receive the entire bounty of Belli's estate. Her attorney Patrick Hallinan told of her determination. "She's a classy lady," he said. "She's like a boxer in the eighth round—she has taken a lot of punishment, but she's still on her feet. She really loved Mel, and took good care of him."

Nancy's claim was also suspect, since the will she produced was written in both pencil and ink. The will was in Belli's scribbled handwriting, written on a piece of notepaper ripped from a binder. Kevin McLean, Caesar Belli's partner, questioned its validity during a hearing on the matter. At this, Nancy's lawyer threw a fit, saying, "You have been a scavenger on the bones of Melvin Belli since he died."

The court was thus faced with deciding between a scribbled will containing mistakes and one written in a felt-tip pen with the date in pencil. The latter contained no mention of the dogs, which caused Caesar to comment, "Look at that. Nancy even screwed the dogs out of the will."

Caesar told the *Examiner*, "She certainly doesn't have what it takes to be a Belli. I mean, ask yourself, did you ever see Mel with an ugly woman?" Caesar's wife, Gretchen, chimed in, "What sort of a woman goes to Tijuana, of all places, to get a face lift?" In fact Nancy had traveled to Mexico with Belli for his medical treatment, not cosmetic surgery.

Two years later the stress from the death of his father and the subsequent estate battle apparently took its toll on Caesar. He and wife Gretchen divorced. Meanwhile, Caesar had been suspended from practicing law for mismanaging sister Melia's trust fund. He was ordered to pay $116,000 in damages.

Faced with a potentially huge malpractice damage award against him in Wisconsin, Caesar claimed he had filed bankruptcy. Suspicious, the judge checked in San Francisco and discovered that Caesar had not, in fact, done so. A damage award of nearly $4 million was entered against him.

When Caesar finally emerged to practice law again, those who contacted him at his office heard, "This is Melvin Belli, attorney at law," on his voice mail. Certainly Melvin Caesar Belli had a right to use his first name if he wished. To do so simply to take advantage of his father's fame seemed shallow to those who remembered the harsh comments he'd made about his father during Belli's final days.

Later, he wrote, "For the record, I use the name and have used the name Melvin Caesar Belli since the day my dad told me to. It is my name. . . . I get the impression that you have heard many unfavorable things about my relationship with my Dad from those people who might still be envious or have an ax to grind. . . . Our arguments were quite the scene as we always argued extensively. That's the way he taught me. However, at the end of the day, we were always father and son."

In the months following Belli's death, Nancy fought Caesar to gain control of the dilapidated office building at 722–728 Montgomery Street. The building was identified as "Historical Landmark No. 48." A tattered gray-and-white striped awning above the front door read "Belli, Belli, & Belli," a tribute to better days.

The building had been severely damaged by an earthquake in 1989. Belli had been at the Giants/A's World Series game at Candlestick Park when the earthquake shook San Francisco. Private investigator Jim Licavoli recalled that Belli and his entourage arrived for the game on Belli's yacht, the *Adequate Award*. When the earth shook, Belli was calm, saying, "Let's have another glass of Port."

In 1997, Nancy finally paid more than $450,000 dollars through Caesar's bankruptcy court for his share of the building. She purchased the other one-half interest from Melia.

In August 1997, a ceremony attended by San Francisco Mayor Willie Brown, was held to dedicate the offices where Belli practiced as a public museum. Nancy promised full restoration of the building, at an estimated cost of $3 million.

Legal hassles prevented reconstruction. While Nancy argued with neighborhood dwellers, the city stepped in with questions about building codes and Nancy's exact plans for the restoration. Finally Melia's attorneys alleged that Nancy didn't own the building and that it should be sold.

As the calendar turned to 2007, Nancy Belli swore she would resurrect the building. She and the city haggled over whether she could follow through at costs that had reach millions, but Nancy was determined to succeed.

Whether the Belli building will become a museum in tribute to the legendary attorney remains to be seen.

Above all, Melvin Belli's legacy was his brilliance in the courtroom. He summed up his life with the famous often-quoted line quoted in the *Los Angeles Times*, "There is never a deed so foul that something couldn't be said for the guy; that's why there are lawyers."

Never was that more apparent than during Belli's last high-profile case. It occurred in November 1995, when he was eighty-eight years old.

The Boggess case originated in Marysville, California. A former student at the local high school had returned to kill three students and a teacher. The killer had also wounded ten other students and held eighty people hostage for nine hours. Belli was representing plaintiffs who argued that the school was liable for the incident.

Belli and associate Alicia Becerril represented ten of the thirteen plaintiffs in the case. Every member of Belli's firm believed the case to be a dead solid loser not worth the time or expense. They pleaded with Belli to drop the case. When he decided to go forward with it, they called him senile.

The skeptics in the Boggess case, Becerril among them, pointed to an inability to prove liability on the part of high school officials and thus the school system, since they had no notice that the killings would occur. But Belli felt differently, and he convinced Becerril that there was a legal strategy to be employed. "He was the only one who believed the case could be won," Becerril said.

Belli's theory dealt with the disclosure that a teacher had noticed the student on campus before the shooting wearing dark glasses and a camouflage outfit. He was carrying two rifles with an ammo belt wrapped around his body. The teacher did not notify authorities or school officials, saying later that she thought the boy was ROTC.

Belli contended that there was an absolute duty on the part of the teacher to act, since teachers were responsible for the welfare of their students. Instead Belli believed that the teacher had dismissed the entire episode as a joke. Doing so was surely negligent.

When Judge John Golden agreed, the war was on. Becerril acted as lead counsel in her first jury trial, with the famed lawyer at her side whispering tips and suggestions throughout the proceedings. Armed with the knowledge that the school's superintendent had ordered school officials not to discuss the case with the defense, and evidence that the deranged student had called the school to warn them, Belli and Becerril marched through their case like Sherman through Atlanta. In the end, the jury decided that yes, the school had breached its duty.

Becerril's experience of trying a case with Belli left a permanent mark on the attractive woman who shared her mentor's passion for the law. "His belief in the 'duty' theory showed just how far ahead he was of everyone else," she said. "He was one step in front, and I was like a sponge soaking up his knowledge. He could evaluate a case on many different levels and he was always attempting to expand the bounds of the law."

"He never thought of himself as old," said Becerril. She was most impressed with Belli's ability, despite his age, to connect with the jurors. "He told me to look into their eyes," Becerril, who shared a front-page photograph in the local newspaper with Belli, recalled. "He believed that was the way you knew what they were thinking."

At the mention of Belli's grandiose voice, Becerril's eyes lit up. "The resonance of his voice displayed the versatility of his personality," she said. "He was such a great trial lawyer and he loved the law and he loved people. That was very clear."

Belli's gift for cross-examination was also apparent to Becerril. "When he cross-examined one witness during the trial," she said, "it was mesmerizing. He had such a command in the courtroom. All eyes were on him."

More than anything, Becerril noted a symbol of exactly what the Belli name meant. "He was so famous that I could tell that those we represented felt that just by having him in their corner, they had a chance to be heard," she recalled. "He was more brilliant than other attorneys could ever be." Bennett Alley, Belli's friend and official photographer, echoed Becerril's thoughts, saying of Belli, "He simply scared everyone to death."

When the favorable verdict was read, Belli, vindicated once again, threw his hands in the air and bear-hugged Becerril. Then it was off to search for other clients who needed his help. Until the day he breathed his last breath, Melvin Belli defended the rights of victims. He was the ultimate legal warrior, and truly was the King of the Courtroom.

EPILOGUE

PERRY MASON CREATOR Erle Stanley Gardner wrote the introduction to Melvin Belli's book *The Law Revolution*. It read, "Melvin Belli is a *great* showman. Moreover, he has all the self-effacing modesty of a steam calliope in a circus parade. These dominant qualities tend to make the casual appraiser fail to appreciate the fact that the man is also a legal genius."

Gardner's assessment of Belli was correct. His imprint on the law is vast and ever expanding. Lawyers and lawyers-to-be continue to study his books and achievements and shake their heads in wonderment at his accomplishments. Certainly no one ever loved the law like Belli.

His innovative courtroom procedures live on in the hundreds or thousands of lawyers he trained and mentored. When Congress debates the issue of multimillion-dollar jury verdicts in personal injury cases, they are doing so because Belli introduced them into the legal landscape.

Perhaps Krysten Crawford of *The American Lawyer* best summed up Belli's life: "Given his tragic ending, it's easy to forget Belli's place in the annals of American law. In his heyday, he was a brash maverick who turned accepted notions of corporate liability on their head. His genius was . . . as a popularizer of daring new trial tactics."

Crawford's article on Belli, titled "Tortious Maximus," began by stating, "The only time I ever spoke to Melvin Belli, he threatened to sue me." Recalling that Ralph Nader once called Belli, "the Babe Ruth of the plaintiff's bar," Crawford wrote that Belli "trained scores of plaintiff's lawyers, judges and civilians about the evolution of tort law."

Journalist William Flynn once said, "Melvin Mouron Belli does more than practice law. He makes it, and while blazing new trails in the evolution of the ancient and honorable English Common law, he combines the best of John Drew, John Barrymore, Maurice Evans, and Richard Burton to provide the audience with a theatrical performance that seldom is equaled in the history of the modern theatre."

Part genius, part comedian, Belli was one-of-a-kind. Richard Alexander, a former associate, said, "Mel was much like the best professors. Yes, he was knowledgeable and informative, but he conveyed so much excitement that he was entertaining as well. He was the ultimate storyteller." F. Lee Bailey had a different viewpoint, saying, "He was a superb craftsman in the courtroom." Upon his death, the *New York Times* called Belli "an impresario of a lawyer."

Belli once told the *San Francisco Examiner*, "I was nothing until I became a screwball." He said, "My biggest contribution has been to bring my imagination to bear on the practice of law." He added a final note, so fitting it could have been inscribed on his tombstone: "What I really wanted to do was force the system [of justice] to make good on its promises and bring due process of law to all the elements in our society, not just the rich and powerful."

The legal pioneer certainly had a great sense of humor. He loved to laugh and he loved making people laugh. When a television reporter asked him whether he was a "gadfly," he responded, "You know, when there are so many horses' asses pointed in your direction, you have to twist their tails in order to get their attention."

On another occasion, he wrote, "I think the greatest asset that I have as a trial lawyer is that I am for hire. I'll take either side—I hope with equal facility. As long as I'm for hire, as long as you can buy me, and once you've bought me, I'm completely honest to your side. I think that's the greatest attribute the trial lawyer has. Because then you know you have a champion in your corner."

He said, "A lawyer's job is to criticize. I think a lawyer's job is to be controversial. I think a lawyer's job is to be a leader, to stir up controversy so that there will be light on controversial subjects."

Regarding the court system, Belli told *Playboy* magazine, "We're just damn lucky that we live in a country where the Supreme Court protects the stumblebum sleeping under the railroad bridge as zealously as it does the president of the railroad sleeping in his private car."

The day Belli died, attorney Tim Palm paid tribute to him in a special way. During a recess of cases in San Francisco Superior Court, Palm rose and suggested a moment of silence in Belli's tribute. The judge reluctantly agreed.

Today there are few tangible remembrances of Melvin Belli. Boalt Hall at the University of California at Berkeley, Belli's alma mater, honored him with the Belli Commons Student Center. He and wife Nancy attended the ribbon-cutting ceremony shortly before he died.

The Montgomery Street Belli building that was so famous now stands in shambles, reconstruction pending. Even though San Francisco has honored favorite sons Jack Kerouac, Caesar Chavez, and Herb Caen, among others, by naming streets after them, there is not a street or monument in San Francisco, or his birthplace Sonora, to honor Belli.

Despite being ignored during his final days, Melvin Mouron Belli was a man of courage who truly knew justice. He stands in the company of the greatest lawyers who ever lived, the ones who helped others and were crusaders for justice. Much of what he said, and did, should never be forgotten.

Quoting Oliver Wendell Holmes, Belli once wrote, " 'A man must share the passion and the action of his times—or run the risk of not having lived.'" He added, "I have shared. I have lived." He certainly had.

BOOKS BY MELVIN BELLI
(PARTIAL LIST)

Captain Fred Reckenbiel 1949
The Voice of Modern Trials 1950
The Adequate Award 1951
The More Adequate Award and the Flying Saucers 1952
Modern Trials—Five Volumes 1954
Trial and Tort Trends—Four Volumes 1954
The Modern Trial Lawyer 1956
Blood Money: Ready for the Plaintiff 1956
Ready for the Plaintiff: A Story of Personal Injury Law 1956
Modern Trial Law 1957
Modern Damages 1959
Belli Looks at Life and Law in Japan 1960
Trial and Tort Trends—Four Volumes 1960
Modern Trials Supplement 1961
Tort and Medical Yearbook 1961
Criminal and Medical Yearbook 1961
Belli Looks at Life and Law in Russia 1963
Dallas Justice: The Real Story of Jack Ruby and His Trial 1964
Justice in Dallas 1965
Ready for the Plaintiff 1965
The Belli Building: San Francisco 1966
Trial Tactics 1967

The Law Revolt 1968

The Law Revolution Civil 1968

The Law Revolution Criminal 1970

Angela: A Revealing Close-up of the Woman and the Trial 1971

My Life on Trial 1976

The Urologist and the Law 1979

The Successful Opening Statement 1981

Product Liability Breach on Liability, the Blue Chip of Damages 1981

Potpourri on Current Trial Law 1983

The Belli Files: Reflections on the Wayward Law 1983

Everybody's Guide to the Law 1986

Belli-Krantzler Book of Divorce 1986

Melvin Belli: For Your Malpractice Defense 1986

Classics of International Law—Two Volumes 1986

MEMBERSHIPS

International Bar Association (patron)
International Academy of Trial Lawyers (cofounder, fellow, member of
  board of directors, dean emeritus)
International Academy of Law and Science
Associate Internationale des Juristes Democrates
International Legal Aid Association
Inter-American Bar Association
American Bar Association
Federal Bar Association
American Trial Lawyers Association.
American Judicature Society Office League of America
American League to Abolish Capital Punishment (member of board of
  directors)
American Academy of Forensic Sciences
National Association of Claimants Compensation Attorneys (chairman
  of aviation section and torts section)
American Institute of Hypnosis
Authors Guild
Association Nacional de Abogados (Mexico; honorary member)
Société de l'Honneur et de la Droit (president), California Bar Associa-
  tion
Municipal Motorcycle Officers of California (honorary member)

Northern California Service League
Criminal Trial Lawyers Association of Northern California
Tuolumne County Historical Society
Plaintiff Trial Lawyers Association of Los Angeles County
San Francisco Bar Association, Beverly Hills Bar Association
Hollywood Bar Association
Barristers Club of San Francisco (past member of board of directors)
Lawyers Club of San Francisco
Phi Delta Phi
Delta Tau Delta
Masons (Shriners)
Scribes
Islam Shrine (California commander)
San Francisco Press Club
Union Club, Olympic Club
Commonwealth Club
Tuolumne County Reunion Association (past president)
E. Clampus Vitas (honorary member).

ACADEMIC HONORS

Legion of Honor (Cuba)
LHD, Columbia Institute of Chiropractic, 1970
PhD, University of Houston, 1970
JD, New England School of Law
Named dean emeritus of College of Law, University of California, Riverside
Grand Collar of Order of St. Brigidia

BIBLIOGRAPHY

Abell, Tyler, ed. *Drew Pearson Diaries*. Holt, Rhinehart, and Winston, 1974.

Belli, Melvin, and Maurice C. Carroll. *Dallas Justice*. New York: David McKay Company, 1964.

Belli, Melvin, and Danny R. Jones. *Belli Looks at Life and Law in Russia*. Indianapolis: Bobbs-Merrill, 1963.

Belli, Melvin, and Robert Blair Kaiser. *My Life on Trial*. New York: William Morrow and Company, 1976.

Belli, Melvin, and Mel Krantzler. *Divorcing*. New York: St. Martin's Press, 1988.

Belli, Melvin. *The Law Revolt*. Bellville: Trial Lawyer's Service, 1968.

Belli, Melvin. *The Law Revolution*. Kingsport: Kingsport Press, 1968.

Belli, Melvin. *Modern Trials*. Indianapolis: Bobbs-Merrill, 1954.

Belli, Melvin. *Trials and Tort Trends*. Indianapolis: Bobbs-Merrill.

Cohen, Mickey. *Mickey Cohen: In My Own Words*. New York: Prentice-Hall, 1975.

Cole, Tom. *A Short History of San Francisco*. San Francisco: Lexikos, 1981.

Conrad, Barnaby. *The World of Herb Caen*. San Francisco: Chronicle Books, 1997.

Crichton, Robert. *The Great Imposter*. New York: Random House, 1959.

Dempsey, John Mark, ed. *The Jack Ruby Trial Revisited, the Diary of Jury Foreman Max Causey*. Texas: University of North Texas Press, 2000.

Flynn, Errol. *My Wicked, Wicked Ways*. New York: G. P. Putnam & Sons, 1959.

Gertz, Elmer. *Moment of Madness: The People vs. Jack Ruby*. Chicago: Follett Publishing, 1968.

Graysmith, Robert. *Zodiac*. New York: Berkeley Publishing Group, 1976.

Haley, Alex. Interview with Melvin Belli, *Playboy,* June, 1965.

Hunter, Diana, and Alice Anderson. *Jack Ruby's Girls*. Atlanta: Hallux, Inc., 1970.

"Jack Ruby on Trial." History Channel Special, April, 2001.

Joesten, Joachim. *Oswald: Assassin or Fall Guy?* London: Merline Press Ltd., 1964.

Kantor, Seth. *Who Was Jack Ruby?* New York: Everest House, 1978.

Kurtz, Michael L. *Crime of the Century*. Knoxville: University of Tennessee Press, 1982.

Lake, Steven R. *Hearts and Dollars*. Chicago: Chicago Review Press, 1983.

Manchester, William. *The Death of a President*. New York: Harper and Row, 1964.

Ragano, Frank, and Selwyn Raab. *Mob Lawyer*. New York: Charles Scribner and Sons, 1994.

Sheresky, Norman. *On Trial*. New York: Viking Press, 1977.

Various issues *San Francisco Chronicle, San Francisco Examiner.*

Wallace, Robert. *Life and Limb*. New York: Doubleday, 1955.

Warren Commission, *Report of the President's Commission on the Assassination of President John F. Kennedy*. Washington, DC: U.S. Government Printing Office, 1964.

Wills, Gary, and Ovid Demaris. *Jack Ruby*. New York: New American Library, 1967.

ACKNOWLEDGMENTS

WRITING A BIOGRAPHY of Melvin Belli has been an honor, but it would not have been possible without the tremendous support and assistance of the many people who chose to share their stories about the legendary attorney. Others read various drafts of the book, giving insight and suggestions that improved the text.

To all of them, I say thank you. They include Jasper Watts, Maggie Quinn, John Hill, Mike Guta, Mike Stipher, Joanie Green, Scott Montross, Martha Moyer, Larry Hancock, Jerry Bales, Tom Peterson, Becky Howard, Anne and Mike Horri, Terri Browning, Sami Baxter, Tourism Coordinator, Tuolumne County, Dythe-Mary Egleston and Anne Williams, Genealogical Society, Tuolumne County, Wendy Sanguinetti, Richard Adler, David Bradlow, Rudy Crabtree, Steve Jacobs, Owen Mullin, Donna Stouder, Kelly James, Martha Moyer, Betty Windsor, Debra Conway, Jerry Dealey, Larry Hancock, Gary Mack (Curator, 6th Floor Museum), Hal Verb, Les Sebring, Kelly James, Pat Riley, Mary Beth Ramey, Allison Anderson, Jack Lupton, and Joe DiSalvo.

Special thanks go to Nancy Ho Belli, Joyce Revilla, and Seymour and Suzanne Ellison for their insight into Belli and their cooperation with the book. Bob Lieff, Gretchen Diandi, and Tricia James are also thanked, as are Hugh and Pearl Campion for their friendship and suggestions.

Laurie McGinnis, assistant to Gerry Spence, is thanked for her assistance with coordinating an interview with the attorney. Like Belli,

Spence has been a true pioneer in altering the legal landscape.

A list those who are responsible for this book and for honoring the memory of Melvin Belli would be incomplete without mentioning Lyle Stuart, president of Barricade Books. When Mr. Stuart, who knew Belli, first examined the manuscript, he was interested but only if major revisions were made to the text. With his guidance, these changes were made, resulting in a book that accurately pays homage to one of the greatest lawyers who ever lived.

Thanks also to Carole Stuart, who has carried on the great tradition of Barricade Books in her husband's absence, to Ivy McFadden for her dedication in streamlining the text resulting in more clarity and organization, and to Christine Scarfuto, whose assistance with production has been invaluable.

On a personal note, this author is indebted to his wife Wen-ying Lu, his family and friends including longtime mentor Jack Lupton, and his Labrador, Black Sox, for his companionship at 5:00 am. Most important, this book would not have been published without the continuing love and grace of the Good Lord, who makes all things possible.

Mark Shaw